# Praise for *Augmented Lean*

"Essential reading for CEOs, masterfully structured, clarifies the pivotal role of technology in the lean domain without resorting to hyperbole. Cleverly balances visionary insight with great implementation guidance."

—**PASCAL BORNET**, Author of *Intelligent Automation*, and LinkedIn Top Voice in Tech

"Tech entrepreneur Linder and futurist Undheim brilliantly argue why augmentation is better than automation. This book provides a clear direction for next-gen operational excellence. If you're in search of manufacturing excellence, search no more: *Augmented Lean* is the thing to do and this book tells you how."

—**PROF. DR. TORBJØRN NETLAND**, Chair of Production and Operations Management (POM), Department of Management, Technology, and Economics, Swiss Federal Institute of Technology, ETH Zürich

"The world is changing towards a platform-based economy. This book gives perfect answers about augmented work and how it multiplies the effects on human ingenuity and automation on each other. The book guidelines the bridge between the digital and physical perspective and will promote future understanding on developments in industry towards platforms. A must read!"

—**CHRISTIAN THOENES**, Chairman of the Executive Board, DMG MORI

# AUGMENTED LEAN

# AUGMENTED LEAN

## A HUMAN-CENTRIC FRAMEWORK FOR MANAGING FRONTLINE OPERATIONS

NATAN LINDER

TROND ARNE UNDHEIM

WILEY

Published by John Wiley & Sons, Inc., Hoboken, New Jersey.

Published simultaneously in Canada.

*Library of Congress Cataloging-in-Publication Data is Available:*

ISBN 9781119906001 (Hardback)
ISBN 9781119906018 (ePub)
ISBN 9781119906025 (ePDF)

Cover Design: © Tulip
Cover Images: © kornkun/Adobe Stock, © kuroksta/Adobe Stock

SKY10035151_082622

# CONTENTS

# LIST OF FIGURES AND INTERVIEWS

# LIST OF TABLES

# ACKNOWLEDGMENTS

To our families for giving us the time to do this book on weekends. To our excellent and diligent executive editor, Bill Falloon at Wiley, for believing in the project from the start and for providing strategic guidance on content and marketing. To VP and publisher Shannon Vargo for her go-ahead. To managing editor Purvi Patel for keeping us on schedule and getting us to the finish line. To publicity manager Amy Laudicano for positioning our book for success through a wide reach. To editorial assistant Samantha Wu for coordinating the practical aspects of publishing, which is no small lift.

To all our colleagues at Tulip, who constantly remind us why we are trying to transform manufacturing. Beyond Tulip's co-founders, Rony Kubat and Pattie Maes, especially Eddy Atkins, Elise Jones, Erik Mirandette, Gilad Langer, Gillian Catrambone, Jen Dyment, John Klaess, Madilynn Angel, Mark Freedman, Olivier Néron, Rony Kubat, Roy Shilkrot, Saul Lustgarten, and Yuval Marcus, who took part in countless brainstorms, provided introductions and advice, and/or tirelessly read early drafts of the manuscript even when it had obvious shortcomings. A special thanks to talented writer, editor, and educator John Klaess, who read and commented on the entire manuscript, and to the creative team led by Elise Jones and Jon Vergara with Harshey Girish and Elaine Chung, for designing the book cover and for designing our fabulous book website and to Joshua Richard for coding it to perfection.

To Tulip's business partners, notably DMG MORI and Stanley Black & Decker, for being so generous with your time and sharing your experience with digital transformation and management challenges with us, including the status of your work to integrate Tulip deeply in your product.

To all the interviewees included in the book, namely Lena Jaentsch, Francisco Betti, Mark Freedman, Edward Atkins, Rick Bullotta, Jon Hirschtick, Marius Schmiedt, Damir Hrnjadovic, Dan Ron, Enno De Boer, Marc Nash, Çağlayan Arkan, Babi Mitra, Elisa Roth, Kel Guerin, Sarah Boisvert, John Klaess, Jon Sobel, Rony Kubat, Elisabeth Reynolds, Roy Shilkrot, Pattie Maes, Dayna Grayson, Shahin Farshchi, Robin Dechant, Jeff Immelt, Hilarie Koplow-McAdams, Arun Kumar Bhaskara-Baba, Andy Burton, Yossi Sheffi, William Bruey, Dave Evans, Kathryn Kelley, Brian Mathews and Kim Knickle, who also made themselves available as guests on the Augmented podcast.

To Kyle McCord with Atmosphere Press, who did a significant job as a developmental editor consultant at a crucial juncture in the book-writing process.

To our developmental editor at Wiley, Kim Wimpsett, for her clarity and constructive criticism.

To our copy editor at Wiley, Cheryl Ferguson, for her accuracy, on-time delivery, and knowledge of the *Chicago Manual of Style*.

To Pascal Bornet, Brad Feld, John Hart, Jeff Immelt, Torbjørn Netland, Klaus Schwab, Nassim Nicholas Taleb, and Christian Thoenes, who endorsed the book and found it worthy of a wide readership.

# ABOUT THE AUTHORS

**Natan Linder**, PhD, is a pioneering entrepreneur of industrial tech, co-founder and CEO of frontline operations platform Tulip, and co-founder and chairman of the board of Formlabs, the pioneer and industry leader in professional desktop 3D printing. Formerly with Jerusalem Venture Partners, Samsung, Sun Microsystems, and Rethink Robotics, he aims to fuse design and engineering to create novel human experiences. He is a *Forbes* columnist and earned a PhD from MIT Media Lab. He is based in Cambridge, MA.

**Trond Arne Undheim**, PhD, is a futurist, scholar, podcaster, venture partner, nonresident Fellow at the Atlantic Council, co-founder of Yegii, and Lead Ecosystem evangelist at Tulip. Formerly with MIT, WPP, Oracle, and the EU, he is the author of *Health Tech: Rebooting Society's Software, Hardware, and Mindset* (2021), *Future Tech: How to Capture Value from Disruptive Industry Trends* (2021), *Pandemic Aftermath: How Coronavirus Changes Global Society* (2020), *Disruption Games: How to Thrive on Serial Failure* (2020), and *Leadership from Below* (2009). He hosts two podcasts, Augmented and Futurized, and is a *Forbes* columnist. His PhD was on the future of work and artificial intelligence. He is based in Wellesley, MA.

# INTRODUCTION

When Lena starts her shift at a mid-sized manufacturing firm, a manufacturer of self-adhesive label application systems, she often reflects about the future. Situated in Germany's Baden-Württemberg, a leading economic region in Europe, she is often reminded that all regions should be on a continued path of opportunity. She is mobile, eagerly exploring opportunities. She earned her engineering degree in Sweden. When we speak with her, she's rapidly advancing, already with a leading role in the production of industrial labels at her firm. Yet, she is deeply committed to her factory job. She loves seeing the product come together, and enjoys the complexity of the process. She likes seeing results right away.

For now, economic life is dominated by the middle-class. The region, home of cuckoo clocks, Black Forest gateau, and the headquarters of Porsche and Mercedes-Benz, is a producer of high-value-added industrial products such as leather goods, musical instruments, medical instruments, food, agricultural produce, and hardware. Lena's employer produces labels and is instrumental in producing the labels used for the COVID-19 vaccine. She is a young, female digital-manufacturing advocate in a male-dominated industry. Her thoughts will contribute to the reshaping of the region over time. Her mindset is continuous improvement, making use of novel technologies and tools, and always digitizing if she can. She is keenly aware of the huge landscape of tools, hardware, and software emerging and now available to manufacturers. And yet, she misses a community of people who think like her who she can talk to. She sees herself as a lone wolf. A lone, female wolf in the Black Forest (see Interview I.1).

**Interview I.1** A Female Fighter in a Manufacturing SME. Episode 16. Interview with Lena Jaentsch, Business Development Specialist at HERMA Group. Augmented podcast.

Manufacturing industries account for 64% of global R&D spend, according to the World Bank. A great deal is spent on tech, although mostly on product development rather than process development. Emerging technologies that matter in manufacturing include AI, Augmented Reality, Robots, Sensors, and Wearables. Many white papers, books, and speeches have been written on these emerging technologies, but most are infected by hype and technological determinism. While effective rhetoric to argue more resources and attention to tech is needed, that view is not useful for long term transformation of manufacturing operations. In fact, we would argue it is counterproductive to the interests of the workforce to see things that way. As we know from history, greater distance between managers and shop floor workers is fodder for distrust, inefficiency and, at times, revolution and revolt. Instead, we offer the view that augmenting operations can happen now, with technologies we already possess.

# WHO ARE THE FRONTLINE WORKERS?

Industrial frontline workers stand at the core of manufacturing. Whether on the shop floor or working in a transitory manner, they embody both the challenges and the opportunities of industrial production. According to the US Bureau of Economic Analysis (2018), manufacturing accounted for about 11% of GDP in the economy and 13.5 million people were employed full- or part-time in American manufacturing (NAM 2022). According to Gartner, frontline workers make up to an estimated 2.8 billion from the global workforce (Allen 2021), although that definition includes a wide variety of professions outside the traditional scope of manufacturing and also includes service workers. A study by Emergence claims 80% of the global workforce working in industries such as construction, manufacturing, and agriculture is "deskless," and that "little of the $300 billion that is spent on business software each year has gone to these workers" (Emergence 2018). Whichever way you slice it, representing a good chunk of the productivity in any economy, the frontline worker is always the first to be asked to step up and deliver more. This type of worker is also typically the last to leave the work shift in order to execute within an ever-changing and increasingly complex environment. For example, faster product cycles, global supply chains, and meeting customer demands in light of competition all tend to fall on the frontline worker.

At the heart of this book is how to make operational decisions around technology. Equally important, those decisions are directly related to making decisions about humans. To be blunt: if the goal is performance improvement in all its dimensions (through sustainable digital transformation), frontline workers need first-class tools. It is not enough to keep introducing just increasingly complex flavors of automation across the factory in order to reap short-term productivity gains. How to empower humans to better leverage everything at their disposal? This is not an easy feat. But it starts with acknowledging that humans are essential for industrial production and will be for some time. The challenge is to make better use of each – technological and human capability – as an ensemble.

Frontline workers, knowledge workers in operational environments, do not necessarily have a desk. In fact, being deskless is almost what defines them. They may have a shared workstation, but their time there is fleeting and they don't always have the luxury of customizing it to their needs. Even more importantly, they do not have the professional tools they should have to carry out their work, the kind of work that society depends on. These days, they may have a privately owned smartphone, but typically not yet enabled with apps that would make them execute their workday with the same efficiency as they book their hair appointments or conduct their online shopping. How can this be? This is untenable. As a society, we have to treat those who make stuff, fundamental products that we depend on, much better. Mobile technology, the internet, advanced software, cloud computing, and networks are all available at a consumer level in most societies.

If you are a decision maker at any level in any type of organization – executives, engineers, operators, policy makers – we are speaking to you. You should be more aware of how good intentions around fostering productivity, whether it be profit, efficiency, throughput, or resource maximization, hits frontline workers. In fact, frontline workers, properly enabled, should also be decision makers in their own right. For that reason, technology is not, in itself, the tool of choice. If the goal is sustainable digital transformation that adapts to technology and continues to skill humans, the best engine of work is (still) human. Even as we attempt to enhance the work process, any changes should be measurably humanistic. Forget that at your peril!

## The Augmented Lean Imperative

Frontline workers are knowledge workers in operational environments, working with tacit knowledge, data, information, and machines to assemble, install, check, or repair products, and make stuff that society needs and depends on, or move parts and products around (logistics) – often with subpar digital tools (for decision-support, process control, reporting, and feedback) – especially compared to office workers.

Finding skilled manufacturing workers is a challenge (Selko 2021). How is the workforce evolving in a period of rapid technological acceleration? When are thorny, global challenges felt by individuals on the front line? What are the challenges faced by frontline workers themselves? How do we deal with the leadership challenges? In an era of thoroughgoing workforce transformation, how do we even define frontline work?

Briefly, during the pandemic, a frontline worker was crudely understood as someone who was a service worker who was exposed to a lot of others – most stereotypically a food service worker or perhaps a firefighter. While that was a useful definition for a tiny aspect of frontline work, it is by no means exhaustive.

*Frontline workers* is our term for the folks on the shop floor, whether they manage a production line or are shift workers making it hum. In industrial settings, process engineers are frontline workers. They may be planners or plant operators, but their remit and responsibility is people, processes, technologies, and tools. Frontline workers are the first to bear the brunt of change. The impact of any tool, technology, or new process that is introduced to increase productivity will first be felt by frontline workers. Many times, changes are introduced without considering all the consequences. Frontline workers, whether attempting to manage the change or simply being subjected to it, are indeed in the line of fire (see Figure I.1). They are truly at the front lines, in many countries, at the mercy of whatever is going on there, although in Germany and Scandinavia there are rich traditions for worker participation through councils and unions (Logue 2019).

**Figure I.1** The Frontline Workers on the Shop Floor.

For hundreds of years, industry has steadily marched toward automation. Over time, sentiment has swung between techno-pessimism and an unchecked faith in the power of innovation to improve life. Authors have cataloged automation's role in mass layoffs, unequal regional economic development, and worker apathy and fatigue, and automation's contributions to massive productivity increases and worker safety gains. There's a perceived opposition between human labor and mechanical automation in this worldview that misses the ways that human ingenuity and automation multiply the effects of the other. When technology takes over repetitive, dull, or dangerous jobs, humans with creativity and agility are free to do different things that create even more value and make them happier. However, automation is about to be met with a powerful force for worker empowerment – augmentation. What technologies should be doing in this decade and in the time to come is to *give working people superpowers, transforming frontline workers into knowledge workers.* Exactly how augmentation works, and can work even better if understood at scale, is what this book is about.

Whenever a product is being made, wherever there is any kind of operational environment or physical infrastructure required to create, deliver, or sell that product, there typically is a person involved. That person is a frontline worker. The main characteristics of frontline work – as juxtaposed with office work – are that it is highly mobile, typically executed standing up or at least not at one particular desk, and involves physical manipulation of machines, equipment, and goods.

The paradigmatic form of industrial frontline work is carried out on the shop floor or in a factory. Warehouses, construction yards, transportation vehicles, ships, the shop floors within them, and even the factories themselves are currently undergoing dramatic changes in physical configuration, status, and with the role they play in work and society. As factories become inhabited by designers, engineers, and other highly trained personnel, the perception of the space, its status, and its importance in the economy starts to transform. A similar thing also occurs as frontline jobs themselves become highly specialized, tech-intensive, and require in-demand, custom-trained labor. As more and more factory-relevant work can be carried out remotely, that also changes the dynamic between workers and managers.

However, even with the influx of industrial automation, there are frontline workers involved in some parts of production. This is true even if the product is enabled by software and data: setting in motion a process, monitoring machines, or fixing problems. Frontline workers are present at various stages of conception and production along the supply chain – even managing the sales process, consumption, return, or recycling of a product.

# WHAT IS AUGMENTED LEAN?

As the manufacturing industry evolves, the role of its workforce also changes. *Augmented Lean* is a book about getting the people/technology-dimension right in the transition to smart manufacturing. We believe what has become known as Industry 4.0 is a misnomer. To be clear: this is NOT an Industry 4.0 book. We have enough of those! The term may have served the purpose of pointing out that industrialization is entering a new phase with more intense interaction between technologies and where factories need to change dramatically. However, as we will get to, most accounts of Industry 4.0 are technology deterministic. That means they are overly concerned with one side of the equation and miss important qualifications. Industry 4.0 overstates the role of technology, but also misunderstands its role, which is, of course, pivotal. The last few decades have not been just about fostering another industrial revolution fueled by technology. Instead, what we see is an ongoing industrial revolution to bridge the digital-physical divide, transform frontline work toward knowledge work, and foster a renaissance in manufacturing.

The notion of "waves" of technology washing over industry so workers and factories need to adapt, is misleading. In fact, thinking in terms of waves is the wrong metaphor because changes overlap and many things remain constant. *Lean production*, a term coined by John Krafcik (1988), who was affiliated with the MIT International Motor Vehicle Program, has always been tied to the way lean was operationalized by Toyota over 30 years ago, and it is here to stay (with some tweaks). The core insights are valid across new generations of factory technologies. It is an operational mindset, a way to run any operation well, and it has been widely adopted for good reason.

Instead, the industrial challenge is to augment workers through means that empower them to not just make industrial products more efficiently.

Taking Merriam-Webster's dictionary, relevant synonyms of augment are amplify, boost, and build up. But what we should be trying to augment is not just the quality, speed, and power of a work process. We should simultaneously be sure we are boosting each worker's sense of worth. To do that, the technology used must be fit for the task but also fit for the person. In fact, we believe humanistic technology is the critical lynchpin for operational success.

Counterintuitively, one way to get the people-dimension in manufacturing right is through the use of software. This is counterintuitive because technology isn't often seen as a humanizing force. However, in the last 30 years, software developments have shifted emphasis from simply improving the efficiency of task execution to extending the capability and creativity of users. Entire job functions from marketing and sales to HR and finance have been transformed by software, cloud computing, and networks as utilities that allow business users – not IT or software development professionals – to create novel solutions to the problems they face every day. Crucially, this new breed of software is generative. It allows a user to create something, whether a process automation, component, or a user interface, that didn't come with the license. Generative software gives control and generativity to users and fundamentally transforms the way a given job function works.

To date, these innovations have been limited to traditionally white-collar work. And for good reason: It's hard enough to get sales and marketing software to play nicely together. Frontline work has the added complexity of occurring in the physical world, and spanning devices and machines and software from a variety of eras and communicating over a variety of protocols. No two operations are alike. No two operations are static. Very necessary adaptations are needed before software-centric approaches can be fully deployed on the shop floor. We know, because of the work we did at MIT keeping an active dialog with industry. We then spun out core technology into the market, commercialized a frontline operations platform (called Tulip), and are now reaching industrial scale. We know this: it took us years tweaking our software to fit the most important shop floor use cases: production visibility, machine monitoring, connecting information back to systems of record, Andon lights, and, most importantly, dynamic work instructions, knowledge apps, and real-time quality detection dashboards that directly augment the frontline worker. No worries if you do not know what all of these features mean: we will explore how to work with them throughout the book.

Broadly, the book outlines industrial tech opportunities, equips you with the vocabulary of change – on a societal and business level – and enables you to understand future developments across the industry. The book will also help you build specific skills: tap into emerging manufacturing innovations – and create some yourself. It will enable you to not only understand, but to act on change by starting to use the manufacturing augmentation toolkit, and giving you the ability to leapfrog traditionally educated engineers or operations professionals (or update your skillset). The book is also written for you, an operator in industry. If you are an executive, even better, you are learning the language of no-code. Being fluent in no-code is akin to speaking the "foreign language" of your employees – and mastering the secrets of productivity. We call it *augmented lean* (AL), a new management framework that is equally valuable for operators and executives.

The road to zero-training-required interfaces in industry is a long one, but we are on the journey. What won't go away so fast is the fact that building a business process requires deductive logic, being aware of what inputs matter, which transformations would be useful, how to use data to achieve them, and what kind of output is required.

The frontrunners in industry are embarking on an era building on the lessons of *lean*, but beyond simple *automation*, making use of *agile and iterative collaboration principles*, and so much more than *digital lean if that only means Lean + Digital "on top."* This new era of software driven manufacturing will favor manufacturers that are able to manage complexity by embracing a new breed of software-driven manufacturing. New, adaptive technologies encourage decentralized decision making and flexible operations yet maintain the ability for manufacturing engineers, and senior management, to carry out connected problem solving. Why? Because they have access to complete real-time data about the essential aspects of production (Mirandette 2019). Those who do so will have a sustained competitive advantage over industry laggards clinging to the twentieth-century notion of a centrally controlled and executed operation. In our vision, frontline operations will support any shared, interoperable, functional form factor that improves human work performance.

*Augmented Lean* is a human-centric framework for managing industrial operations. Welcome to the era of barebone *human cognitive augmentation,* where fewer special tech skills or complex gadgets are required. For sure, other skills, including the ability to interact with machines and sensors are required.

Work is neither dangerous, nor dull, nor dirty. Work might be automated, but never without meaning, metrics, and context. With plug-and-play components from your neighborhood electronics store and a more than average clear head you can become an augmented frontline worker whose career opportunities are promising. Subscribing to a new stack of cloud-based software that integrates no-code aspects, a manufacturer, regardless of size and scope, can become an innovator with very little sunk cost. An operator without a software degree can become an app developer and create lasting efficiencies. Because of the groundwork made by frontline operations platforms, simple steps you take can now bridge the cyber-physical divide. All that's required is a *learning mindset* and being adaptable to change. We live in exciting times, where simplification is in sight, but where the details on how to make headway, are still complex.

# HOW IS THIS BOOK ORGANIZED?

The book is structured around four parts: (I) The Evolution of Industrial Lean, (II) The Coming of Augmented Lean, (III) Engineering, Tech, and Skills, and (IV) Augmented Lean Operations.

## Part I: The Evolution of Industrial Lean

This section's four chapters provide an overview of the management, techniques, and tools leaders typically have used to implement effective organizational dynamics throughout industrial transitions. The section leads into the current challenge: how to empower operators, those crucial mid-level managers who facilitate the work of frontline workers, to transform their organizations for the better using augmented lean methods.

In Chapter 1, "The Evolution of Frontline Industrial Work," we briefly trace the evolution from Industry 1.0 (seventeenth century), the era of mechanization, through to Industry 2.0 (eighteenth century), the era of mass production, Industry 3.0, the era of automation (twentieth century), and Industry 4.0 (twenty-first century), the era of connectivity. We think the more apt name would be the era of augmentation, but will instead describe that phenomenon as Industry 5.0 (mid-twenty-first century). The beginnings of this era is already manifesting itself through cobots (in addition to robots) and other forms of man–machine systems (including most current forms of AI) that integrate the capabilities of each or complement each other.

In Chapter 2, "From Classic Lean via Agile to Digital Lean and Beyond," we consider how the wildly impactful production paradigms of manufacturing are integrating the lessons of other industries' digital transformation. Today, manufacturing workers do not design the process, engineers do, and that legacy has led to alienation, especially if the process is not agile enough to pick up needs and wants. Here, the engineers design the process, but the ultimate promise is for frontline workers to own and shape more and more of their work environment, a point that the human relations school of management has hammered in, and which the best lean practitioners also appropriated – but which is still not mainstream. Agile principles derived from the software engineering process that, in turn, originate from lean methodology in the automotive sector, are making it full circle back into operations. As a result, frontline industrial workers are empowered and processes are changing for the better.

In Chapter 3, "The State of Play in Industrial Tech Software," we track how the 1960s with industrial control systems gained industrial adoption throughout the 1970s, the 1980s brought the digitalization of engineering design (in 2D) as well as powerful visualization tools, and by the 1990s, the internet platform brought remote control systems as well as next generation design tools in 3D. The late 2000s brought the first manufacturing execution systems and throughout the decade and beyond, a plethora of such systems had emerged and their functionality (and integration cost) had ballooned. However, legacy systems didn't go away and are still present in today's factory floor control rooms. The gradual advancement and adoption of cloud computing is a key shared component across industry and government. Many think it will become a new utility. So far, cloud computing is poorly understood among policy makers and is not properly regulated. Once it is, one would hope that it would become a truly shared resource where migration on or off private or public clouds could happen in an interoperable manner.

In Chapter 4, "The Journey Past Digital Lean," we reflect on the fact that empowering industrial work will not happen by itself. Rather, it is a journey with explicit actions needed by workers, management, and the organization as a whole. New, lightweight technology to complement humans better than legacy systems is also part of what makes this possible.

Digital transformation is seldom a painless process. As much as the technologies allow for innovation, they also challenge the production process and the leadership principles of control that used to prevail. Adding to that, in a regulated environment, digital processes must be standardized to a fault, must be traceable, secure, and provably reliable.

At Tulip Interfaces, an industrial tech startup, we have experienced what it means to take much larger companies through a deep digital lean journey, both challenging notions of what it means to make improvements, but also witnessing how shockingly easy some parts of the process might turn out to be.

# Part II: The Coming of Augmented Lean

This section's three chapters describe the emergence of a new management framework in industry. The approach builds on bottom-up reskilling and digital transformation efforts. These efforts are enhanced by no-code platforms: enabling the technology interface to stay in the background; letting operators shine as facilitators; and fostering frontline worker empowerment across the organization. We try to show how augmentation replaces automation, and interpretable data replaces big data once we shift to an *augmented lean* management approach built on a humanistic approach to technology where reskilling needs are minimized.

In Chapter 5, "The Augmented Lean Framework," we for the first time, present what's next, after the transitory ways that "post-lean" or "digital lean" approaches have been implemented in the manufacturing industry. Our distilled framework, augmented lean, aims to clearly communicate how the company we work for, Tulip, has learned and appropriated a humanistic approach to technology and adapted it to manufacturing. The result is a novel approach to implementing industrial tech for maximum value that is inclusive, scalable, and still aligned with the constraints of a physical environment for the entirety of human workers who are not "blessed" with a desk (or an office). One might soon be able to say that the desk was hardly an ideal workplace compared to the emerging cadre of augmented industrial frontline workers.

These workers are transient, mobile, yet still deeply in need of advanced knowledge worker capabilities, both at individual, organizational, and supply chain levels, throughout their workday, and increasingly 24/7 when other shifts are complementing work and need to carry it out with the same precision.

The ever-simpler production enhancement techniques and tracking systems ensure less alienation, better use interfaces, and greater work satisfaction. We think of it as a framework of a few elements that include a set of human traits (a hacking mentality), organizational enablement (tools, techniques, technologies), a leadership mindset (augment, decentralize, and empower – led from below), and systemic awareness (understanding – and respecting – all levels of the system).

This framework is not hard to understand intellectually, but it is tricky to execute because one group of people does not control all the variables. We offer practical suggestions to overcome that challenge – whether you sit at the top, the middle, or even at the frontline. In many ways, the tables are turned, and the top management will need to rely on well-executed actions across the organization – and beyond. Up until this point, we have been focusing on describing the world of manufacturing as it is emerging, with small takeaways at the end of each chapter. In this section, starting with this chapter, we will look at how augmented frontline operations can be implemented at an organizational level.

In Chapter 6, "How to Roll Out Industrial Technology the Right Way," we tackle the practical challenges of industrial tech innovation in a wide range of industries and settings, from life science to manufacturing, and across both discrete and continuous, process-based workflows, which may well coexist within the same organization, or even at the same worksite.

There is room for both top-down inspiration (Lighthouses) and bottom-up experimentation and growth (Greenhouses) in order to roll out industrial tech. Discovery of best practices, however, is only one component. Successful change needs to address inertia, deal with pilot purgatory, and avoid misuse of ROI too early.

In Chapter 7, "Democratizing Operational Technology Using the Dynamic Capabilities of the Organization," we take a fresh look at the so-called "IT vs. OT divide." The informatics (IT) vs. operations tech (OT) power dynamics are intensifying as they clash or need to interoperate. Gartner's notion of the "citizen developer," developed by Gartner analyst Ian Finley back in 2011, is rapidly becoming a reality a decade later. IT is complicated, and big enterprise systems often fail, are subject to major implementation delays, or become more expensive than planned. You never hear "success by IT," just "death by IT." Low-code or no-code as a democratizing force changes what the workforce should demand from its organization because it enables the dynamic (internal) capabilities of the firm as opposed to relying on third parties.

# Part III: Engineering, Tech, and Skills

In this section's three chapters, we describe the need to foster a skillset appropriate to augmented lean. Making the industrial engineer fully digitally literate is a key component, but engineering-like tasks need to be dispersed across the organization, too. The operational value of data will increase, but the process takes work.

In Chapter 8, "The Emergence of the Digitally Literate Industrial Engineer," we explore how engineers are becoming increasingly digital regardless of their subfield. As systems get deployed in real contexts, software engineers are also learning industrial realities. Engineers are learning to work closer together with the huge and important part of the workforce who have "middle skills" – those in between high school and college degrees. Despite the fact that the manufacturing industry is rapidly digitizing, few industrial engineers have software as their primary or secondary expertise. Instead, they are experts on systems-thinking, discrete manufacturing techniques, and statistical methods. Is that a problem? Will it change anytime soon? How can the industrial engineer operate fully digitized operations without being software literate?

In Chapter 9, "Training the Process Engineers of the Future," we specifically look at training needs, requirements, and promising approaches to hyperscaling training. Training engineers must increasingly happen on the job – standing up, not sitting down. Curricula, approaches, and learning goals need to change. Training is social and community enabled. The process engineer of the future will ideally come prepared from some type of college training. Even if not, tomorrow's training is likely to take place on the job. Given the gargantuan upskilling needs of the industrial workplace, the best way to train engineers (or any employee) is through a community approach, not formal training or even apprenticeships. The chapter looks at some such approaches and documents Tulip's own experience building a community of learners based on our client needs. We also look closely at the challenges of elite universities such as MIT as well as the quite different challenges faced by huge land-grant colleges with thousands of students per cohort or even by dispersed community colleges in the US and around the world.

In Chapter 10, "From Automation to Augmentation," we sharpen our argument that not only is continued mindless automation shortsighted from a long-term perspective, it is also counterproductive in the short term. Automation took care of the low-hanging fruit. But by its very nature, simple automation solves problems by taking people out of the equation. However, at low volume, the cost to automate doesn't always make sense. The most pressing challenges manufacturing faces today cannot be solved with automation. For the remaining problems too hard for a robot to solve, you must rely on the most powerful computer on the shop floor: humans. These problems include: creative problem-solving, teamwork, complex assembly, safety checks, and real-world testing.

# Part IV: Augmented Lean Operations

This section's three chapters spell out how C-suite senior management, and most of all, crucial mid-level operators, can create conditions conducive for *Augmented Lean* to emerge in such a way that it both benefits the bottom line and empowers the workforce. Realistically, this type of process cannot be forced, it just needs to emerge. How then, to answer the leadership question: How do I design my organization?

In Chapter 11, "The Potential Augmenting Power of Operational Data," we take a look at one of the most powerful forces for change – structured information that is widely available and can be acted upon. The quest for speed and scale has fostered rapid prototyping for production lines. Making products faster and scaling manufacturing is a product of data + process + apps + artificial intelligence and machine learning (AI/ML) as the icing on top. Data is the centerpiece that makes these technologies so powerful. But making data operational is a difficult task. It takes a focus on process and technology that puts humans, not machine efficiency, at the center.

In Chapter 12, "Facilitation over Control: How the Industrial Systems of the Future Might Emerge," we muse on the ways we think industries of the future could play out: (1) Networks of firms and stakeholders who collaborate with each other with no clear lead (mutually dependent supply chain networks); (2) Oligopolies that control their own affiliate networks (the Asian conglomerate model) or ecosystems of scale (e.g., the Android model); or (3) Constantly shifting sets of companies that dominate for a few years each before new disruptors take over and dethrone the former kingmakers (an intensified version of the current IT industry). The system we have in mind, as the industrial system of the future, unlike manufacturing execution systems of the past, is wide-ranging, flexible, and rewards proactive, competent individuals, not only organizations and large corporations. Most importantly, for cyber-physical systems to work, executives, operators, workers – and machines – must work together.

In Chapter 13, "Reconfiguring Global Supply Chains," we do a deep dive into supply chains, a topic few outside the field cared much about before the pandemic. At this point, everyone knows about supply chain disruptions in the early stages of the pandemic, and the real bottleneck-induced shortages induced by the later stage of the pandemic. The end-to-end perspective (from idea to user) is now part of product development and has become a concern for all of the industrial workforce. But putting the supply chain on the cloud has yet to happen, although startups are leading the way.

# Conclusion: Augmented Lean Management of the Emerging, Frontline Industrial Workforce

We conclude by reflecting that the emerging workforce will need to look radically different than before. Due to the scale of the challenge, the many actors with a stake in the game, and the pace of change, it won't be an easy feat to accomplish. Reimagining training will not be enough. Industrial organizations will have to change. They will have to become true learning organizations. Humanistic technology can do some of the work – automation alone is not the answer. Augmentation is far more effective, yet harder to pull off. Early experiences need to be collected, understood, adapted, and scaled up. There are lessons here for executives, engineers, operators, and policy makers far beyond the industrial sphere.

# REFERENCES

Allen, J. (2021). Gartner Hype Cycle Frontline Worker Technologies Recognizes Coolfire Solutions. https://www.coolfiresolutions.com/gartner-frontline-worker-hype-cycle/ (accessed 12 March 2022).

Emergence (2018). The rise of the deskless workforce. https://resources.dynamic signal.com/youtube-all-videos/rise-of-deskless-workforce-webinar (accessed 12 March 2022).

Krafcik, J.F. (1988). Triumph of the Lean Production System. Sloan Management Review. 41. https://www.lean.org/downloads/MITSloan.pdf (accessed 19 May 2022).

Logue, J. (2019). Trade unions in the Nordic countries. *Nordics Info* (18 February). https://nordics.info/show/artikel/trade-unions-in-the-nordic-region (accessed 19 May 2022).

Mirandette, E. (2019). Manufacturing is finally entering a new era. World Economic Forum [blog]. (21 March). https://www.google.com/url?q=https://www.weforum.org/agenda/2019/03/manufacturing-is-going-digital-it-s-about-time/&sa=D&source=docs&ust=1647092814353665&usg=AOvVaw2xQYuFEwebp ZmNC8-EtdGG (accessed 12 March 2022).

Selko, A. (2021). The skilled labor shortage threatens manufacturing's full recovery, says study. *Industryweek* (July 14). https://www.industryweek.com/talent/article/21169565/the-skilled-labor-shortage-threatens-manufacturing-sectors-fully-recovery-says-study (accessed 9 February 2022).

U.S. Bureau of Economic Analysis (2018). https://www.bea.gov/ (accessed 9 February 2022).

NAM (2022). Facts About Manufacturing. https://www.nam.org/facts-about-manufacturing/ (accessed 9 February 2022).

# PART I

# THE EVOLUTION OF INDUSTRIAL LEAN

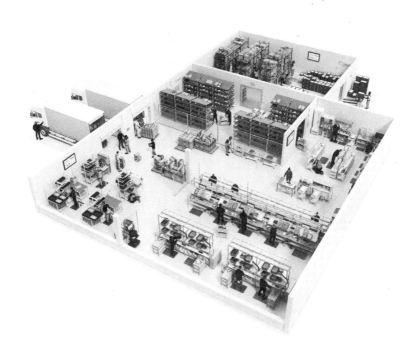

# CHAPTER 1

# THE EVOLUTION OF FRONTLINE INDUSTRIAL WORK

Francisco Betti, a soft-spoken but effective Italian man with a classic Humphrey Bogart hairstyle and chiseled looks, heads up the
World Economic Forum's global Platform for Shaping the Future of
Advanced Manufacturing and Value Chains, an endeavor involving more
than 200 firms, startups, consultants, and academic collaborators. To him,
the "fourth industrial revolution" became real throughout the COVID-19
pandemic. This concept was originally developed as "Industry 4.0" through
strategy efforts of the German government in 2011 (Dima 2021) and got
popularized by the founder of the Forum, Klaus Schwab (Schwab 2013),
through the broader framework of the "4th industrial revolution," with the
ambition of creating change at all levels of society. It escalated the efforts

to work with regional networks of manufacturers, including small and medium enterprises, and with fast-growing companies and startups who could inspire change into the forefront.

Faced with a myriad of challenges, including a global pandemic, climate change, and geopolitical tensions, a digitally enabled stakeholder capitalism emerged, providing new efficiencies, collaborations, and a surprising coalescence around fairly ambitious sustainability targets. Betti found himself in the middle of a whirlwind where manufacturing was back at the core of the global economic agenda. As Betti said on the Augmented Podcast (2021; see Interview 1.1):

> The pandemic showed that manufacturing still plays a major role in the global economy and society [...related to megatrends part of. . .] the fourth industrial revolution referring to the blurring lines in between the operational technology (OT) and information technology (IT) that are transforming, not just where companies operate, but probably even who we are and what we do as human beings.

**Interview 1.1** The Fourth Industrial Revolution post-COVID-19. Episode 9. Interview with Francisco Betti, Head of Advanced Manufacturing and Production, World Economic Forum. Augmented Podcast.

For Betti, this is not just a technological challenge:

> Together with the climate change imperative for sustainability combined with the geopolitical trends [and] the tensions that we have seen over the past five years, the concept of stakeholder capitalism started

to gain traction, where one realized the need to create and deliver a new type of value, not just to shareholders, but to shareholders, worker, society and the environment altogether. [If that process is to run its course,] we probably need to start by asking, "What can manufacturers do to get closer to the general public?" and [contemplate] things like opening up facilities so that people can see them, not just imagine or have demonstrated to them the factory of the future, but really understand what the factory of today looks like. [...] I'm sure that the younger generations will get very excited by [such exposure]. Manufacturing has traditionally been operating behind the scenes. We need to change that.

The World Economic Forum's Global Lighthouse Network, a best practice initiative, also inspires the next generation of manufacturers (see Resource 1.1).

**Resource 1.1** World Economic Forum's Global Lighthouse Network.

Manufacturing has always been the engine of economic growth, and was recognized as such in the popular media. In reality, we should point out, manufacturing really never faded in societal and industrial importance; policymakers and business leaders just perceived it as "boring" or "outdated," which trickled down to parents, teachers, and eventually to new talent. Meanwhile, the operational improvements which did take place due to deeper and deeper digitalization took significantly longer, but are kicking in slowly, and piecemeal. When they kick in across the board, the world will be in a whole other place, but not in the place most people imagine.

In 2020, the frontline worker again took center stage, a pattern similar to the popularization of laborers during previous industrial revolutions. Indeed, this resurgence in interest in manufacturing has made it necessary to draw boundaries between industrial frontline work and frontline workers writ large. The term *frontline worker* entered our collective vocabulary during the pandemic alongside a companion term, *essential worker,* which encompassed a wide variety of functions, including grocery store clerks, nurses, cleaners, warehouse workers, and train and bus drivers, among others. It's easy to conflate the two, especially because the folks who hold these jobs tend to be "overworked, underpaid, under-protected, and underappreciated," and are disproportionately women, people of color, and low-income (Rho, Brown and Fremstad 2020). These groups were typically unable to work remotely, and were generally poorly supported by productivity tools or technology. While there is a massive case for building the digital tools that would make these kinds of frontline service workers more efficient (and empowered), we will, in this book, largely focus on *industrial frontline work* specifically tied to production sites and supply chains.

# INDUSTRIAL FRONTLINE WORKERS AND TECHNOLOGICAL REVOLUTIONS

Industrial frontline workers are staffing factories, shop floors, machine shops, labs, and warehouses and are present all along the global supply chain, wherever a process needs to be manually moved along or facilitated.

These workers generally have little safety training and poor access to upskilling or even basic training programs. Precise work instructions and expert knowledge transfer improves safety, employee productivity, and training efficiency. Digital evolution has a lot to do with it, because it makes information easier to share in principle. But while the internet is rolling out digital transformation across every industry under the sun, frontline workers are being left behind.

As active participants in this latest "wave" of industrial transformation, we feel it is imperative that industrial technology does not repeat itself – not just because it slows down progress but because it isn't right. And, this time, paying little or no attention to worker training is definitely not necessary or beneficial – neither for technology pioneers' business models to work out nor for manufacturing sector incumbents to maintain their (relative) operational freedom. To understand what can and what should happen in the next decade, it is instructive to glance quickly at what lessons we can glean from the past few centuries. Otherwise, despite so-called technological progress, the history of workforce exploitation might repeat itself, only with more sinister consequences for the workforce and for humanity itself.

In order to chart a path forward, we need to know where we've already been. It is less about avoiding repeating the past and more about pondering the implications of realizing how little we know at any given time in history when faced with implementing technology or indeed confronting any kind of disruptive opportunity. That awareness should not stop progress but should lead to balancing experimentation with caution and foresight.

With technological shorthand, which we don't necessarily applaud, Industry 1.0 (eighteenth century) was the era of mechanization, Industry 2.0 (nineteenth century) was the era of mass production, Industry 3.0 was the era of automation (twentieth century), Industry 4.0 (late twentieth century) was the era of digitalization, and Industry 5.0 (twenty-first century) begins with the era of intensified automation driven by machine intelligence (AI/ML), with robotics and connected machines as the hardware and is evolving toward human augmentation. As we ponder what's next, some might even start to envision an Industry 6.0 (mid-to late twenty-first century into the twenty-second century) will begin an era of full augmentation and might evolve into the capability of creating fully autonomous, regenerative systems. In Table 1.1, we have sketched how familiar shorthand descriptions might help clarify the needed skills, work instructions, and machine monitoring efforts part of each era – except that such a schematic is wildly misleading if we think of it as complete transitions. The opposite is the case; these practices are wildly overlapping and everchanging, even within countries and sites.

**Table 1.1  From Automation to Regeneration**

| | Needed skills | Work instructions | Machine monitoring |
|---|---|---|---|
| **Industry 1.0** | Physical stamina | Oral | Not accessible to individuals |
| **Industry 2.0** | Structure, discipline | Written | In person, expert on call |
| **Industry 3.0** | Information processing | Digital | In person by specialists |
| **Industry 4.0** | Broad tech skills | Prioritizing machines | Mix of remote and on premises |
| **Industry 5.0** | Polymathic skills | Empowering people | Decentralized, edge device, on cloud |
| **Industry 6.0** | Holistic skills | Empowering nature | Regenerative machines |

Popular accounts of industrial history often stop there because they want to point to a linear progression toward ever more perfect technology and progress. From that perspective, all we are waiting for this decade is the perfect augmented reality (AR) device. However, reality is more complex. First off, we are sticking with a numbering system for these transitions only because it is established practice. We actually disagree with such an approach the way it is typically done because it is overly simplistic and masks how key traits survived each era and continue to impact us today.

In these types of archetypal descriptions of the industrial revolution, the main emphasis is on productivity increases and not on worker empowerment. We see that as a fundamental flaw in the narratives, and argue that human perspective must be front and center in any effort to adopt new technology. What exactly happened to industrial work, and the industrial worker, in the four industrial revolutions from the eighteenth century until today?

Viewed from that perspective, the eras look slightly different. Industry 1.0 (eighteenth century) was more accurately the era of exploitation (which material conditions theorist Karl Marx pointed out). Industry 2.0 (nineteenth century) was the era of alienation (and social science forefather Emile Durkheim said as much). Industry 3.0 (twentieth century) was the era of "rationalization" from the perspective of managers but neglect from the perspective of the individual worker. Industry 4.0 (late twentieth century) was the era of mediation, meaning various types of media (control systems, computers) came into play to alter the direct relationship between workers and what they are working on. A more apt word for that might be *interference*.

But unfortunately, exactly like Canadian media theorist Marshall McLuhan (1964) famously said about mass media, all digital media (even in the workplace generally and to an increasing extent in industry) became "the message" and focal point, not the communicator and the recipient. Industry 5.0 (twenty-first century) is, from this perspective, still the era of augmentation. However, we should disregard the somewhat-empty notion of augmented reality for the sake of commercial exploitation. We are not saying AR will not improve or will not become useful. It will, over time. We are saying it is currently still maturing and it will take time, while mature internet-based technologies are here and available now. Moreover, true transformation happens in the way industrial processes carried out by human workers can be improved. Superimposing digital layers deepens the visibility of the tasks. If we can supply in real time the analytics that sensors and machines generate, the worker can adjust what he or she is doing and achieve a smoother, more optimized workflow.

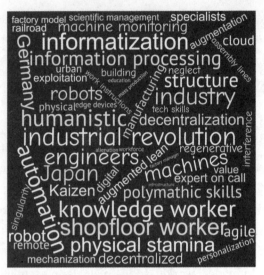

**Figure 1.1** What Industrial Revolutions Are All About.

# INDUSTRIAL REVOLUTIONS THROUGH HISTORY TO THE FUTURE

Considered in this light, the progression through industrial history reveals a profoundly human story that helps us better contextualize the relationship between industrial work and technology in our present moment.

## The First Industrial Revolution's Urbanization, Automation – and Exploitation (18th Century)

The first industrial revolution, characterized by the big project of building the transcontinental railroad and by the invention of electricity, transformed work from agricultural and rural to industrial and urban. Adapting to urban lives proved challenging for many, but also created new opportunities for leisure for those lucky enough to carve out some spare time. Work itself was physically demanding but sufficiently rewarding that the accumulation of assets among the working classes began for the strongest and most able. It was very much a survival-of-the-fittest environment. Not only that, this era was marked by the quite ruthless exploitation by industrialists and entrepreneurs who were given near free range by the weak (by contemporary standards) governments that ruled at the time. There were no industrial policies to speak of, no workers' rights, no discrimination laws, and no history of technology being scrutinized for its adverse consequences. The field of science and technology studies was not even in its infancy.

The key theorist of the era, Marx, mostly focused on the most egregious differences in material conditions and lack of wage differentiation and realistic wage ladder by which one could move up in the world. However, that was only one set of issues, and became politicized (by Marx and his followers) in a way that has forever made it difficult to fully understand this era for what it is, without the lens of socialism vs. capitalism, which at least to us, seems outdated and blinding in light of the need to provide a deeper, more granular analysis of the subtle changes that technology introduces over time.

To claim that the industrial revolution(s) led to worker exploitation is not a socialist argument, it is the broad lens that history provides, considering what is common sense today. Labeling the first industrial revolution as an era of exploitation is, as a first pass, descriptive and does not necessarily pass moral judgment on individuals who were part of that era (although one could do that, too). Why is it important to point out the exploitative side? Because it bore the seeds of what was to come, which is an antagonistic relationship within capitalism. It unnecessarily put a wedge between what could have been equals carrying out different functions – specialist labor and management of that labor. It attached greater value to efforts that were

31

(at the surface) easier to scale, and temporarily deemphasized such essential qualities of work as craft, originality, purpose, and origin story. These are elements that only now have been brought back. These values are back because, viewed differently, they have intangible but sometimes greater value than pure quantitative scale. Also, as it turns out, with contemporary tools and management paradigms, even craft can be scaled, which is one of the reasons why decentralized, mass personalization is poised to take off in the coming decade. We will elaborate more about the augmented "farmers' market" in Chapter 13, as we reflect on what lies ahead.

# The Second Industrial Revolution's Mechanization, Industrial Education – And Alienation (19th Century)

The second industrial revolution, characterized by the factory floor and the invention of steam power and mechanized work, confined workers to specific spaces and put them on the clock. In the late nineteenth century, the United States saw a vast expansion of its industrial plants and quadrupled output, fueled by machines that were capable of mass production, a process first pioneered by British textile manufacturers.

It was also during this period that German industrialists decided to create the Gymnasium, the world's first full-fledged basic educational system. It was designed to create the optimal factory manager, someone who would feel at home with discipline and would be able to develop new skills to keep pace with the introduction of new work processes in evolving factories that just kept increasing in size and ambition. Having said that, the history of education, both in Europe and in the United States, is far more complex than a "factory model" and has (luckily) always had elements of critical thinking embedded in it, and each type of technology brings its own challenges in that regard, even today (Watters 2015).

Toward the end of the second industrial revolution, the father of scientific management, Frederick Taylor, who had worked his way up the job ladder (laborer, shop clerk, gang boss, foreman, and finally chief engineer), wanted a solution to the problem of how to run these corporate behemoths. He found his solution in reducing variability. In *The Principles of Scientific Management* (1911), he outlined efficiency measures in work method, process, and operations such as standardizing work based on time and motion studies (aka Taylorism) but ignored organizational practices and behavioral effects of those methods. He explicitly criticized any arbitrary restriction of output, such as the bricklayer's union at the time restricting their men to "275 bricks per day when working for the city and 375 per day when working for private owners." According to Taylor, his "scientific" approach also applied to homes, farms, small businesses, churches, philanthropic institutions, universities, and government. At the core, Taylorism argues that each element of work needs to be broken down for scientific study in order to optimize it, even down to the "habit of resting at proper intervals," and claims "half of the problem [of 'initiative and incentive'] is up to the management." In a rare moment of realism, Taylor notes that too fast of a change often is met with trouble, strikes, and failure.

Henry Ford, starting in 1910, created his assembly lines with continuous flow of production by conveniently (to employers) arranging people, machines, equipment, tools, and products. His Model T automobile made him the richest man in the world. However, his system, and his own stubbornness, left him open for competition as market demand craved new models, colors, and product varieties. His poor handling of labor unions throughout the 1920s also didn't help his cause. As a result, by the 1930s, GM started dominating the automobile market.

33

The Taylorist, industrial approach to the workforce did provide generations of docile workers. It also had its share of challenges. Workers who took the tradeoff of being confined to cramped quarters in cities suffered in uncomfortable housing arrangements that cost them most of their wages. By the same token, by tacitly accepting severely restrictive factory conditions that took their health, destroyed their morale, and, in the end, devalued their humanity, some workers, simultaneously, started to experience a new phenomenon – social alienation. The structures of society were now arranged in such a way that some individuals felt maladapted, separated from their group (even from those suffering the same conditions). Ultimately, they did not feel part of the progress gospel their employers were preaching. Understandably, under these conditions, the growth of unions provided social bonds and a voice – and successful strikes did at least temporarily improve labor conditions for some unionized workers. However, it was the economic disarray of the 1930s that cemented the notion that labor unions would be equal partners at the negotiating table with industrial employers (Chaison 2005).

Industrial automation through mindless implementation of AI-enabled robotics is not innocuous. The allure of short-term wins is alluring. The fix is in embracing and regulating the conditions around business models where that kind of development is not only discouraged but also not as profitable as the augmentation path. This will require algorithmic oversight on behalf of industry-wide ecosystems or standards bodies (perhaps even by government agencies) coupled with interoperability interventions as well as defining infrastructure roadmaps that govern industrial platforms. Algorithmic oversight refers to governance of the autonomous selection principles glued into our IT systems, telling machines what to do, and affecting anything from what gets recorded and valued to what gets done and how. If we think algorithms that govern social media and news flows are important, we should spend even more energy on manufacturing algorithms. What we make and produce is what we are as human beings.

# The Third Industrial Revolution's Informatization, Automation – And Neglect (20th Century)

The third industrial revolution, characterized by electronics and the invention of information technology, started to measure productivity and began to radically automate the work process so that mass production could begin. After the Second World War, the Toyota Production System, with terms such as lean, Kaizen, and its American corollary, Six Sigma, greatly facilitated automated production by emphasizing quality and accuracy. Joseph M. Juran (1951), the Romanian-born American engineer, invented a range of quality management techniques. The third industrial revolution, characterized by robotic automation, advanced analytics, and sensors, brought velocity, scope, and systems impact to industrial production.

In the post-war years, Toyota pioneered the *Japanese lean manufacturing* methods (e.g., *JIT, Kaizen, Kanban*), evolving Ford's flow of production concept and GM's mass production of the 1920s to 1940s. *Kanban*, a Japanese word meaning signboard, sign, or card, primarily uses visual cues to signal when an action should take place. For example, a card listing specific information can be sent from the shipping department to the assembly line requesting a certain number of products or parts. Kanban was first used in manufacturing environments by Taiichi Ohno of the Toyota Motor Company in the mid-twentieth century. Ohno had studied American supermarkets' stocking techniques, which took cues from real-time, in-store consumer demand, instead of only relying on demand-forecasting using historical data. The Toyota Production system relies on quickly identifying waste (Muda) as whatever does not add value to customers. The "Toyota Way" (Liker 2004) has resulted in high-quality cars with few defects, using fewer man-hours, less on-hand inventory, and half the floor space of its competitors (full disclosure, Trond has owned three Toyotas and Natan owned two).

Garden varieties of these *lean* approaches were, again, copied by both the Americans and the Europeans, with mixed results. According to Japanese experts in lean methods, it takes 10 years to fully learn and implement across an individual factory. Kanban is now commonly used in hospitals, offices, and warehouses across the world, who all use visual cues to trigger action such as moving materials, completing items sequentially in a workflow, replacing products, triggering emergency action, or combining information to start a task and move the finished material to the next stage of production.

The barcode was first invented in 1948 at Drexel University for the supermarket industry and patented in 1952. However, it only worked in the lab (Silverman 2015). It was not until the 1970s that electronic barcode scanners from the British company Plessey enabled Kanban to be implemented at industrial scale in the form of barcode labels. In electronic Kanban systems, barcodes are placed on items, on materials, or in specific locations. When more of something is needed, scanning the barcode sends a signal (nowadays an email or text) to the correct person or department to fill the request or send orders to external suppliers.

Kaizen, a Japanese term for "change for the better," began after World War II when Toyota first implemented quality circles in its production process, but only emerged as a business philosophy in the 1980s. By that time, it aimed at capturing and stimulating employee engagement through cultivating a long-term, organizationally shared, culturally aware focus on eliminating waste, tidiness, and standardization. Although the idea is philosophical in nature, the measurement tools are supposed to be quantifiable, and there is heavy emphasis on training. The famous five steps of this methodology (5S): Sort, Set in Order, Shine, Standardize, Sustain (from Japanese: *Seiri, Seiton, Seiso, Seiketsu, Shitsuke*) is a systematic, visual management approach whereby you go through everything in a space, decide what's necessary and what isn't, put things in order, clean, and set up procedures for performing these tasks on a regular basis.

Kaizen was singlehandedly introduced to a world audience by Masaaki Imai in his 1986 book, *Kaizen: The Key to Japan's Competitive Success* (Imai 1986), building on a business fad that had begun decades earlier at Toyota. In the American experience, this became translated into continuous improvement both at individual and factory levels, but lost the community aspect so important in Japanese business culture. In the end, American companies are more results oriented than process oriented, so any process improvement would seek validation through visible short-term results. Imai (1986) contrasts Kaizen with western companies' innovation focus.

Six Sigma, introduced by American engineer Bill Smith while working for Motorola in 1986, doubles down on gathering technical data, targeting process improvement to optimize the quality of the final product. The six "sigmas" (a standard deviation away from the mean in statistics) in question, Define, Measure, Analyze, Improve, and Control (DMAIC) map to a defect rate where three are above the mean and three below, yielding an extremely low defect rate.

Famous implementers of Six Sigma include Fortune 500 companies such as 3M, Bank of America, Caterpillar, General Electric, Honeywell, and Microsoft (Mbizm 2021), although few results are systematically documented beyond sketchy case studies. Today, a slew of organizations provide Six Sigma certification, including the American Society for Quality (ASQ), the Chartered Quality Institute (CQI), the Institute of Industrial and Systems Engineers (IISE), and a plethora of universities around the world (mostly in the US and Germany). A myriad of Six Sigma "Black Belts" with vested interests run around as itinerant change agents, either as free agents or as part of systems integrators and management consulting firms.

The trouble with Six Sigma, however, appears to be that it is narrowly designed to "fix an existing process" and arguably does not help so much in "coming up with new products or disruptive technologies" (Richardson 2007). It might also stifle creativity. Six Sigma lends itself to obsessing on perfecting a process and misusing inferential statistics to validate an exploratory model of how things should work as opposed to focusing on getting it right the first time. In short, Six Sigma's, at times, excessive metrics obsession is based on a narrow, bounded technical rationality and not on a human-centric understanding of workplace dynamics that includes being aware of the existing organizational culture or team dynamics.

> With the advance of industrial automation and shop floor machinery, particularly in the form of robots, some would say a dystopian future came a step closer, since robots threaten to replace a good percentage of jobs. That notion, however, is debatable, given that many of the jobs being replaced are not enormously desirable. Rather, many of the jobs most easily replaced by robots tend to be those commonly viewed (by those who don't want to do them) as "dangerous, dirty, and dull." The term originated from the Japanese expression 3K: *kitanai, kiken, kitsui* (respectively, 汚い "dirty," 危険 "dangerous," and きつい "demanding"). In some iterations, the third expression is not dull and not demanding, but rather, demeaning – adding a moral component.

The Israeli scientist Eliyahu M. Goldratt introduced his Theory of Constraints in his immensely popular industry novel, *The Goal*, and later in a book dedicated to the topic (Goldratt and Cox 1984; Goldratt 1990). Goldratt showed that systems typically are limited by a small number of constraints, where the "weakest link" can adversely affect the outcome, most detrimentally by stopping the assembly line. This simple yet immensely powerful finding serves as a warning to anybody trying to improve operations that have both humans and machines in the mix. Goldratt's warnings clearly apply to the fact that it's tough to apply robotics to any process, because what they do and don't do changes the work dynamics elsewhere in the production process.

Paradoxically, robotization places a greater emphasis on cognitive, organizational, and creative skills to compete for the jobs that are left. The jobs to be done also change. For one, it impacts those of us who find constant challenge and improvement a stressful element of work rather than a bonus. Adding to that, we cannot automatically assume that intensifying demands for knowledge work leads to an increased pool of desirable jobs. Some will be left behind. The workforce will start to self-select for the kinds of competencies that are in high demand. There will continue to be tiers within the workforce, perhaps less based on the physical versus mental characteristics of the job and more on the cognitive demands of the job.

Interestingly, so-called dull, demanding, or demeaning jobs that are not automated because that is too hard to do, may bring higher wages. Such jobs in high demand will, at times, be filled by migrant workers looking for higher wages than in their home country. However, what is dull to one person is not dull to another. What is demanding depends on your skills, attitudes, and physical readiness. Even what is considered to be demeaning is culturally specific, and even personal. All depends on context, culture, situation, economic imperatives, and legal context. To be clear, we don't think robots are a bad idea. It should be okay to take away jobs that humans never should have been doing in the first place. Still, humans will continue to be needed for our cognitive skills. The thing to bear in mind is that there is no war between humans and robots. In fact, in an operational context, they are not to be seen as separate things. To work well, there has to be operational symbiosis between humans and robots. That symbiotic relationship became possible through the increasing digitalization of the interface between humans and machines allowing for a richer set of information exchange.

# The Fourth Industrial Revolution, Digital Systems Acceleration – And Interference (Late 20th Century)

In Klaus Schwab's (2016) classic account, the "velocity, scope, and systems impact" is what characterizes the breakthroughs we have been witnessing over the past decades. Arguably, every industry is being impacted by AI, IoT, robotics, autonomous vehicles, knowledge access, drastically increased processing power, and mobile devices fusing together. The impact on workers is clearly a need for reskilling at an enormous scale, given the pace of new technologies that is constantly being adopted by industry.

Yet, as much as digital technology promises to accelerate work, human work does not necessarily accelerate at the same pace. At least, it is not a given. This was something many implementers, managers, employers, and executives got wrong, and some are still getting wrong, in the fourth industrial revolution. For example, accelerating data collection by novel machine monitoring software does nothing for someone who cannot access that information, who sees it every two weeks, or who only hears about it as a controlling move from their supervisor. Even those asked to collect data in the form of key performance indicators (KPIs), a set of quantifiable measurements used to gauge a company's overall long-term performance, might experience unneeded stress. Nothing is worse than garbage in-garbage out KPIs. If you measure too much, or measure the wrong thing, then you create what lean methodology calls "waste." As pointed out long ago in Peters and Waterman's (1982) book *In Search of Excellence*, becoming "data rich and information poor" (DRIP) is detrimental. In manufacturing, you then become a slave to automation. The content of any spreadsheet needs to be defended, contextualized, and justified. If people believe they measure the right thing, there's a chance they might be motivated to improve. If not, KPIs become your worst enemy.

What matters to individual workers – at any level in the organization – is the degree to which they have autonomy in their daily work tasks and have a feeling that they control the (to them) essential aspects of their own work habits (Fuller et al. 2019). Just allow us to make one comparison at this point. Consider for a moment the introduction of ATM machines, which automated the process of depositing or withdrawing money, and the next iteration, which was online banking. Both were sold to consumers as conveniences, but neglected to emphasize that it also entailed the loss of a relationship with your local banker, a community function. At the end of the day, few people cry many tears over the loss of local bank branches (although some still do). But now consider remote work. If it is a privilege to work from home, which you have to apply for and only is given to 10% of the workforce upon merit, it might be viewed as a perk.

The mediation that digital technologies bring with them is not innocent in the sense that it is neutral. AI, IoT devices, robotics, autonomous vehicles, and the algorithms that govern them, none are value agnostic. The creators of each embedded these technologies, gadgets, devices, and systems with physical form factors, languages (written in a certain computer code perhaps), personalities, and typical usage scripts that can (and will be) deviated from but not without consequences. You want to implement warehouse robotics? You will be purchasing a domain-specific robot that works best for a certain set of use cases. Your shop floor better look similar to the one the robot was trained on – if not, you need to spend a lot of time implementing and adapting it. You want to automate your shop floor completely? Historically, you had to fence off most industrial robots because they were deemed dangerous to humans (and some were). Contemporary sensor technology is changing this with the advent of built-in sensors that give the robot ambient awareness. There are even co-bots, robots built to collaborate more effectively with human workers. There is a branch of AI, labeled emotion AI, that aims to read facial expressions and respond adequately to human moods.

Yet for all this progress, we are still stuck in the fourth industrial era. Technology, as we observe it on the factory floor (or in offices), is still built to control, measure, and speed up industrial processes. Technology does not do a good enough job at transforming those processes into human-centric work where meaning, empathy, cultural connection, and team spirit are key elements in the equation. The medium became the message. The tool dominated over the toolmaker and certainly was detrimental to the craftsman's autonomy. We traded long-term sustainability for short-term efficiency. As a result, the 4.0 mindset is not just techno-deterministic; it is also, ultimately, destructive for humans.

In rugby, a scrum, deployed as a means to restart play after an interruption, is formed by the players who are designated forward binding together in three rows. The scrum then engages with the opposition team so that the players' heads are interlocked with those of the other side's front row. Ken Schwaber and Jeff Sutherland co-developed the Scrum framework in the early 1990s to help organizations struggling with complex development projects with a big backlog to still prioritize and complete the most valuable tasks. In a scrum, the team picks tasks and uses a sprint (usually two to four weeks) to complete its work, but it meets each day to assess its progress. The Scrum Master keeps the team focused on its goal, which is to turn the backlog into shippable products. After that, the team does a quick retrospective and picks another sprint. Scrum Alliance (www.scrumalliance .org), founded in 2001, is now a membership organization of more than one million professionals on a mission to "create agile workplaces that are joyful, prosperous, and sustainable."

The first group to recognize that there was a better way to develop engineering products was the software community. In the early 2000s, a small group of software industry leaders met in Snowbird, Utah, agreeing to what is now known as the "Agile Manifesto" and founding the Agile Alliance, today a diverse community of more than 72,000 people (aka Agilistas). The main idea behind its 12 principles was to quickly build working software and get it into the hands of end users in order to get rapid feedback on the software's scope, direction, and usability. Baked into this idea was the willingness on the part of software developers to make changes as they learned more about how their software was being utilized. This was in contrast to what in engineering methodology is known as *waterfall* methodology where teams complete one step before moving on to the next in a sequence.

As these ideas caught on, the manifesto soon became the "Agile movement," and a decade later, in 2011, consultant to Chrysler, Kent Beck, presented new ideas on how to accelerate software delivery through continuous delivery of code, which he labeled "extreme programming." In 2016, the *DevOps Handbook* (Kim et al. 2016) was published, where four software engineers led by Gene Kim iterated how to create "world class agility, reliability and security in technology organizations" by cleverly integrating product management, development, QA, IT operations, and information security functions to bridge the so-called "IT vs. OT divide," which we will discuss throughout our book, through "flow, feedback and continual learning."

But while *DevOps* goes in the right direction, it is not a fully human-centric system. Instead, software-centered principles rule the day instead of usability as well as workforce considerations. Moreover, the measurement systems, and the metrics involved, favor technologists and managers rather than workers. To start reversing that historical mistake, a thorough revision of basic principles is needed, which is what the fifth industrial revolution should have been all about, but does not yet seem to be (which is why we earlier alluded to that reflection process as a possible sixth industrial revolution). Either way, that revolution also must start to address important issues such as how work actually gets accomplished. Trust cannot be assumed in an environment built on antagonistic worker-manager relationships. Despite decades of studying workplace sociology, our understanding of why people get stuff done is limited. Because of that, knowing how to fix problems or become more efficient at it, often eludes managers. What seems clear is that step one is to tailor frameworks to reality and the context shop floor teams, factories, and organizations are facing as opposed to tailor work challenges to frameworks (Perrow 1986).

# The Fifth Industrial Revolution's Decentralized Augmentation – And the Risk of Leaderless Management (21st Century)

With COVID-19, which changed industry priorities overnight, we are arguably about to complete the fourth and perhaps move into a fifth industrial revolution, which is nearly completely digitized. The next advancement is not further automation, but human augmentation. Robots evolve into co-bots that increasingly can work alongside humans in the workplace. Sensors throughout the workplace can deliver data to human controllers. Frontline operations platforms provide visibility and give control over the work process back to the shop floor workers in significant ways.

The industrial use cases of augmented reality technologies have started to accelerate in military and automotive sectors. Microsoft recently won a huge contract for its Hololens technology for the US military (Gregg and Greened 2021). Finnish AR maker Varjo's industrial grade mixed reality is training astronauts to dock at the International Space Station (ISS) and helping car maker Volvo develop new cars by enabling them to experiment with many new prototypes in realistic online environments before pushing the production button on an (expensive) physical prototype (Undheim 2021). Even so, the industrial augmentation that will have the largest impact within this decade is of a much more subdued kind: it consists of industrial software developed to enable frontline industrial workers to do their job better, with more autonomy, and whilst retaining meaning, control, and pride in their work.

When this type of augmentation is completed, we will arguably be left with a certain amount of decentralized production as well as consumption, leading some to assume that remote work might near term become a reality even for frontline industrial workers. It is our view that this will take a long time. For now, we are left with a transitional period where adjusting to a fully digitized workday will entail continued engagement with the physical shop floor, face-to-face interactions at work, and coordination that blends online and offline work – a hybrid situation where computers, systems, machines, and robots need to blend together to accomplish the tasks at hand. On the bright side, real-time data and analysis is the "new gold" and allows for less control. The control is transformed to data-driven decision-making and thus puts the people who do the work with higher ability to make good decisions, resulting in less of a need for old-school leadership.

At this early point in our exposition of what augmented means and might become in the emerging sixth industrial revolution, we have to admit the following: as positive as we feel the general thrust of augmentation has the potential to become, there are also significant risks.

One key risk is leaderless operations at the lower tiers of management and among entry level supervisors as a result of complete decentralization of production. In economic terms, you could call it disintermediation, or cutting the important intermediaries that used to provide context, trust, and explanation across geographical distance. Imagine a global business without a salesforce and management, where manufacturing starts to resemble e-commerce even for complex industrial products and infrastructure. Who will truly be in charge? Will the number of management layers finally shrink as has been predicted with every new industrial and technological era? Moreover, as augmented workers start to dominate the workforce, there is also the potential for discrimination based on cognitive impairment or lack of entrepreneurial or polymathic skill or disposition. We wanted to flag these risks to point out that even if technology somehow becomes our friend, business and society are still left with all the organizational and societal factors that inhibit perfect communication between humans, such as cultural diversity, class, status, and cognitive variability. Technological augmentation may, even in its most humanistic implementations, still serve to highlight such differences as opposed to hide or make them insignificant.

If the "deskless" workforce represents up to 80% of the workforce, the truly industrial component of that may still represent a significant proportion. Yuval Marcus's reanalysis of US Bureau of Labor Force Statistics shows that frontline operations represent 23% of total employment (Marcus, personal communication). This includes maintenance occupations; technicians (excluding health); natural resources; construction; production occupations; laborers; freight, stock, and material movers; stockers; and order fillers. While this figure includes construction and cleaning services, it excludes many other "frontline" fields like healthcare, education, foodservice, and transportation.

Workers have been severely discriminated against for almost five centuries of the industrial era, and almost certainly for countless centuries before that. Even if the working conditions become more humane and motivating, the differences in salary, status, and opportunities between senior leaders and shop floor workers are likely to persist. Yes, technology is empowering humans. However, that strong potential is there to be realized – it is not a given. When you take workers who did not finish high school and give them a computer with data and training, you are showing them they can play in society today through their job, and that is truly humanizing technology. Technology is empowering humans only when it facilitates social mobility or at the very least makes individuals and teams happier, wealthier, or more fulfilled. You cannot use a company's share price, productivity, innovation capability, or meteoric rise to fame as a proxy for such social effects. However, when you make workers out of dropouts who did not even finish high school, give them a work challenge, a context, and a computer with data and training, you are showing them they can play in society today, not tomorrow, through their job. When that happens, we are watching truly humanizing technology at play.

# The Sixth Industrial Revolution – Singularity, or What Happens Next (22nd Century)?

We are currently only at the beginning of the era of augmentation. It is important to realize that it will take time. Therefore, it is perhaps not possible at this stage to reflect on what this will mean when augmentation comes to fruition, and is (potentially) complemented by yet another advancement, but we have to try. The reason is urgency. It is becoming evident that we don't have much time before the degradation of our biosphere will catch up with all of these generations of previous extractive industrialization.

Current advancements in energy efficiency generation are not enough to achieve emission neutrality and technology is not there to build fully autonomous systems that begin to regenerate the biological ecosystem. While we can make great strides, and should, those are next generation systems that will need another few decades to achieve the kind of systemic impact that this decade's augmentation can have already – especially if we are talking about large-scale biological machines that carry out present day industrial tasks. We would then quite likely be near the level of technological prowess where a bounded type of singularity is achieved for multiple key tasks, meaning that artificial intelligence becomes smarter than humans for things such as factory operations, preparatory decision-making collateral, and even systemic self-repair, where robots can carry out their own restoration to factory conditions given that material resources are made available to them.

In our estimation, this next era won't be happening any time soon. We need step change improvements in an array of fields, and synthetic biology must be a fully understood innovation platform integrated with materials science, which might take several decades, perhaps more. First, we are likely looking at 20–50 years, perhaps more, of humans and machines working together and honing each other's skills in unison. This is why we are writing a book on *augmented lean*, a paradigm likely to shift our intention to the right challenges. If a pervasive focus on augmented lean does not happen across industry, we would not get to this next paradigm shift even in the next century, that we are fairly certain about. Simultaneously, we have to handle supply chains, which need to be completely reconfigured. Just-in-time was a nice idea but global disruptions, wars, pandemics, and other $x$-factors now means nearshoring is not only more economically viable, but an imperative fail-safe that needs to be baked into our thinking.

Realistically, even with surprise innovations, as well as significant momentum and joining of forces between public and private investment, this is the next century's challenge. That is not to say that we shouldn't prepare for it, just that other challenges and opportunities that will occur on the way there, such as the near collapse of existing biological systems and an ongoing irreversible reduction in biodiversity, mitigating fallout caused by previous industrial revolutions, is what we need to focus on now.

# CONCLUSION

Today's industrial frontline workforce, with a global footprint of over 350 million workers, has been underserved by technology. This is a paradox, considering that five decades of industrialization has been almost singularly focused on scaling production using machines.

In the next chapter, building on the historical foundation we established in Chapter 1, we will take a fresh look at the industrial productivity paradigms, from *classic lean* via *agile* to *digital lean*, the latter being the latest but still highly underestimated change that will determine the fate of the Industry 4.0 and likely the Industry 5.0 eras. As these are management paradigms, we will still mainly focus on the role of leaders. Throughout the following chapters, we work our way toward the approach we recommend to truly embracing the reality of a workforce that is asserting itself and where its, at times radical empowerment is the main source of competitive advantage. Our approach is *augmented lean* and it entails *significantly* more than *lean* plus *digital*.

# REFERENCES

Chaison, G. (2005). *Unions in America*. Los Angeles: Sage.

Dima, A. (2021). Short history of manufacturing: from Industry 1.0 to Industry 4.0. *Kfactory.eu*. https://kfactory.eu/short-history-of-manufacturing-from-industry-1-0-to-industry-4-0/ (accessed 12 March 2022).

Fuller, J., Wallenstein, J., Raman, M., de Chalendar, A. (May 2019). *Future Positive*. Published by BCG, Harvard Business School.

Goldratt, E.M., and Cox, J. (1984). *The Goal*. Croton-on-Hudson, NY: North River Press.

Goldratt, E.M. (1990). *The Theory of Constraints*. Croton-on-Hudson, NY: North River Press.

Gregg, A. and Greene, J (2021). Microsoft wins $21 billion Army contract for augmented reality headsets. *Washington Post* (31 March). https://www.washington post.com/business/2021/03/31/microsoft-army-augmented-reality/ (accessed 22 October 2021)

Imai, M. (1986). *Kaizen: the Key to Japan's Competitive Success.* New York: McGraw-Hill Education.

Juran, J.M. (1951). *Juran's Quality Handbook.* The University of Michigan.

Kim, G., Humble, J., Debois, P., and Willis, J. (2016) *The DevOps Handbook.* Portland, Oregon: IT Revolution Press.

Liker, J.K. (2004). *The Toyota Way.* New York: McGraw-Hill.

Marcus, Y. (2022). Personal communication. Re-analysis of Labor Force Statistics from the Current Population Survey. https://www.bls.gov/cps/cpsaat11.htm (accessed 12 March 2022).

MBizM (2021). Companies that have successfully implemented Lean Six Sigma. https://www.mbizm.com/companies-that-have-successfully-implemented-lean-six-sigma/ (accessed 25 October 2021)

Perrow, C. (1986). *Complex Organizations: A Critical Essay.* New York: McGraw-Hill.

Peters, T.J., and Waterman, R.H. (1982). *In Search of Excellence.* New York: Harper and Row.

Plant Automation Technology (2021). Top 10 Largest Manufacturing Nations in the World in 2020. *Plant Automation Technology* (accessed 25 November 2021)

Richardson, K. (2007). The "Six Sigma" factor for Home Depot. *Wall Street Journal Online* (7 January). https://www.wsj.com/articles/SB116787666577566679 (accessed 26 October 2021)

Rho, H.J., Brown, H., and Fremstad, S. (2020). A Basic Demographic Profile of Workers in Frontline Industries. *The Center for Economic and Policy Research (CEPR).* (April 7). https://cepr.net/a-basic-demographic-profile-of-workers-in-frontline-industries/ (accessed 22 March 2022).

Schwab, K. (2013). *The Fourth Industrial Revolution.* New York: Penguin.

Schwab, K. (2016). The Fourth Industrial Revolution: what it means, how to respond, *World Economic Forum* (14 Jan): https://www.weforum.org/agenda/2016/01/the-fourth-industrial-revolution-what-it-means-and-how-to-respond/ (accessed 22 October 2021).

Silverman, L. (2015). Barcodes: A Brief History. TrackAbout (19 November). https://corp.trackabout.com/blog/barcodes-brief-history (accessed 26 October 2021).

Taylor, F.W. (1911). *The Principles of Scientific Management.* New York: Harper & Brothers.

Undheim, T.A. (2021, ep. 9). The Fourth Industrial Revolution post-COVID-19. Episode 9/. Interview with Francisco, Betti, Head of Advanced Manufacturing and Production, World Economic Forum. *Augmented Podcast.* https://www.augmentedpodcast.co/the-fourth-industrial-revolution-post-covid-19/ (accessed 29 November 2021).

Undheim, T.A. (2021). Industrial-grade Mixed Reality. Futurized podcast. https://www.futurized.org/industrial-grade-mixed-reality/ (accessed 22 October 2021).

UNIDO (2020) UNIDO's Competitive Industrial Performance Index 2020: Country Profiles published. UNIDO. (September 7). https://www.unido.org/news/unidos-competitive-industrial-performance-index-2020-country-profiles-published (accessed 25 November 2021).

Watters, A. (2015). The invented history of "The Factory Model of Education." *Hackereducation* (April 25). http://hackeducation.com/2015/04/25/factory-model (accessed 5 January 2022).

WEF (2020). Global Competitiveness Report Special Edition 2020: How Countries are Performing on the Road to Recovery. *World Economic Forum.* (December 16). https://www.weforum.org/reports/the-global-competitiveness-report-2020 (accessed 25 November 2021).

World Economic Forum Global Lighthouse Network (2021). https://www.weforum.org/projects/global_lighthouse_network (accessed 29 November 2021).

# CHAPTER 2

# FROM CLASSIC LEAN VIA AGILE TO DIGITAL LEAN AND BEYOND

W hen Mark Freedman graduated from the University of Vermont in 2009, he had studied biology and engineering. However, in the workplace, he rapidly found himself as an operations excellence engineer driving continuous improvement through the Japanese-inspired kaizen approach. He was certainly no software developer. *Kaizen* is Japanese and means change for the better, or in better English it would mean continuous improvement, from *kai* meaning change and *zen* meaning peaceful, relaxed, and aware. Freedman says: "To me, [doing kaizen] means having the mindset of continuous improvement, being honest and transparent about your problems, making things visual, and then solving them and being willing to fail" (Augmented 2021, ep. 22). Freedman says, "with all change we have to respect the current state." In other words, before we start to change something, we have to take in what is and recognize why it is that way.

Lean is about designing a process to tackle inefficiencies in process, people, stock, or quality. The core concepts are, of course, waste reduction and efficiency. Lean privileges quick paths to value over the waterfall model of optimal planning, for the simple reason that an operational environment will never be perfect and that the search for perfection could be detrimental to everyday operations. The only operational way to integrate a lean approach as an integrated process improvement approach is to create awareness across the teams involved about the need to stay active to discover and act on inefficiencies (Drew et al. 2004, pp. 18–22).

Right before Freedman discovered the app-based approach to digital manufacturing (e.g., through the startup Tulip), he was about to suggest to his employer that he would build something like it himself. Having himself ordered one of Tulip's factory kits and experimented with it for a few days, he quickly decided to jump ship. Why work at arm's length when this product seemed to be exactly what he had been looking for? Without deep digital skills, Freedman had been able to create an application that made a difference on the shop floor. Within weeks of joining, he became a resource at Tulip, merging *classic* lean with digital skills (see Interview 2.1). He started to embody a digital lean attitude that is contagious and exhilarating: "I'm so passionate about all these new technologies that are available, specifically around *no-code* stuff. How could you use software in kaizen now that we have all these cell phones in our pockets and you can do so many things with them? You swipe on your cell phone and just with your finger and a pizza arrives or something like this, and you go to manufacturing and it's not like that" (Augmented 2021, ep. 22).

**Interview 2.1** Freedman's Factory: What Is No-Code? Interview with Mark Freedman. Episode 22. Augmented podcast

Freedman's engagement with customers stimulates them to think out of the box and to keep the focus on finding the best approach, with an open mind as to which tools might be needed to implement. He says:

I love best practice. I go to a factory and literally my favorite thing to do is to walk around together. I'll talk with the managers, the people who are a couple levels above the operation, but then, I'm like, can I just run, or walk around for a while? Can I just talk to people? Do you mind? So, I just stroll about and talk to water spiders [in Japanese: *Mizusumashi*, e.g., a person in a warehouse or production environment who is tasked with keeping workstations fully stocked with materials, thus controlling the continuous flow of productivity] and look at [kanban] boards. And I find there's always people who are making it work, who are facing problems every single day and covering them up, addressing them. If those people aren't there, then the factory has a problem.

When imagining a problem and a solution, Freedman does not go straight to the tech. He goes to the people first. After that, the processes emerge naturally. He says: "I don't care what we use to solve problems. The simplest solution is what I want to do. I want something that's gonna make an impact quickly that people can get behind and is going to sustain.

To Freedman, discovery by walking about (see Peters and Waterman 2004) even applies to solving problems with enterprise resource planning (ERP) systems (see Interview 2.2):

> I think the approach that you'll find I most often take is what is, I want to be as close to the floor as possible when looking at this. So, as I'm looking at an ERP, we could talk about the schema of the database and its table structures and so forth, because I've definitely spent time looking into these and trying to make sense of them. But none of that really matters at that level of detail on the floor. People just want to know: "What am I supposed to do right now? What is this part that just showed up in my system? What is this?" So I care more about the people on the floor. What's their way of dealing with things? Whether the supervisors or planners or hourly associates, whoever's dealing with the actual work that needs to be done, how do they experience the ERP? That's what I care about. I always care about that person.

**Interview 2.2** Freedman's Factory: Introduction. Interview with Mark Freedman. Episode 15. Augmented podcast

# WHAT IS DIGITAL LEAN?

The next generation of lean management has had the potential benefit of digital tools. Digital lean allows for real-time improvements because changes are logged digitally and at times autonomously and are immediately available to adjust the work process. Through standardizing technology, you may be able to spot overproduction, inventory, defects, waiting time, and a host of other problems on the shop floor (Laapher et al. 2020).

Is digital lean simply a continuation of efficiency efforts, amplified by automation? Or is it the beginning of a new era of augmented operations that is distinct, empowering, and still evolving? How does digital lean manifest itself on the shop floor? The answers to these questions have revolutionary potential. If you go wrong with digital in a manufacturing environment, it has detrimental consequences, it is expensive, and it is not always fixable. If you get it right, it has positive spillover effects across society because production and supply chains move across to enterprises and eventually to consumers and in the end affects all of us. IT moved at the speed of the internet, too fast to spot a revolution. In operational technology (OT), for example, industrial process technology monitoring industrial equipment, assets, processes, and events (Gartner 2022), there is a massive tectonic shift happening, and it is accelerating.

While digital lean in and of itself can be powerful, it all depends on what type of digital tools are available. A common objection many lean practitioners have to technology is that it just becomes another form of waste. In traditional manufacturing execution systems (MESs), digital oversight comes at a cost. The reason is that the system might be complicated to implement, expensive to run, and does not yield the real-time data directly to the workers who would need it to adjust their day-to-day operations. In fact, by many lean practitioners, a MES itself is considered waste. Workers have to use extra non–value-add time to serve the system with information. It is a managerial control system, albeit in digital form. When digital lean is implemented and run top-down, you lose a lot of the benefits of lean management, and you risk simply running a digital operation, not really a lean operation. This is at the heart of many implementation failures in the deployment of large, complex organizational IT systems.

# BEYOND DIGITAL LEAN: HOW INDUSTRIAL NO-CODE EMPOWERS OPERATORS

Building on what we have come to know from contemporary software applications that don't have a (long) learning curve, industrial *no-code* attempts the same thing, but with software written for the physical world, which is immeasurably harder to do because production cannot go down and you don't get second chances. We learned from Mark Freedman that Tulip's deeply humanistic approach to no-code is rooted in the shop floor experience and in trying to reflect, but also question, factory floor behavior while respecting the "current state." This is, of course, another way of saying that technology, and frameworks, must respect company culture, people, teams, individuals, and context, not the other way around.

There is an ongoing technology revolution in manufacturing, and it is turning the industry upside down. We are in the midst of it and are watching centuries of competition wither and new giants rise (Gartner LCAP 2021), including manufacturing applications such as Power Apps by Microsoft, Mendix by Siemens, Salesforce, Oracle Application Express (APEX), and Appian. Many of these tools were not initially created to address manufacturing or even operational challenges but are now offering such tools.

Software-driven manufacturing (Mirandette 2019) will favor manufacturers who encourage decentralized decision making to access complete real-time data about the essential aspects of production. *No-code* gives tools to the people who actually do the work so they themselves may create their own workflows. This is democratizing access to the technology, and is helping organizations transform bottom up. With proper implementation of *no-code* tools, you can implement them quickly. The advantage is

58

that you can collect as much information as you want and if you analyze it once, it will refresh automatically, yielding exponential uplift on process oversight. In contrast, MES does not require engineering work where you typically end up mapping everything and uploading it to a system of record. Then, you need to write down all process flows, build the rules, and act as if you have more control than you actually do, because meanwhile, the actual production system on the floor changes quickly. Typically, an MES is on-premises software. This introduces additional constraints in an otherwise cloud-enabled supply chain.

*Low-code* and *no-code* (where industrial users can deploy apps to their operation with little to no software knowledge) and 3D printing give engineers new tools to engineer faster, better, and more creatively. However, this is all quite new. It wasn't until 2014 that "low-code" platform was coined (by industry analyst Forrester), as platforms that "enable rapid delivery of business applications with a minimum of hand-coding and minimal upfront investment in setup, training, and deployment." From there, there has been a rapid evolution toward "no code" (e.g., platforms accessible to any business user that allows non-software folks to create software). Rapid visual tools produce apps and allow for data manipulation and collection. As a result, scores of workers can collaborate to get a result that is integrated with other systems, machines, and sensors. The biggest learning curve with such low-code environments is not the tools themselves, but the governance. There always needs to be rules and agreements on how to use the tool within a company's existing tech and product stack.

However, there is still an array of differences between the early, diversified technology companies with their own enterprise software platforms and components (e.g., SAP's enterprise resource platform, EPIC's digital health records, Oracle's database, IBM's cloud environment) that have evolved in the last few years, including low-code (e.g., Mendix) and *no-code* platforms (e.g., Airtable, Bubble, Pipefy, Torq, Tulip, Y24, Wix, Workato), which require hours, not months, of training. Some of them are generic and started as office worker productivity tools; others have more of an industrial flavor. What happens to the pressures of productivity, leadership principles, and best practice? Do the core principles of lean stay the same with new, increasingly digitized operations? What is the difference between traditional information technology (IT) development and operational technology (OT) development, which entails programming a physical–digital environment?

# Cloud-Native Workplace Tools

Salesforce, Google Workspaces, Netsuite, Workday, Atlassian, Slack, Zendesk, and Hubspot can be said to represent the cloud-native group of software platforms of the 2020s era. Each of them comes with a software-as-a-service (SaaS) business model. Each is helping redefine the contemporary workplace. The pivotal role to be played by such systems as they increasingly permeate the industrial workplace, too, and simplify and adapt to those requirements, are bound to be profound.

So far, these companies may be used among office workers across industries, but their software has limited impact in operational environments and particularly among the deskless industrial workforce. The reason is that even though they have mobile apps, too, their software is (for the most part) tethered to the knowledge worker who has access to a desk, monitor, and keyboard at work and at home, and who can use a laptop when commuting or traveling. In fact, the vast majority of dollars spent on developing innovative new software over the past decade has been spent on one valuable category of worker, the "white collar" digital knowledge worker as opposed to on another valuable category of worker, the "blue collar" cyber-physical worker. This is despite the fact that industrial work has gotten much more knowledge intensive in this same time period, and, in principle (if not always in practice) relies on the same plethora of advanced technologies, including AI/ML, AR/VR, IoT, cloud, edge, robotics, and more. We will spend quite a bit of energy trying to not only understand what this discrepancy has meant for industrial progress, but also how it affects productivity overall.

Industrial tech was slow to embrace cloud-native tools. By cloud-native, we mean tools that were built with cloud computing in mind as opposed to being onsite software that has to be installed on physical machines in a distinct location – with one exception. Founded in 2012, OnShape was based in Cambridge, Massachusetts (USA), with offices in Singapore and Pune, India, and it took on the charge of putting CAD on the cloud, setting off a fire in industrial companies that are used to onsite solutions. The leadership team includes several engineers and executives who originated at SolidWorks. Co-founder Jon Hirschtick: "I saw what was happening with Google Docs [2006], Salesforce [2009], NetSuite [1998], Workday [2005], and Zendesk [2007]. [They were rethinking] the whole app. The data and the tools live in one place in the cloud and everyone accesses it. You eliminate all this hardware crap, license codes, and service packs [...] by design" (Augmented 2021, ep. 23). These early advances deploying cloud-computing in manufacturing replaced work done on manual drafts. These workers never look back, and this is what is happening in operations today at full force, across a myriad of operational areas (e.g., work instructions, quality management, process execution).

# Connected Worker Tools – Point Solutions to a Larger Problem

Connected worker platforms aim to give industrial companies the tools they need to collaborate on manufacturing processes and supply chain operations with increased efficiency, better safety, and higher worker satisfaction. It is the beginning of what the World Economic Forum (2022) calls the augmented workforce, in which business is beginning to harness Industry 4.0 technologies for workforce empowerment (WEF 2022). The trend is that companies are emerging to fix the core inefficiencies created by legacy systems by starting with point-solutions (small parts of the bigger problem) that are relatively easy to create and that are at least marginally better than incumbents. What they have going for them is their ease of use, which is no small feat.

The emerging startup space in manufacturing includes a few other startups that have started to chip at the notion of digital thread and worker connectivity for industrial workers. Michigan-based eFlex Systems, founded in 1988, developed one of the earliest work instruction software platforms. However, even though the company serves customers globally with installations on four continents and in 20 countries, it has not gained global, industrywide traction. We had to wait until 2015–2020 for the true explosion of connected worker tools for industry brought by startups. These days, US startups Instrumental, Parsable, Poka, and Vention, stand out as connected worker tools for industry.

Instrumental, a manufacturing optimization startup founded in 2015 by ex-Apple product design engineers, aims to proactively discover, root cause, and remediate manufacturing issues, strongly emphasizing user needs and workflows that have previously been neglected. Its cloud and AI tools support global engineering and operations functions as they eliminate waste and deliver better products.

Lawrence Whittle, CEO of San Francisco-based Parsable, founded in 2013, says that the connected worker market is a multistage process: "Stage one, which is table stakes, is creating digital versions of static work instructions. [...] Stage two is when you can start to capture data that's not currently captured by any systems in real time" (O'Donnell 2020).

Poka, a Canadian startup founded in 2014, is focused on connecting factory workers to their colleagues, the machines they operate, and the data and systems that support production. Vention, a next-generation digital manufacturing platform for machine design founded in 2016, enables manufacturing professionals to design, order, and assemble custom factory equipment in just a few days.

Point solutions often don't aspire to be true platforms or in any event have a long path to get there. As a result, they cannot be reasonably expected to provide full solutions to complex production challenges across industrial operations as a whole. Despite contributing valuable tools to an emerging reality of connected workers on the factory floor, many of these startups remain clever tools that don't fully connect across the value chain in a company. This is not just because these startups are young – understandably, such breadth takes time to develop – but also because they, as a strategy, attempt to automate and connect "on top." However, providing surface level insight, derived from monitoring what humans do, does not by itself improve operational dynamics.

The contrast would be against MESs that typically excel at so-called machine monitoring, or collecting data from machines, but are "built for machines, not humans." As we have pointed out, the era of building systems that cater more to machines than to humans should be over. The connected worker approach works for some initial big wins against stodgy MES, but has the potential to introduce problems later. What these tools typically don't do is incorporate logic into workflows, connect apps with tables, and use that to build powerful, clickable real-time dashboards. Most importantly, while some of these tools might be easy enough to implement, they don't always enable engineers on the client side or on the shop floor to themselves create apps for solving problems.

What these startups show is that the efforts by existing industrial systems attempting to modernize their solutions is not proceeding fast enough. As a result, companies are emerging to fix the core inefficiencies created by legacy systems.

# BEYOND
# POINT SOLUTIONS

We will now briefly explain the company we know best, Tulip. We are attempting to overcome the point-solution trap that startups face. Instead, we provide a platform that addresses legacy problems with simplicity and interoperabil-ity, designed as a first-class tool for frontline engineers and workers. The chal-lenge Tulip took on was to build a solid foundation that, over time, can scale to most industrial use cases covered by traditional manufacturing execution sys-tems. Tulip is not a point-solution (e.g., akin to a connected worker platform). Rather, Tulip creates a new, broader category, a frontline operations platform. The platform fully integrates with legacy software, is generative, and allows users to create applications that fit their use cases, whatever those may be.

Some successful companies create their own product categories. Extraordinary companies lead movements. For that, it is often the case that it is "Better to be first, than be better" (Ries and Trout 1994). Salesforce created the cloud category and led the "no software" movement. Hubspot created the marketing automation category and led the inbound market-ing movement. Tulip has announced it is creating the category of front-line operations platform, empowering industrial engineers to change the way their businesses operate. That is possible because Tulip is built using *no-code* software. Using cloud-native apps that connect both directly to workers and to machines as well as sensors on the shop floor frees them up from awaiting the IT department to deploy sophisticated and simple solu-tions. However, only a few companies every decade can pull off creating categories or leading movements. Could it happen to Tulip? The thought experiment is exciting.

Tulip is a growth startup spun out of MIT Media Lab in 2014 in the midst of an epic industrial change that was, at that time at least, only fully understood in university labs and not yet in the industrial marketplace. Tulip is a connected frontline operations platform that connects the people, machines, devices, and the systems used in a production or logistics process in a physical location. Our own estimate is that about one in five global workers are frontline operators who are fundamentally deskless. Others have come to a far higher ratio (Emergence 2020). Their work envi-ronments are highly complex with work cells, sensors, benches, conveyor belts, and back-end systems in what constitutes a physical and digital environment, and they need a platform that is just as dynamic to support all the moving pieces. Just like knowledge workers, frontline workers need access to the right tools to get the data they need to stay competitive and to future-proof their operations.

Before we go further, we should be clear about our obvious bias in describing this company. One of the authors, Natan, co-founded and is CEO of Tulip, and the co-author, Trond, was instrumental in launching Tulip – through MIT – to its first enterprise customers, and has now spent a year interpreting Tulip's impact on the world through hundreds of interviews with employees, partners, competitors, investors, and clients, and is also working as an investor in the industrial space. Tulip's two other co-founders, Rony Kubat, the CTO of the company, and MIT Media Lab professor, Pattie Maes, both bring a perspective deeply steeped in the experience of experimenting with cyber-physical systems through a human lens. What matters is to always think of how to best empower humans, engineers, and workers, not inventing technologies that are looking for a user. Tulip is based on intelligence augmentation (IA), not augmented and/or artificial intelligence (AI) (see Chapter 9).

Tulip addresses numerous Frontline Operations use cases, including backend processes (work orders, connections to ERPs, BOMs), guided workflows (guided work instructions), real-time metrics (from people, machines, devices, sensors, and cameras), as well as process-data and insights (see Figure 2.1). It is a true *no-code* platform, meaning it takes no programming skills, and limited training even for engineers with little IT system user experience to build even sophisticated apps. If you can use PowerPoint and Excel, or Google Docs, you can use Tulip.

The distinctive feature is that Tulip augments and optimizes human-centric processes that match the client's workforce and existing approach. Tulip creates a system of digital continuous improvement where you can improve operations by digitizing paper processes, replace legacy software,

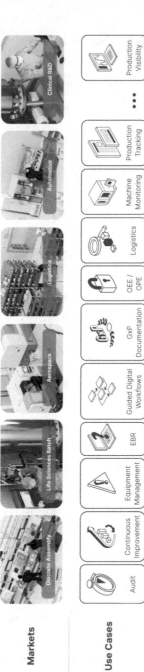

**Figure 2.1** Tulip Use Cases.

connect and monitor your machines, sensors, and smart tools, as well as augment and extend your databases or systems of record. A distinctive feature is the media-rich digital workflows you can easily create, which can allow you to alert shift supervisors to issues in cells with SMS messages or Andon lights. However, you can also connect systems all the way to ERP systems and shipment along the supply chain. Tulip serves clients in life sciences, discrete manufacturing, industrial (machine shops, automation), automotive, food and beverage, and luxury goods.

Tulip, and frontline operations systems to come will act as the system of engagement (with the workers) even though it could also be a system of record for the company (if there is none already). Tulip has a set of training tools, but aims to require days, not months, of training to get going, depending on initial familiarity with digital systems. That's the way *no-code* software (Hubspot, Workday, Slack) works in the nonindustrial sphere more familiar to desk workers. A process engineer is typically needed to build an app, but this person does not need to be a software engineer. The process engineer just needs to know how to understand the context of their process and translate it to a Tulip app and workflow. This is a challenge of its own because engineers don't always build the most user-friendly interfaces. Instead, what's important is to enable a true sandbox environment where things can adapt. Because little time is spent building, much more time is spent tweaking, experimenting, and innovating. Building *no-code* systems for industrial operations takes effort but is, undoubtedly, the way most industrial systems will work in the coming years.

In 2020, former McKinsey consultant Eddy Atkins, now at Tulip, held a day-training for 40 McKinsey ex-colleagues on their manufacturing practice team. They built a basic app taking a use case from a McKinsey implementation project and built it in 90 minutes. Atkins's take on lean is to "iteratively uncover small problems, solve them, standardize and share best practices in quick sprints" (Augmented 2021, ep. 36). Sounds simple, no? In reality, of course, it is a bit of an art more than it is a process you can simply copy. Atkins points out that even with *no-code*, you still need lean behavior. Without sharing improvements and giving management support, you may not break the prevailing mentality of "good enough." His take is that consulting firms' well laid plans often lead clients into pilot purgatory because the iterative loops are not run by the clients themselves, but strongly monitored by process consultants. Even the lighthouse approach of looking to best practices, is quite use case specific. In contrast, the tech gap is being closed by Tulip allowing process engineers to build apps themselves and experiment with the results (see Interview 2.3).

**Interview 2.3** Digital Lean.
Interview with Edward Atkins.
Episode 36. Augmented podcast.

# THE EMERGENCE OF FRONTLINE OPERATIONS

Even though information technology has been part of shop floors, factories, and manufacturing settings for decades, we don't think this technology (yet) has dramatically altered the reliance on age-old manual practices or tribal knowledge. This is perhaps an extreme view.

However, we can say that, because over the past decade, Natan and co-founder Rony Kubat have spent ample time at factory sites discovering that beyond the obvious need for advanced automation, a stunningly high number of low-hanging fruit is still there to pick for the right solution, manager, or lean improvement initiative (see Figure 2.2). From the business process perspective, the use cases include material management, kanban replenishment, exception handling, and overall equipment effectiveness (OEE; OEE n.d.), all of which may be relevant from an operational perspective and could influence the value chain if managers have access to that information. In fact, there is literally an IT tool (or many) already available for each of the following operational tasks: manufacturing, lab, quality, maintenance, logistics, R&D, engineering, planning, or service. However, they are seldom interconnected, or they take enormous amounts of resources, time, license fees, and systems integration work to put in place. This is a cost that only huge sites can afford (and are loathe to spend energy on).

**Figure 2.2** Frontline Operations Are Everywhere: On Shop Floors, in Labs, and at Warehouses.

However, even more stunningly, most of the existing tools are not made available or easy enough to access for the vast majority of manufacturing workers, those without office desks, who are itinerant, on the move, oscillating between activities that include process monitoring, assembling, fabricating, training, supervising, testing, material handling, quality control, quality assurance, disassembling, analyzing, servicing, or repairing. From the human operator's perspective, such use cases include formalizing (digitalizing) work instructions, chasing efficiencies in numerous other existing paper trails along the assembly line (and beyond), audit, and quality inspection.

In fact, over the past decade it has become obvious (to us) that industrial operations have begun to (radically) change with the advent of a confluence of sweeping developments – notably, advances in information technology across software and hardware, intensified globalization (as well as nationalist backlash in key industrial countries), supply chain disruptions (due to COVID-19 or just bottlenecks at innovation averse ports), and consumer expectations to see increased customization as they review, buy, and receive products through e-commerce, sustainability concerns, and more.

However, it is a gradual change without fully taking on board the opportunities that stem from deep digitalization that has occurred in other sectors of society, and indeed in the IT industry. One could argue that, in some sense, the sector has actually taken a step back, by, at times, adopting technologies that have cemented outdated business processes or the opposite, that force changes in business operations because of the rigidity of the technology solution.

What is needed is a new generation of solutions that build on the benefits of *low-code* and *no-code*, as outlined above, to unlock operations. To do so, it would be imperative to build in the flexibility of not relying on software programmers to tweak the solutions. That lets your team or whoever is closest to production adapt to new challenges. They are the best people to solve the problem, but whether they are engineers, machinists, CI, quality managers, or even the IT department, they more often than not can't (or have been taught not to because of prior misfortunes with self-built tools) code their own software or tools.

Decades of business as usual from cloud-only-in-name legacy systems have ignored the needs of industrial workers and created massive inefficiencies in precisely the areas they promised to improve. There's now an army of point solutions that fix small epiphenomena of that core inefficiency, but none of them address the root cause.

Jason Dietrich, head of commercial operations at Tulip (Augmented 2022, ep. 73; see Interview 2.4) said:

Think of frontline operations as a connected data and process management tool that connects people, systems and things, [including] machines, sensors, and scales where data is captured and needs to be represented [...] with a library of applications, as well as the ability [for a citizen developer] to build applications quickly that meet very specific needs. [Building apps] is an iterative process, with quick wins and a fail fast mentality, not a sequential, V-shaped deployment curve.

**Interview 2.4** The Challenge of Frontline Operations. Interview with Jason Dietrich, Head of Commercial Operations at Tulip. Episode 73. Augmented podcast.

A frontline operations platform deploys a Platform as a Service (PaaS) business model that allows people in industrial companies to build digital content with *no-code* (Apps + Data + Collaboration) to solve industrial challenges. Frontline operations represent a massive market opportunity. Using the weighted average share of industry as a percentage of GDP in 2008–2011 for 40 countries would put the frontline operations category at up to 27% of global GDP (Bolt and van Zanden 2020).

More broadly, according to IDC (2021), organizations are forecast to spend nearly $656 billion on future of work technologies in 2021, shifting work to a model that "fosters human-machine collaboration, enables new skills and worker experiences, and supports a work environment unbounded by time or physical space" and as they are "seeking automated decision support and virtual collaborative approaches, discrete and process manufacturing, the two largest spenders on Future of Work technology over the forecast period, are investing in key use cases like collaborative robotics, operational performance management, and 3D and digital product design and review for improved cost control and higher process efficiency." Increasing spending is good but not sufficient. For us, democratizing frontline operational technology is much more pressing than simply increasing focus, attention, and spending on the general area of productivity IT (Linder 2021).

# CONCLUSION

The path from classic lean via agile to digital lean is not as straightforward as it would seem. Digitalization is not the same across industries and certainly is more complicated in manufacturing settings because it exposes the lacking physical–digital interconnect in most off-the-shelf software solutions. Add to that the long-standing technological determinism among software vendors who haven't thought deeply enough about creating platforms and solutions tailored to people, teams, organizations, and contexts, rather than optimizing systems to communicate with machines, and you have the perfect storm.

In our view, manufacturing has evolved (comparatively) slower than other segments of society in the past few decades both because it is sufficiently complex that new innovations and technologies take time to mature and adapt into the sector, but also because legacy issues (technologies, mentalities, regulations, and more) prevent fast adoption. What's the solution? Rethinking how manufacturing again can lead through lean practices that cut across society, empower the workforce, and transform productivity across the board, the way pathbreaking industrial paradigms have tended to do throughout the centuries. We have, for now, called this emerging paradigm digital lean and have resisted to lean too much on established (yet evolving) terminology around "connected worker" or "augmented worker," which we will come back to in Chapters 5–8. For now, we want to hammer in that even though the humanistic angle, and awareness of workforce training is at the core of the challenge, it is a systems dynamics problem, not just a "technology issue" or a "people issue."

In the next chapter, we will explore the state of play in industrial tech software, a history of legacy software and machines that create a cyber-physical systems infrastructure that complicates innovation at the speed of software development.

# REFERENCES

Akella, P., and Prager, D. (2018). The state of human factory analytics. *Kearney* (October). https://www.kearney.com/digital/the-state-of-human-factory-analytics (accessed 27 October 2021).

Arctern Ventures (2021). ThinkIQ. Digital Manufacturing Transformation SaaS. Arctern Ventures Portfolio company. https://www.arcternventures.com/portfolio/thinkiq/ (accessed 27 October 2021).

Augmented (2022, ep. 73). The Challenge of Frontline Operations. Jason Dietrich, Head of Commercial Operations at Tulip. Episode 73. *Augmented podcast* (January 19). https://www.augmentedpodcast.co/the-challenge-of-frontline-operations/ (accessed 14 March 2022).

Augmented (2021, ep. 15). Freedman's Factory: Introduction. Interview with Mark Freedman. Episode 15. (May 12). https://www.augmentedpodcast.co/15 (accessed 26 October 2021).

Augmented (2021, ep. 22). Freedman's Factory: What is no-code? Interview with Mark Freedman. Episode 22. *Augmented podcast* (July 5). https://www.augmentedpodcast.co/freedmans-factory-what-is-nocode/ (accessed 26 October 2021).

Augmented (2021, ep. 36). Digital Lean. Interview with Edward Atkins. Episode 36. *Augmented podcast* (Aug 18). https://www.augmentedpodcast.co/digital-lean/ (accessed 26 October 2021).

Augmentir (2020). Augmentir – AI for the Connected Worker. *Augmentir*. You-Tube channel. https://www.youtube.com/watch?v=c2C5VCrEYY8 (accessed 27 October 2021).

Bolt, J., and van Zanden, J.L. (2020). Maddison style estimates of the evolution of the world economy. A new 2020 update. Working Paper WP-15. *The Maddison Project*. (October). https://www.rug.nl/ggdc/historicaldevelopment/maddison/publications/wp15.pdf (accessed 26 October 2021).

Brunelli, M. (2014). A quick history of PTC and PTC Creo. PTC.com (14 August). https://www.ptc.com/en/blogs/cad/a-quick-history-of-ptc-and-ptc-creo (accessed 26 October 2021).

Drew, J., McCallum, B., and Roggenhofer, S. (2004). *Journey to Lean*, London: Palgrave.

Drishti (2021). Drishti Trace™: Video traceability for manual assembly lines. Drishti. Products. https://drishti.com/products/trace (accessed 27 October 2021).

Encyclopedia.com (2021). Autodesk, Inc. https://www.encyclopedia.com/social-sciences-and-law/economics-business-and-labor/businesses-and-occupations/autodesk-inc (accessed 26 October 2021).

Emergence (2020). The Deskless Workforce. Emergence https://www.emcap.com/deskless-workforce (accessed 5 January 2022).

Gartner (2022). Operational Technology (OT). *Gartner Glossary*. https://www.gartner.com/en/information-technology/glossary/operational-technology-ot (accessed 12 March 2022).

Gartner LCAP (2021). Enterprise Low-Code Application Platforms (LCAP) Reviews and Ratings. Gartner https://www.gartner.com/reviews/market/enterprise-low-code-application-platform (accessed 26 October 2021).

GMI Insights (2020). SCADA Market Size. Global Market Insights (Jan 2020). https://www.gminsights.com/industry-analysis/scada-supervisory-control-and-data-acquisition-market (accessed 26 October 2021.

Griffith, E. (2015). Exclusive: SolidWorks vets raise $64 million for Onshape. *Fortune* (March 6). https://fortune.com/2015/03/06/exclusive-solidworks-vets-raise-64-million-for-onshape/ (accessed 26 October 2021).

HR News Desk (2021). Augmentir Announces New Product Features to Extend Leadership Position In AI-Based Performance Optimization for Frontline Work. *HR Tech Series* (August 5). https://techrseries.com/artificial-intelligence/augmentir-announces-new-product-features-to-extend-leadership-position-in-ai-based-performance-optimization-for-frontline-work/ (accessed 27 October 2021).

IDC (2021). Organizations Are Forecast to Spend Nearly $656 Billion on Future of Work Technologies in 2021, According to New IDC Spending Guide. IDC (June 30). https://www.idc.com/getdoc.jsp?containerId=prUS48040921 (accessed 26 October 2021).

Kolb, D. A. (1984). *Experiential learning: Experience as the source of learning and development* (Vol. 1). Englewood Cliffs, NJ: Prentice-Hall.

Laapher, S., and Kiefer, B. (2020). Digital lean manufacturing. Deloitte. (August 21). https://www2.deloitte.com/us/en/insights/focus/industry-4-0/digital-lean-manufacturing.html (accessed 26 October 2021).

Lamb, F. (2015). Wonderware. *AutomationPrimer* (April 26). https://automation primer.com/2015/04/26/wonderware/ (accessed 26 October 2021).

Linder, N. (2021). Why Manufacturing Needs Citizen Developers. *Forbes*. https://www.forbes.com/sites/natanlinder/2021/03/23/why-manufacturing-needs-citizen-developers/?sh=65b48a477168 (accessed 12 March 2022).

Linder, N. (2020). A New Stack for Industrial Operations. *Forbes* (9 December). https://www.forbes.com/sites/natanlinder/2020/12/09/a-new-stack-for-industrial-operations/?sh=7da4120314f3 (accessed 12 March 2022).

Masterton, A. (2021). Poka Raises $25M in Investment to Connect and Empower Factory Workers. Poka. Blog (June 7). https://blog.poka.io/poka-raises-25m-seriesb-for-connected-worker-platform#.YL400A9-VjI.twitter (accessed 27 October 2021).

Mirandette, E. (2019). Manufacturing is finally entering a new era. *World Economic Forum* [blog]. (21 March). https://www.google.com/url?q=https://www.weforum.org/agenda/2019/03/manufacturing-is-going-digital-it-s-about-time/&sa=D&source=docs&ust=1647092814353665&usg=AOvVaw2xQYuFEwebpZmNC8-EtdGG (accessed 12 March 2022).

Mitra, S. (2020). Serial Entrepreneurship in CAD: SolidWorks and Onshape Founder Jon Hirschtick (Part 4). One Million by One Million Blog (July 15). https://www.sramanamitra.com/2020/07/17/serial-entrepreneurship-in-cad-solidworks-and-onshape-founder-jon-hirschtick-part-4/ (accessed 26 October 2021).

O'Donnell, J. (2020). Time is right for connected worker platforms. *TechTarget*. (August 20). https://searcherp.techtarget.com/feature/Time-is-right-for-connected-worker-platforms (accessed 26 October 2021).

OEE (n.d.). Free resources and fresh perspectives on OEE: Master the art and science of OEE, https://www.oee.com/#:~:text=OEE%20(Overall%20Equipment%20Effectiveness)%20is,possible%2C%20with%20no%20Stop%20Time.

O'Hanley-Clayton, B. (2017). A Brief History of SolidWorks *Scan2CAD*. https://www.scan2cad.com/blog/cad/solidworks-history/ (accessed 26 October 2021).

Peters, T. J., and Waterman, R. H. Jr. *In Search of Excellence: Lessons from America's Best-Run Companies* (New York: HarperBusiness Essentials, 2004).

Plant Automation Technology (2021). Top 10 Industrial Automation Companies in the World. *Plant Automation Technology* (accessed 25 November 2021).

Poka (2021). Standardizing Work Instructions with Poka. *Poka*. Blog. https://www.poka.io/en/solutions/work-instructions (accessed 27 October 2021).

Ries, A., and Trout, J. (1994). *The 22 Immutable Laws of Marketing: Violate Them at Your Own Risk!* New York: HarperBusiness.

Slavin, R.H. (1997). *The Wonder Way*. Lake Forest, CA: Wonderware.

Tulip (2021). The Ultimate Guide to Manufacturing Execution Systems. Tulip. E-book. https://tulip.co/ebooks/manufacturing-execution-systems/ (accessed 27 October 2021).

Verilli, R., and Magruder, M. (2021). Manufacturing Software Market Update. *Madison Park Group* (MPG) https://docsend.com/view/6z3sun9juii8772i (accessed 27 October 2021).

WEF (2022). Augmented workforce: Empowering People, Transforming Manufacturing. White Paper in Collaboration with Cambridge University. *World Economic Forum* (January 2022). https://www.weforum.org/whitepapers/augmented-workforce-empowering-people-transforming-manufacturing (accessed January 28, 2022).

# CHAPTER 3

# THE STATE
# OF PLAY
# IN INDUSTRIAL
# SOFTWARE

There are not that many industrial tech startup stories that define a 30-year evolution (see Figure 3.1). On the contrary, manufacturing is the epitome of industrial companies but also of many small suppliers. It is a space that historically favors consolidation and scale. The history we will quickly touch on in this chapter is shaped by many things: a small set of companies that had outsized impact; complex industrial ownership constellations that drove value for acquirers (or not), but not always for the clients; and a small number of innovations that follow set pathways, given that "everything" has to work together (or, it does not and creates

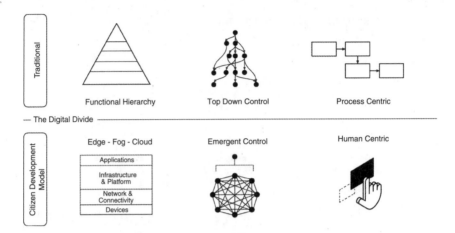

**Figure 3.1** The Paradigm Shift in Industrial Software from Top Down to Bottom Up.

parallel workflows, which, at times, is worse than no system). Precisely because of the lack of interoperability, industrial tech is a particularly complex affair: competitors with incompatible approaches that cannot be combined, legacy and newer systems, hardware and software systems, and systems that started out doing different things but gradually need to interact. Most of all, expensive, grueling, time-consuming customizations make executives believe these systems are as valuable as the pain they caused to implement. For all these reasons, a manufacturing execution system (MES) is hard to turn off.

The story starts with United Computing, founded in 1963, which bought some industrial tech code from a company called MGS in 1973, which became the foundation for a product known since 1975 as Unigraphics. After a metamorphosis where it got acquired by aerospace company McDonnell-Douglas (now part of Boeing), it got into the computer-aided design business, subsequently got acquired by EDS (then part of General Electric), before it was renamed UGS, and then was sold to private equity companies Bain Capital, Silver Lake Partners, and Warburg Pincus. Finally, in 2007 it was acquired by German electronics giant Siemens for USD $3.5 billion and is now called Siemens PLM Software, where PLM stands for product lifecycle management (PLM). PLM systems manage product strategy from the initial idea through prototyping, product launch, retirement, and disposal.

This story is important because it foreshadows why we know so little about the history of manufacturing. It is complex, it is not always sexy or straightforward, and it involves twists and turns, acquisitions, name changes, a plethora of three-letter acronyms, and nearly always consolidation. Importantly, PLM systems are often currently used alongside (and at times integrate with) a wide range of ERP and MES systems. In an ideal world, some would say companies would have the budget and resources to have all three solutions, fully integrated and sharing data, but that's not always the case.

Public visibility is not all that matters in industrial development. A relatively unknown industrial tech precursor, OSIsoft, LLC, was a manufacturer of application software for real-time data management ("the PI System"). Founded in 1980, OSIsoft was privately held and headquartered in San Leandro, California. OSIsoft has installations in 127 countries and is currently widely used across manufacturing, energy, utilities, pharmaceuticals, life sciences, data centers, facilities, and the process industries, as well as the public sector and the federal government. For example, 100% of the Federal Energy Regulatory Commission's (FERC) Independent System Operators and Regional Transmission Organizations use it to ensure the security and stability of the US power grid. Its systems also play a part in ensuring global supply of vaccines.

PI System's strength is time–series data. If the data has a value at a given time, OSIsoft collects, stores, and shows it to customers whenever they need it. More precisely, the system enables collecting, historicizing, finding, analyzing, delivering, and visualizing industrial data from dispersed sources such as control systems, lab equipment, calculations, manual entry, or custom software. As recently as 2021, AVEVA, a leader in industrial performance applications where Schneider Electric owns a

60% stake, acquired the operational data platform for $5 billion. OSIsoft stuck to their moat and built a relatively dominant market position over 40 years, remaining majority-owned by OSISoft's founder, J. Patrick Kennedy, a chemical engineer by education and systems control engineer by profession. Even the specialty media does not always manage to cover these important industrial stories and what they mean. As a result, new entrants to the field – investors, executives, operators – often have to trace these dependencies themselves. Schneider now owns 20,000 industrial client relationships, and an ecosystem of 5,500 partners and 5,700 certified developers around the world (LinkedIn 2022). However, it comes at the cost of having to support intricate legacy software that has been updated and tweaked many times over.

Autodesk was founded in 1982 in Mill Valley, California, by computer programmers John Walker and Dan Drake, and they took the company public in 1985. Autodesk built a 2D drafting system called AutoCAD for the IBM PC that had just come out. It was so popular for drafting that computer-aided design (CAD) increased in popularity by an order of magnitude. Says industry veteran Jon Hirchstick: "Where Autodesk hit the nail on the head is they had a product that they made to work well enough for drawing. And the market of people who made drawings was ready. Then came the go-to-market of selling through dealers and affiliates and bundling it with the PC. It just came together and worked in this magic formula" (Augmented 2002, ep. 23). By 1986, Autodesk had 60% market share and was the largest design automation software company in the world. Today a near $4 billion revenue company, Autodesk makes software products and services for the architecture, engineering, construction, manufacturing, media, education, and entertainment industries. Autodesk's flagship product is its CAD software, which provides two- and three-dimensional digital prototypes of designs for users but today develops a broad array of solutions. The company's manufacturing software is used in several manufacturing segments, including industrial machinery, electro-mechanical, tool and die, industrial equipment, automotive components, and consumer products (Encyclopedia.com 2021). Autodesk also has a significant role in the emerging augmented reality (AR) space, powering media and entertainment applications for Hollywood films and exploring extended reality (XR) immersion for industrial collaboration (Autodesk 2022). However, most of these use cases are at the piloting stage.

In 1985, Boston-based PTC entered the scene, founded by Russian immigrant and mathematician Samuel P. Geisber, and initially written out as Parametric Technology Corporation. A few years later, it was the first to launch industrial-scale 3D modeling. Legendary heavy equipment manufacturer John Deere becomes its first client. Construction giant Caterpillar became PTC's biggest client in 1992. By 1998, PTC surpassed 25,000 customers (Brunelli 2014). Rockwell Automation made a $1 billion equity investment in PTC, acquiring 8.4% ownership stake in PTC on June 11, 2018. Today, the global technology company has over 6,000 employees across 80 offices in 30 countries, 1,150 technology partners, and over $1billion in revenue with products and services that include internet of things (IoT), augmented reality (AR), and collaboration software, as well as with an active consulting, implementation, and training business. PTC's Vuforia AR solutions, although still experimental, are starting to create valuable impact in the areas of documentation, training, operations, and analytics (Forrester 2019). For example, it can quickly capture and scale expertise to help frontline workers get their jobs done quickly and accurately.

# AN OUTLIER RESHAPING THE INDUSTRY

Once in a while, an industrial automation startup comes along that reshapes the industry. In the 1990s, WonderWare was such a company, producing a range of software products to address production operations, production performance, manufacturing intelligence, business process management, and collaboration (Slavin 1997). Arguably the first well-known company in the industrial software space, the two co-founders, Dennis Morin and Phil Huber, had recognized the value of PC revolution and Microsoft Windows, and they harnessed it to maximum effect. Morin had envisioned a software product for monitoring factory operations that would be fun and easy to use and enlisted Huber and started the company with a $100,000 investment.

Known for outrageous marketing strategies by manufacturing standards, they "chartered cruise ships, hired bands and lingerie models and otherwise hyped the company to the normally conservative engineering audience" (Lamb 2015). Rick Bullotta, an early employee at Wonderware, says: "There wasn't anybody in the industry that didn't know the name. Go to a trade show. This is a company, to put some perspective, I think the first year I was there, we did about 20 million in revenues. We spent about a million five on a party" (see Interview 3.1). You could say they were a dotcom before that term existed. They rapidly gained a major market share in the Supervisory Control and Data Acquisition (SCADA) market, which had evolved from the 1970s onwards into the USD $30 billion market it is today (GMI Insights 2020).

A human–machine interface (HMI) is a user interface or dashboard that connects a person to a machine, system, or device to help carry out an industrial process. By inputting commands into machines you earn feedback about their status. Every SCADA has an HMI. If you have seen the interface of an early SCADA system, the Windows-based navigation system must have been a godsend. Bullotta says:

What Dennis and Phil did was really twofold. And this, I think ties into a lot of the innovation we're seeing today, is they democratize the ability to build applications. They made it easy and fun. So the whole experience wasn't coding. It was very visual. It leveraged kind of a drag and drop experience. You didn't need to understand software to apply it. You could build these incredible applications, like literally in minutes or hours, connect them to the physical world. (Augmented 2021, ep. 10)

**Interview 3.1**  A Brief History of Manufacturing Software. Interview with Rick Bullotta. Episode 10. Augmented podcast.

Wonderware was sold to British-based engineering giant Siebe plc in 1998, which, in turn, merged with BTR plc to form Invensys, which merged with French multinational Schneider Electric in 2014, and is now sold as (previously mentioned) Aveva. Wonderware represented a true industrial shift, according to Bullotta:

This is the shift to empowering two main groups: process engineers inside manufacturing companies and secondly, a new breed of systems integrators that were very focused on this automation domain. Historically they may have done the physical automation, the PLCs, the actuators, the sensing distributed control systems. Now that we were able to take on this role we could make other things happen. Just prior to the advent of things like Wonderware, that user experience was physical gauges and push buttons and things like that. And sliders, now they also became digital. I mean, this was in a way, this is almost like magic at the time. Right? It's virtual reality.

No wonder, then, that Wonderware was (and to some extent still is) used as a synonym for computer-based machine interfaces and you would run into it quickly, just as with Allen-Bradley (now owned by Rockwell Automation) and Siemens.

Wonderware has had an outsized effect on manufacturing automation and is a precursor of what is now happening across the world. Today, it constitutes a collaborative, standards-based foundation that "unifies people, processes, and assets across all facilities for continuous operational improvement and real-time decision support" (Aveva.com). That's one side of the story. The other is that today, Wonderware is more valuable as a storied brand (being carefully retired) and for its client relationships than for its legacy technology, the original Wonderware plant operations software (Whiting 2020).

SCADA is essentially an industrial controls system implemented in a combination of hardware and software that allows industrial organizations remote control of operations, real-time monitoring, gathering and processing of data and directly interacting with sensors, valves, pumps, and motors through a human–machine interface. SCADA is used by most industrial sectors from manufacturing through to oil and gas, transportation, power industries, and more. Before SCADA systems, manufacturing floors and industrial plants had to be operated by personnel onsite, no matter how remote they were situated. Two giants of the industrial automation world are Rockwell Automation, which is dominant in North America, and Siemens, which is dominant in Europe and Asia, with Schneider Electric, Emerson Electric, General Electric, Omron, ABB, Yokogawa Electric, Honeywell International, Partita, Toshiba, and Mitsubishi Electric as other major players. The emergence of intelligent remote terminal units (iRTUs) is currently fueling market growth through aid in collecting and analyzing local data and taking the initiative to report data, provide alarms, and reduce the load of center handling data, and facilitating unmanned supervision and control at remote locations, reducing costs significantly (GMI

Insights 2020). Growth is mainly driven by the oil and gas industry with the energy industry's smart grid evolution a close second, and government-fueled smart cities a third future factor (GMI Insights 2020).

# THE ADVENT OF 3D COMPUTER-AIDED DESIGN

We previously mentioned how Autodesk and PTC competed fiercely in the 1980s and outgunned many other contestants in the CAD space. How was it then possible that they also were surpassed by a startup? This is the story of SolidWorks.

In 1993, SolidWorks, a "solid" modeling computer-aided design and computer-aided engineering computer program that runs primarily on Microsoft Windows was co-founded by Jon Hirschtick and Scott Harris and developed out of Hirchtick's Winchester, MA home. Initially unable to get Boston venture capital, he funded it in the first year from the $1 million he had made from his time with a winning streak on the MIT BlackJack team and volunteer friends jumping in as coders. SolidWorks eventually convinced Atlas Venture and then Polaris and raised a $3.8 million A-round followed by a $9.2 million B-round. Hirschtick was quoted as saying: "We were building SolidWorks in my house. My wife got pregnant the day I got the term sheet. We get venture capital. We ship the product. Immediately, it starts to sell like crazy. The fax machine was running out of paper" (Mitra 2020).

The SolidWorks software could be used for planning, visual ideation, modeling, feasibility assessment, prototyping, and project management in the initial phases of a project. Moreover, it could also be used for the design and building of mechanical, electrical, and software elements. The unique value of SolidWorks, set against the other players in the field at that time, was the sophisticated 3D models and simulations that could be used to create machine parts in 3D and simulate their physics and motion. The manufacturing industry's multitude of challenges include the difficulty of ensuring your design is perfect before the prototype stage. SolidWorks brought users the ability to eliminate interferences, produce automatic estimates of part manufacturing costs, and eliminated the need to import or export between design and CAM (O'Hanlon-Clayton 2017).

SolidWorks grew to 2 million users. As of 2013, two million engineers and designers at more than 165,000 companies were using Solid-Works. Hirschtick stayed on board for the next 14 years in various roles (Griffith 2015).

SolidWorks was sold to Dassault Systemes (DS) in 1997, for $310 million in stock and has since operated successfully as a subsidiary. Hirschtick says that it's hard for people to relate to the different speed at which computing and digital technology evolves relative to physical technology. If cars had gotten faster at the same rate as computers have, they would be going 50,000 miles an hour today. He says, "Change happens when it happens. It doesn't happen on the schedule of the entrepreneur. It happens because there's a combination, like a storm of certain conditions comes together, and it's like magic and then boom: it happens" (Augmented 2021, ep. 23; see Interview 3.2).

**Interview 3.2** Digital Manufacturing in the Cloud. Interview with Jon Hirschtick. Episode 23. Augmented podcast.

Another precursor, this time making use of the emerging web interface, was Lighthammer, an Exton, Pennsylvania-based software startup
founded in 1997, that streamlined interfaces to shop-floor production systems. An information portal of sorts for manufacturing, its "Collaborative Manufacturing Suite" provided, for the first time, a unified view of
what was going on, enabling (more) complete workflows. Lighthammer
was acquired by SAP in 2005, and got integrated with SAP's own analytical
manufacturing dashboards.

Bullotta came on as an investor and advisor, with characteristic
realism:

> The unique thing about the industrial space, I like to say, is that every-
> thing's legacy the moment it gets put in, right? Everything had propri-
> etary APIs and interfaces and protocols. My approach has always been
> to solve hard problems because you're gonna have fewer competitors
> and the value's there. All these different, crazy systems that were scat-
> tered around. The objective was unified visibility. But then when we
> realized, if people can see that information, why can't other systems?
> It rapidly progressed from just empowering people with information
> to empowering another line of business systems. So your supply chain
> systems, warehouse systems, ERP systems can now be informed with
> real information in a timely manner. And that was what got us on SAP's
> radar. Because you started discovering the importance of standards.

Lighthammer brought SAP another advantage that put them on their
radar, initially as an ecosystem partner, says Bullotta: "We had something
that had a license cost per worker, not just a new module for their ERP
system. In addition, there were manufacturing site costs. The scale and size
of the deals were pretty substantial and there was real value being created."
What we are now beginning to uncover, is the bundling of software and
hardware that suddenly started to happen in the manufacturing industry
in the early days of digitalization.

In 2009, ThingWorx, founded by Bullotta, saw the light of day, offering a software platform that allowed developers to build and run machine-to-machine and IoT-based applications (the term wasn't yet IoT, but that's what it was). Machine-to-machine didn't mean anything to people yet, either. The secret sauce was remote connectivity. However, factories and power plants required different levels of connectivity requirements to fleets of trucks, MRI machines, and light towers. One's 98% on prem and needs to be reliable, one's 99.9% cloud, intermittent, and, at the time, unreliable. Says Bullotta: "We (initially) built a platform to serve both of those tasks. In retrospect, we probably made compromises along the way to accommodate that. But maybe there is something about the industry itself that lends itself very easily to [consolidation]."

ThingWorx was later (in 2003) acquired by PTC, Bullotta said, "after we met with them and it turned out that they had been trying to develop something similar in house" (Davis 2021). ThingWorx targets a broad range of industries; however, a significant coding background is required to create industrial IoT (IIoT) apps with ThingWorx. It is primarily a tool for developers, systems integrators, and the IT department. Due to these features, ThingWorx is typically adopted in a traditional top-down manner and pricing is opaque and subject to specific development with considerable professional services costs.

# THE EMERGENCE OF MANUFACTURING EXECUTION SYSTEMS

Industrial tech has been an endless evolution of systems that do not always work well together. As industrial processes themselves evolved, so have the systems. *Manufacturing execution systems* is a more recent label that takes into account how these systems have taken on important operational functions.

According to Gartner's Magic Quadrant (2021), MESs are computerized systems used to track and document the transformation of raw materials to finished goods, and includes leaders such as Parsec, Dassault Systèmes, Siemens, Honeywell, Critical Manufacturing, Korber, and AVEVA, as well as challengers such as Tulip, Rockwell Automation, GE Digital, and Oracle (see Resource 3.1). In short, these systems manage, monitor, and synchronize the execution of real-time, physical processes involved in manufacturing operations.

**Resource 3.1** Gartner's Magic Quadrant Manufacturing Execution Systems, 2021.

An MES captures the data, processes, and outcomes of the manufacturing process, both for regulated and unregulated industries, with numerous benefits, including to improve efficiencies, share best practices, reduce downtime, and increase the consistency and safety of manual processes. Often, this is achieved through enabling paperless and to a large degree uninterrupted workflow, which maintains a worker's concentration and efficiency during crucial procedures. Another key outcome is the near eradication of just-in-case inventory.

We don't know if a readable introduction to MES systems exists (we haven't found a good one that is honest), but, if not, we aim for this segment to be the first. The reason is that seldom has such a fundamental piece of software been so misunderstood, misconstrued, and mislabeled. What do we mean? The essence of such systems should be (and often is) wider than manufacturing. The system in question always aims for more than "execution" (whatever that means). Lastly, they are rarely systems, but rather bundles that consist of usable and nonusable parts. Each part is typically too big and expensive to handle. As a result, a market for systems integrators and consultants has opened up.

That said, an MES should excel at shop floor management, across a wide range of industrial use cases, and should optimize the use of shop floor resources, assist with scheduling minute to minute (not just by day or shift), and should at the very least be an excellent "system of engagement" where it ties up loose ends for mobile workforce along assembly lines, shop floors, or across factories. A MES is typically optimized for complex production processes with frequent bottlenecks (the bane of production lines), limited capacity (a common occurrence), and as a way to deal with alternative paths in production. At times, it should also be a "system of record," although that role is typically better played by an ERP system. One way to look at it is to consider that MES software is generally used for the "Who, What, When, Where, Why and How Much" facets of work order execution (Lamb 2015).

A MES, by its very design, is not human centric. Worse, it disconnects work from the floor where it occurs. MES solutions typically have a logic built-in to predefined modules. What that means is that the system pre-determines certain ways of doing things, and the shop floor has to adapt instead of the system. Flexibility also suffers when changes have to be made, because a MES typically lacks frontline workflows and nearly always entails programming experience to configure. Even programmers would butt their head against the rigid prebuilt modules and data structures that were supposed to give stability. They might collect data from (big, expensive) machines but will not collect (so much) data from humans or perhaps not from more peripheral custom devices and sensors because they were not built into the first installation. Furthermore, the analysis of data might happen "next day, next week" instead of real time, the way newer machine monitoring point solutions do. Lastly, the biggest issue for many customers is evidently the expensive upfront installation, site license, the system integration services that follow, and the annual contract based on factory floor headcount. Half the fight is to change management's perception of what they are trying to accomplish. Control is never the desired outcome. Deeply understanding what has to be done, comparing that to what is being done, and widening the scope of work so workers can thrive and excel, is.

It is not an industry secret that manufacturers are frustrated with traditional MES systems. A plethora of point solutions have emerged to try to fix parts of the problem. There are one trick ponies for machine monitoring (e.g., companies such as MachineMetrics). GE tried to build a much more ambitious solution with GE Digital's Predix but failed despite massive investments perhaps because software is seldom built by cash infusion absent a clear path of user-centric development (Mann and Gryta 2020). Either way, you find connected worker solutions that can help digitize workflows but don't necessarily tie in to all other systems (Dozuki, eFlex Systems, L2L, Parsable, Poka, VKS). There are generic low-code or no-code platforms that include manufacturing among their target markets but with generic digital solutions (Appian, Mendix). Additionally, industry-specific solutions have emerged, for example for life science (Emerson, Kneat, Körber Werum, MasterControl, Valgenesis), food, beverage, and CPG manufacturers (Redzone), asset intensive industries (Arundo, Cognite), or automotive (Workclout). Lastly, business function–specific solutions also now exist, such as auditing (iAuditor).

# Must Manufacturing Execution Systems Turn Mastodonic?

Discrete manufacturing involves assembling and making distinct things such as manufacturing cars, bicycles, or mobile phones. Process manufacturing involves mixing ingredients according to specific formulas or recipes, such as paints, specialty chemicals, textiles, or pharmaceuticals. Traditional software for manufacturing has always been dedicated to one of these industry modalities. Rarely have software vendors been able to support both discrete and process manufacturing without complicated customizations and workarounds. However, even so, these software systems seem to quickly grow in complexity and license and site costs, and require specialists to implement and service.

If you look at the top 10 industrial automation companies in the world, which includes Siemens, ABB, Emerson, Rockwell Automation, Schneider Electric, Mitsubishi Electric, Yokogawa Electric, Omron Automation, and Danaher Industrial Ltd., many of these companies have either acquired an MES system or have contributed to the success of the space by providing enormous contracts to these systems (Plant Automation Technology 2021). This makes sense, from their point of view, if you think about the complexity of the products they make and the effort it takes to manufacture them. However, their approach slows industrial innovation because it keeps dinosaurs alive, and the marketplace suffers inferior systems as a result.

A MES is, typically, a rigid system and takes time to customize. According to Gartner, the average implementation time for an MES is 15–16 months (Tulip 2021); others estimate 6–18 months (Swanton and Smith 2005). Custom-built MES configurations based on MES tool kits can run high ratios of license-to-service dollars, often upward of 1:5. That means for every $10,000 spent on licenses, you may actually be spending $50,000 in services. The total cost of ownership of custom-built or off-the-shelf MES is high (Tulip 2021). There is near universal frustration with MES systems, but up until recently there have been few realistic alternatives.

A MES does not need to be mastodonic. The ISA-88 and ISA-95 standards do make data transfer between systems feasible. Features can improve faster. Any system that needs to be on premise misses the opportunity to natively and flexibly rely on cloud computing. The big systems that resulted from solutions being patched together over time could be ending. In fact, we predict startups currently providing point-solutions to eventually merge with more complete offerings that have similar functionality without the same complexity. It does not hold the test of agility, especially in build-to-order, high-mix-high-volume manufacturing. MES in its current form is dying. Partly, the infrastructure it is based on is getting old. The Purdue Enterprise Reference Architecture (PERA), a structural model for industrial control system security (e.g., "The Purdue model"), was developed back in 1990, before the internet and cloud computing took off, and will need to be complemented with the flexibility of contemporary Edge systems (Greenfield 2020). The key challenges of Industrial IoT include standardization, connectivity across vendors, and defining data models and digital twins across big industry verticals including automotive and manufacturing. That work is underway.

# Between Lean and Agile

There is a very strong similarity and connection between lean and agile. Continuous improvement cycles are, in fact, largely the same as agile sprints. Back in 1990, agile was interchangeably used for software and industrial processes, that is where agile manufacturing was born, although the Agile Manifesto (2001) dates from a meeting of 17 programming leaders at a ski resort in Utah. Both lean and agile are based on observation of human ways of learning, because we, arguably, learn in experiential cycles (Kolb 1984). The problem is: industrial tech (software and hardware) was never agile, it was stale.

Companies strive for agility (which also means adaptability). They want to optimize their processes. There is a close analogy to natural systems as adaptability as in nature increases not only chances of survival but also chances to thrive. Lean organizations are not necessarily agile. They can break apart when macro changes happen, the way the COVID-19 pandemic broke the lean supply chain. Lean is firmly embedded in manufacturing because the automotive industry introduced it. Agile, on the other hand, is a term that originates in software companies. To show our allegiance, we stick with lean in this book. The term *digital lean* takes us part of the way. However, we feel both digital and operational enhancements are necessary. Notably, the objective needs to be clear: augmenting human work and helping workers optimize their work, hence, *augmented lean*. To excel, you cannot just strive to work more effectively, you must feel fulfilled in what you do. Both content and process must evolve naturally, and in sync with task, team, and evolving cyber-physical constraints. You cannot take productivity software created for desk workers and shove it down the throats of shop floor workers. It simply won't work.

# Startup Innovation Paving the Way for a New Operations Stack in Industrial Technology

Despite years of inferior software developed by well-meaning entrepreneurs entering the manufacturing space from the IT sector, something new is afresh. Dozens of innovative startups are contributing to the broader reshaping of industrial operations. The startups have emerged from Massachusetts Institute of Technology, Stanford, and other technical institutes over the past five years. Our MIT bias makes the following examples a bit slanted, but 3D printing startups (Desktop Metal, Formlabs, Inkbit) are starting to reach industrial scale. Spatial sensor networks (Humatics) complement automation in factories so we can regain control with what our machines do and where they move at any time. Augmented capability such as "emotion AI" is on its way to guide autonomous automotive systems (Affectiva) in a more human way that recognizes human emotions and reactions. We see the emergence of industrial

AR/VR (Spatial), digital factories (Fictiv), interoperable robotics plat-forms (Ready Robotics), and custom tools built-on-demand (Vention). What these startups share is the commitment to interoperable interfaces as well as a focus on bypassing legacy challenges to achieve factors of magnitude operational efficiencies by cloud-based approaches to sim-plifying industrial operations. All of this is not just a list of successful startups. Together with a host of others, they amount to an emerging, new stack for software for operations.

# CONCLUSION

The history of industrial tech software began in the 1960s with industrial control systems (United Computing, SCADA-systems), which gained industrial adoption throughout the 1970s. In the 1980s, the digitaliza-tion of engineering design (in 2D) brought powerful visualization tools (Autodesk, PTC). By the 1990s, the internet platform brought remote con-trol systems (Wonderware) as well as next-generation design tools in 3D (SolidWorks). The late 2000s brought the first manufacturing execution systems (ThingWorx), and throughout the decade and beyond, a plethora of such systems emerged, and their functionality (and integration cost) ballooned. However, legacy systems (SCADA control systems, etc.) didn't go away and are still present in today's factory floor control rooms. Also, most systems have been proprietary (not open source) and have had poor interoperability (and lack of shared standards). That way, the pathways of this short history are very much part of the present, quite often setting limits to what further innovation can accomplish.

In the next chapter, we will explore what the digital lean journey itself might look like from the perspective of manufacturing companies, work-force, vendors, and policy makers.

# REFERENCES

Agile Manifesto (2001). https://agilemanifesto.org/history.html (accessed 5 January 2022).

Augmented (2021, ep. 10). A Brief History of Manufacturing Software. Interview with Rick Bullotta. Episode 10. *Augmented podcast* (July 5). https://www.augmentedpodcast.co/a-brief-history-of-manufacturing-software/ (accessed 26 October 2021).

Augmented (2021, ep. 23). Digital Manufacturing in the Cloud. Interview with Jon Hirschtick. Episode 23. *Augmented podcast* (June 30). https://www.augmentedpodcast.co/23 (accessed 26 October 2021).

Autodesk (2022). The New Possible: Extended reality: Virtual, augmented, and mixed. https://www.autodesk.com/solutions/extended-reality

Davis, T. (2021). Lessons learned from serial founder Rick Bullotta. LinkedIn (May 10). https://www.linkedin.com/pulse/lessons-learned-from-serial-founder-rick-bullotta-tom-davis/ (accessed 26 October 2021).

Encyclopedia.com (2021). Autodesk, Inc. https://www.encyclopedia.com/social-sciences-and-law/economics-business-and-labor/businesses-and-occupations/autodesk-inc (accessed 26 October 2021).

Forrester (2019). Forrester total economic impact: PTC Vuforia. https://www.ptc.com/en/resources/augmented-reality/report/forrester-total-economic-impact (accessed 28 January 2022).

Gartner LCAP (2021). Enterprise Low-Code Application Platforms (LCAP) reviews and ratings. Gartner https://www.gartner.com/reviews/market/enterprise-low-code-application-platform (accessed 26 October 2021).

GMI Insights (2020). SCADA market size. Global Market Insights (Jan 2020). https://www.gminsights.com/industry-analysis/scada-supervisory-control-and-data-acquisition-market (accessed 26 October 2021.

Greenfield, D. (2020). Is the Purdue model still relevant? *Automation World*. (May 12). https://www.automationworld.com/factory/iiot/article/21132891/is-the-purdue-model-still-relevant (accessed 12 March 2022).

Griffith, E. (2015). Exclusive: SolidWorks vets raise $64 million for Onshape. *Fortune* (March 6). https://fortune.com/2015/03/06/exclusive-solidworks-vets-raise-64-million-for-onshape/ (accessed 26 October 2021).

Lamb, F. (2015). Wonderware. *AutomationPrimer* (April 26). https://automationprimer.com/2015/04/26/wonderware/ (accessed 26 October 2021).

LinkedIn (2022). AVEVA. Global leader in engineering and industrial software. https://www.linkedin.com/company/aveva/ (accessed 28 January 2022).

Mann, T., and Gryta, T. (2020). The dimming of GE's bold digital dreams. *The Wall Street Journal.* (July 18). https://www.wsj.com/articles/the-dimming-of-ges-bold-digital-dreams-11595044802 (accessed 12 March 2022).

Swanton, B., and Smith, A. (2005). MES for long-term revenue and market benefits. https://www.ee.co.za/wp-content/uploads/legacy/AMR-MES.pdf (accessed 5 January 2022).

Tulip (2021). *The Ultimate Guide to Manufacturing Execution Systems.* Tulip. E-book. https://tulip.co/ebooks/manufacturing-execution-systems/ (accessed 27 October 2021).

Whiting, R. (2020). Manufacturing app developer Aveva opens full software portfolio to channel partners. CRN. https://www.crn.com/news/channel-programs/manufacturing-app-developer-aveva-opens-full-software-portfolio-to-channel-partners (accessed 28 January 2022).

# CHAPTER 4

# THE JOURNEY PAST DIGITAL LEAN

D MG MORI, the € 2.229 billion (2014) firm with both Japanese and German heritage, is headquartered in Bielefeld, a city in the northeast of North Rhine-Westphalia, Germany. The company is a world-leading manufacturer of high-end precision machine tools, peripherals, and systems. Computer numerical control machines (e.g., CNC machines), which cut metals to medical and aerospace industry demands for micrometer precision and accuracy, are indispensable for all advanced industrial production. DMG MORI has done more than 160,000 installations around the world and exemplifies German precision engineering at its best.

The German side of the firm, Gildemeister, was founded in 1870 as a mass manufacturer of machine tools. The Japanese firm, Mori Seiki, began as a textile manufacturer in Japan in 1948. Starting collaboration in 2009, the two aligned their corporate name in 2013, and the joint structure has 12,000 employees from 48 nations. The user of the machine tool, the "qualified employee," is at the heart of their future strategy.

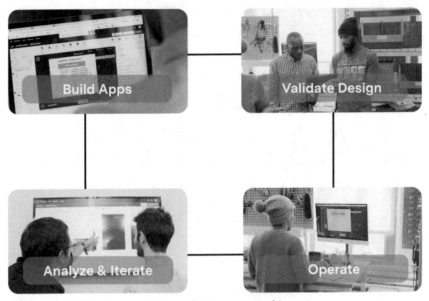

**Figure 4.1** The Journey Towards Augmented Lean.

With its mission to become the world's preeminent machine tool manufacturer with digital and sustainable products, the company serves customers in over 42 industries and 79 countries (DMG MORI 2021; see Figure 4.1). Says Dr. Eng. Masahiko Mori, the son of the company's founder and president:

We are committed to the true nature of the machine tool. It continues to be at the center of our strategic triad of automation, digitization and sustainability." [...] "We are developing software tools that make machine tools more productive, more future-proof and thus more sustainable. And it means that we are digitizing our own value creation chain." CEO Christian Thönes emphasizes the double significance of the machine tool: "On the one hand, it is the nucleus of a more than 150-year-old machine building tradition, and on the other hand, it is the guarantor of DMG MORI's future viability."

Marius Schmiedt, head of operational excellence, is an industrial engineer and MBA with ample experience across production, logistics, quality, and information technologies. Being in charge of 14 production sites, 140 sales organizations, 12,000 employees, and 300,000 machines is, one would expect, not a walk in the park. Says Schmiedt: "One of the first things that I learned was if you want to sell it and give it to customers, we need to test it and use it internally."

# DMG MORI'S INTEGRATION WITH TULIP

The story of DMG MORI's deep integration with Tulip goes further back than this. In October 2018, Ric Fulop, CEO and founder of the metal 3D printing startup Desktop Metal, was bringing a few executives to Boston's manufacturing startup scene. One of them was Christian Thönes, CEO of DMG MORI. Rony Kubat, Tulip's CTO, gave a full demo and caught his eye. Tulip CEO Natan Linder met with Board Member Michael Horn shortly thereafter. Less than a year later, a deal was announced. Says Schmiedt: "We showed Tulip one of our biggest plants in the south of Germany and said: 'They have a pre-assembly area. This is your playground. Show that Tulip works.'" What happened was that the project team digitized this production line in only three weeks, testing different things. They started with worker instructions and went on to create drawings with material information, right at the workstation. Then, they implemented an Andon light system and pick-to-light a paperless fulfillment technology to guide employees in light-aided picking, putting, sorting, and assembling.

On every journey, there are tour guides on offer. Digital change is best led by those who will benefit from the change, not by third parties. DMG MORI's digital journey was not a Tulip-led process. Says Schmiedt: "We believe that the digital journey is only going to work if we involve our own people for all pilots. If you don't know the system, you cannot build systems." DMG MORI Academy developed a training approach in two modules. In module one, employees are trained four times for four hours remotely on how Tulip works, what its components and variables are, and how to connect them. In module two, people can start building advanced apps and tables and learn how to use table records, build the data model behind it, and how to start advancing the apps behind the models. Then, they are ready to run their use case. "People become really good as builders if they have a good use case straight ahead. The use case matters more than the innate skills of the people building it." As Schmiedt says, he is not himself a software developer, but "I can build apps." "Nobody is alone on this journey. They learn how to build apps and they have a network. They know people, we are organizing ourselves to get in touch with others in order to find a solution for their specific [challenge]" (Augmented, 2022, ep. 74; see Interview 4.1).

**Interview 4.1** DMG MORI's Digital Lean Journey. Episode 74. Interview with Marius Schmiedt, Head of Operational Excellence, DMG MORI. Augmented podcast.

Why did DMG MORI succeed? Schmiedt claims their executive saw a huge opportunity in Tulip to digitize the shop floor and that there was a very strong pull from the top. After the initial pilot, they simultaneously launched another pilot in four different plants. After the pilot, they did a bigger training with 40 people in a classroom. Once completed, they let them be the consultants. They gave each of them 10 people to work with and said, "Find your use cases to build apps, every afternoon, go out to the people who work on the shop floor who are going to use it and ask them: 'Do you like it? Is it valuable for you? What should be different?'"

This way, engineers started to learn to link apps together. After two weeks, Schmiedt said, five plants were on the "journey." They went back to their factories and said they have a new tool in their toolbox. He describes the process as "fun, because people liked what they were doing and start to solve their own problems on a very high level of detail." Either way, a very strong momentum is being created. What was striking was how a German, highly structured organization responded to the opportunity. Suddenly, there was momentum, through a group that started building apps without needing detailed instructions. They just wanted to solve their real problems. As a result, it started to grow slowly. Schmiedt said, "After half a year, we had all the plants on board and they keep moving building apps" (Augmented, 2022, ep. 74).

# How Digital Lean Is a Journey Far Beyond Digital

Currently, DMG MORI's engineers have built more than 400 different apps that are already used in production. How did they make it happen? They tend to look 12 months out and see what kind of savings or improvement they can make, looking at the implementation, including internal costs such as license fees. If the savings are higher than the cost you have, we call it a net benefit. "For us, the average ROI is seven to eight months. In a bit more than half a year, the use case is paying back and then it starts bringing value continuously to the organization." [...] "One of the biggest points [for us] is that it should pay back within less than a year. Savings after year one tells people how much potential there is."

Talking about ROI is one thing, but how do you make it part of front-line operations, not just a figure you calculate in the end? DMG MORI tries to link the ROI to operational KPIs. "Say for example, there's an app that is providing support and the preassembly of this specific product or component of this component we have, failure rate or scrap rate or whatever, and we tried to reduce it. This is data we're looking for anyway. From this point, you can start tracking it, so you can continuously control if the app is delivering a positive benefit for the organization" (Augmented, 2022, ep. 74).

What Schmiedt points out is that real-time ROI is far more valuable than post-project ROI, a point that often gets missed in top-down best practice case studies. The journey past digital lean needs to balance technology and people, and the technology has to be properly evolved, timed, and positioned, not just shoved down people's throat:

People are interested in technology. So suddenly I go into a factory, and they say, look at the marvelous things I have here. And they show you some integrative IOT integration with digital calipers. And we bought it from our local supplier and they gave us something to try and now we have implemented it and it directly gives us the values without writing them. It's not all of the standard to the toolbox, but they managed to boot this and implement it. This is where these two things come together. People are evolving. They have a better knowledge and understanding of digitization technology. And then when it comes to bigger challenges, like your product launch operations, strategy, pivot, maybe review of how you want to organize your assembly, then you can bring everything together and you can push these revolutionary improvements.

Digital maturity, as it turns out, is equally important for people as for technology, otherwise, the cyber-physical connection gets lost in chaos.

DMG MORI began an intensive collaboration with the developers of the platform app (Tulip) at a very early stage. The apps are now used in their own production and via the subsidiary DMG MORI Digital, Tulip is also being offered to customers. The tool is a no-code application, which means no programming language is required to work with it. DMG MORI feels the interface of Tulip is reminiscent of PowerPoint: Using modules and elements, the user can organize workflows, integrate instructions, and check quality. Advantages include that paper disappears and that the tool can be connected to machine interfaces, as well as to the applications of the internet of things (IoT). The result is that all processes can be displayed transparently and any errors can be quickly detected. The open concept of the app gives employees a great deal of scope to use Tulip in a way that makes sense for their work. (DMG MORI 2021c).

DMG MORI operates two Technology Excellence Centers for Aerospace and Die & Mold in Pfronten, located on the northern edge of the Allgäu Alps in Germany. With around 1,500 employees and a total area of 149,000 m², Pfronten is one of the most important development and largest production plants of DMG MORI in Europe. Housing the company's milling expertise, the factory alone produces 50 different types of machines from the versatile monoBLOCK series up to the XXL machines. Pfronten offers the capacity for around 1,500 machines to leave the factory every year for global distribution. The company DMG MORI Ultrasonic Lasertec GmbH is also located in Pfronten, and is responsible for advanced technologies in the group. The subsidiary company develops and builds its LASERTEC machines for high-precision applications in the field of laser texturing and drilling in Pfronten (see Video 4.1).

**Video 4.1** Tulip Apps on DMG MORI Machines.

How was the implementation process? Says Musch, managing director of DMG MORI's Deckel-Maho operations: "After four weeks, we gained insight into how we could significantly reduce errors and stabilize production. Our motor spindle line consists of 16 stations. It is important that the operators at each station know exactly which task they need to perform in order to complete the job. Tulip supports this 100%."

What they did, together, is create spindle assembly apps that guide operators through each step of the assembly. These applications eliminated paper forms from the line and provided feedback to the operators in real time. Musch said (DMG MORI 2021):

> Now, there's live information from the operators and stations and we know where improvement is needed in order to reduce errors. Tulip helps us identify the root cause of problems. It is easy to configure with no programming skills required. This helps us reflect daily changes to requirements. Here at the motor spindle line, we've successfully deployed Tulip to significantly avoid internal rework, and reduce our return rate. During the next month, we're going to integrate the entire supply chain from information provided by suppliers to the final assembly of our machines.

DMG MORI has been leveraging Tulip Edge devices to drive operational improvements within their organizations. They currently have

14 Edge gateways at their Pfronten factory site, lightstack for Andon lights and pick by light are in testing. Andon is a Japanese term meaning "light" and derives from a particular paper lantern used in the Edo period (between 1603 and 1867). However, in lean manufacturing, Andon refers to a tool that is used to inform and alarm workers of problems within their production process. They can now connect to the machine for testing when commissioning and can use this capability to test machines on an ongoing basis. Colleagues in Japan have also integrated with devices.

The Famot "Excellence Factory" in Pleszew in central Poland is a pilot plant for new technologies. The unique feature is its continual flow assembly fueled by a driverless transport system. Famot exemplifies what the industry now calls a "digital factory" with direct feedback from the machine or machine workstation, and real-time monitoring of machine and process-relevant data. Even order management, supply chain, and customer relationships all are digitized. The industry is experiencing shorter product cycles and increasing desire for individualized products. "Manufacturers now think in terms of smaller batches and are able to do so without sacrificing economic efficiency – with the aid of digital processes, intelligent algorithms and automated processes" (DMG MORI 2021, p. 50).

Mobile devices and tablets have long since begun their advance in production environments where networking facilitates planning:

An important component of the Excellence Factory is Tulip, a no-code platform for the development of individual apps. They display relevant information for technicians – including machine-specific working plans for each cycle and the material required in each case. Detailed drawings and video instructions support the assembly of newly introduced equipment or special options. With the aid of interactive checklists and inspection plans, the complete assembly process is documented and the quality gates are marked. This enables continuous quality inspection for the team. Further support can be requested directly from the Tulip app, for example in the event of a malfunction. The digital product not only optimizes production processes; it also enables early detection of any errors. This ensures the quality of the machine and enables delivery deadlines to be met. A glance at the production figures shows that the Excellence Factory does what DMG MORI hoped it would: The lead times per model have been reduced by 30%. This has enabled DMG MORI to increase the production capacity from the previous 600 to over 1,000 machines. (DMG MORI 2021c, p.46)

No-code startups are transforming experiences for factory owners like DMG MORI because its shop floor solutions are so easy to implement from the perspective of lean production methods. However, does no-code actually mean that process engineers can become independent from the IT department? Damir Hrnjadovic says DMG MORI power users are able to do that, even though he is quick to point out that not every shop floor operator will create a Tulip application. Damir says he, at times, feels like a time traveler when he encounters paper-based processes on the shop floor when encountering firms in the German Mittelstand of small-and medium size businesses (see Interview 4.2). There is a significant need for

**Interview 4.2** Bottom Up and Deep Digitization of Operations. Episode 14. Interview with Dr. Damir Hrnjadovic, Managing Director, DMG MORI Digital GmbH. Augmented podcast.

upskilling. Clearly, shop floor change is uneven at the moment, depending on whether you heard the right digital gospel and what the attitude of the IT department is to introduce changes that democratize IT. This is not just important for the firm itself because its business depends on its suppliers. Via the customer portal My DMG MORI, the company is currently connected with more than 30,000 small and medium-sized enterprises, linking up 20,000 machines, both projected to double by 2022 (see Case study 4.1).

**Case study 4.1** DMG MORI Uses Tulip to Digitize Their Spindle Assembly Line.

# A DIGITAL BOOST TO MEDICAL MANUFACTURING: ANOTHER JOURNEY

At times, the actions of one person can become the impetus for a whole movement. Those who end up having that role seldom plan for it. Dan Ron, lead quality engineer at Dentsply Sirona, is a dynamic young operations leader with a warm smile and more than a decade's experience in implementing Industry 4.0 concepts improving manufacturing efficiency, project management, and process control. A Six Sigma Black Belt with a background in data analytics, Ron is intimately familiar with classic lean. Before Dentsply, he spent time at GE Aviation, and prior to that he worked as an engineer in a consulting firm. With a degree in mathematical statistics from UMass Amherst, he picked up digital pretty quickly. His reputation as a team player served him well when Dentsply wanted to digitize more deeply. He explains:

> When Tulip first presented us with their products, I think they had one customer and it was a computer manufacturer. Wow. The demo was somebody going through a very standardized assembly process: the computer box. We looked at that and I think I was the only one in the room that said, "Hey, we can use that for this highly customizable, completely ridiculous process that we have." They looked at me and said, "What the hell are you talking about?" (Tulip 2021e; see Interview 4.3)

**Interview 4.3** Digitizing Medical Device Operations. Episode 63. Interview with Dan Ron, Lead Engineer, Dentsply. Augmented podcast.

Dentsply Sirona is the world's largest manufacturer of dental solutions, markets its products in more than 120 countries, and has factories in 21 countries, and revenues of $4.03 billion USD (2019), competing with the likes of Danaher Corp., MMM, and Zimmer Biomet Holdings. Their

*The Journey Past Digital Lean*

comprehensive catalog of preventative, restorative, and cosmetic products are used in practices and labs worldwide, as are their best-in-class dental instruments. Dentsply Sirona's implants division processes thousands of custom orders each day. Since each order is built-to-order (BTO) to the patient, no two orders are alike. There are billions of potential kitting combinations, and executing every order on time demands skilled, attentive operators.

Ron says they already have a digital workflow by the nature of Dentsply's business. They accept digital scans from customers. They make digital restorations and work digitally with customers and clinicians to finalize and approve those designs. "We got 80% of the way by digitizing 20% of our problems. At some point, that was not enough."

However, Ron says the "shadow IT" issue in a larger organization is still real. If a solution or vendor is not approved or if it looks and feels different they're going to say, why didn't you look at Microsoft (or any other big vendor), they've got something similar. But when something unique comes along, "I'm going to say, 'that's the one we're going to allow'" (Augmented 2021, ep. 63).

Before Tulip was involved, in order to assure the quality of their shipments, Dentsply Sirona associates needed to complete six months of training and shadowing before they were qualified to enter production. Further, process engineers lacked visibility into key areas of production, such as which components were shipped. This made it hard to maintain quality control and enable process improvement.

Says Ron:

When we first saw Tulip, our immediate instinct was that we now have a place where we can digitize work instructions. Let's say one particular operation was about 70 pages long, [you could] make your own story book. If this is true, flip to page 13, if that's true, and this is true, we flip to page 28. It's like putting together some enormously complicated

IKEA outfit. It was absurd and training times took forever because some operations were just very [complicated]. Digitizing the work instruction didn't just automate the process, but it served to simplify.

At the same time, Ron says, the new apps didn't require changing too many procedures: "On the whole, we followed existing process steps. From there we then gradually reduced steps, as we could, or eliminated button clicks, if we could."

Today, Dentsply Sirona uses Tulip's machine monitoring solutions, pick-to-light (PtL) bins for picking (and saw the rate of complaints go down a lot), and (web) cameras for quality control (which also led to quicker investigation after customer complaints). As it turns out, "screws are very expensive" especially when they also need to be shipped. At the end of the day, Tulip's apps helped Dentsply Sirona cut training times by 75% while reducing errors in a complex kitting process by digitizing work instructions, monitoring devices, and increasing traceability (Tulip 2021b; see Case study 4.2).

**Case study 4.2** Tulip's Apps Helped Dentsply Sirona Cut Training Times by 75% while Reducing Errors in a Complex Knitting Process. Tulip Use Case: Dentsply Sirona.

Reducing the cognitive load of the operator makes it easier for them to focus on the work they have to do instead of figuring out what they should do. Turning paper-based work instructions into interactive digital apps allows the senior process engineer to streamline new operator training. By following the apps, new operators are able to self-train and learn new skills much faster than before. Using Tulip for training facilitated cross-training with existing workers, letting them continuously gain new skills, operators can be successfully reassigned to areas of the operation where they are needed, when they are needed (Tulip 2021b).

Ron says that from operators to engineers, to managers, to executives, everyone loves to see their ideas count. They want to see improvements that can get done quickly and do not want to wait for software developers that are in process for every three- or six-month release cycle.

There's a lot to be gained in terms of engagement on the front lines from the bottom up. But there's a lot to also be gained from including people in the core of the movement. Ron says:

> When operators see that we can iterate on the fly, the problems that they have can go away very quickly. Managers also like it because now their engineers or their operators or whoever they're managing have the tools to solve problems that weren't available before. The software developers and the IT folks also appreciate it because they can focus their efforts on the core of problems, as opposed to focusing on the user interface. They now have bandwidth to solve a much larger problem.

One of those larger industry operations process problems is called *kitting,* stemmed from Dentsply Sirona's mass personalized products. They make dental restorations from implants. A regular dental implant has the implant itself and goes into the bone. Then the abutment is interfaced with the implant, and the crown is cemented to the abutment. "We make the top to input the abutment. We also make peripheral products to help with the surgery or the procedure." Some of the products are 3D printed and some are mail. Everything is patent specific, and no two orders are the same. After all, since there are 32 teeth in the mouth, you can have 32 possible variations for each implant. There is also a screw that is specific to each implant, with about 70 screw options. So without a product like Tulip, it was information overload.

Dentsply Sirona leveraged Tulip's Edge capabilities to further improve the kitting app and error proof the process. A senior process engineer led the process, not a whole team. The app controls Tulip's Light Kit, a pick-to-light solution, so that the bin with the correct parts illuminates to guide the operator, ensuring he or she picks the right part for each kit. The app connects with a printer that prints a label with the order's information, further preventing mistakes. Finally, the app integrates with a camera to take a photo of the package contents before shipping. This increased the traceability of orders and the accountability of workers involved.

Squeezing the last 20% of value out of their operations is where most global businesses need to go in the time to come. It is not easy. The managed simplicity of no-code apps made the difference for Dentsply Sirona. Gains were made without switching out their existing legacy systems or even the newer systems that likely had been acquired at great cost, and the no-code system simply fits between the cracks. But it wasn't so straightforward to make the case. In fact, when Ron presented his idea to take a completely standardized use case and tweak it to simplify Dentsply Sirona's complexity, his colleagues laughed at him. To turn that around takes strong conviction. At the heart of digital lean lies a deep digital transformation journey.

# CONCLUSION

Empowering industrial work will not happen by itself. Rather, it is a journey with explicit actions required both by workers, management, and the organization as a whole. New, lightweight technology to complement humans better than legacy systems is also part of what makes this possible. Both industrial manufacturer DMG MORI and medical manufacturer Dentsply Sirona chose a no-code, self-serve platform; it was not implementation hand-holding but their own efforts that saved them. Their experiences indicate that with a focus on continuous improvement, the journey is the destination. Those who aim for perfection might meet up with obsolescence. The challenges of deskless workers cannot be solved only with a fancy software approach. It must be developed from the ground up, ideally by those operators who already know what the bottlenecks, challenges, and opportunities are. No system should be allowed to change a company's basic operational principles just because it is convenient for the system and its integrators who stand to benefit.

Digital transformation is, by definition, a painful process. Rather, it is a set of distinct transitions on a longer change journey. The challenges of a manufacturing environment are highly specific, and at times seemingly discrete: how to improve work instructions, how to achieve more efficiency out of industrial machinery, how to build a product with less faults, and, the big operational challenge: how to avoid the manufacturing line shutting down. The emerging digital environment allows clients to order on demand, requesting highly specific build-to-order modifications. As much as the technologies allow for innovation, they also challenge the production process, the leadership principles that used to prevail having to do with exerting a certain control over the workforce, and the production environment. Adding to that, in a regulated environment, digital processes must be standardized to a fault, must be traceable, secure, and provably reliable. We are at a point in manufacturing where lean approaches must be enhanced by digital. At the same time, digital transition must be carried out in a lean way; we cannot have one without the other.

In the next chapter, we will present augmented lean (AL), a management framework balancing the roles of humans, automations, and IT platforms. It is our firm belief that the time has come to merge the classic lean manufacturing frameworks with a human-centered approach to technology. We think implementing such an approach is the logical next step past the trivial digital lean, and companies who realize that will achieve sustainable digital transformation.

# REFERENCES

Augmented (2021, ep. 14). Bottom up and Deep Digitization of Operations. Episode 14. Interview with Dr. Damir Hrnjadovic, Managing Director, DMG MORI Digital GmbH. Augmented podcast. (April 21). https://www.augmented podcast.co/bottom-up-and-deep-digitization-of-operations/ (accessed 29 October 2021).

Augmented (2022, ep. 74). DMG MORI's Digital Journey. Episode 74. Interview with Marius Schmiedt, Head of Operational Excellence, DMG MORI. Augmented podcast. (January 12). https://www.augmentedpodcast.co/74

Augmented (2021, ep. 63). Digitizing Medical Device Operations. Episode 63. Interview with Dan Ron, Lead Engineer, Dentsply. Augmented podcast. (December 8). https://www.augmentedpodcast.co/63

DMG MORI (2021a). Tulip on DMG MORI spindle line at DECKEL MAHO Pfronten.DMGMORI.YouTube.https://us.dmgmori.com/products/digitization/tulip?tax=438344 (accessed 27 October 2021).

DMG MORI (2021b). Pfronten production site. DMG MORI. https://us.dmgmori.com/company/production-sites/pfronten (accessed 27 October 2021).

DMG MORI (2021c). Ideas for Tomorrow. Digital Book. DMG MORI. Unpublished manuscript [update when published]

Edwards, D. (2019). DMG MORI and Tulip partner to offer agile manufacturing solutions. Robotics and Automation. (November 27). https://roboticsand automationnews.com/2019/11/27/dmg-mori-and-tulip-partner-to-offer-agile-manufacturing-solutions/27005/ (accessed 27 October 2021).

Heller, M. (2019. Restructuring IT for growth. *CIO Magazine* (October 23). https://www.cio.com/article/3446697/restructuring-it-for-growth.html (accessed 29 October 2021).

Tulip (2021a). DMG MORI uses Tulip to digitize their spindle assembly line. Tulip. Case Study. https://tulip.co/case-studies/dmg-mori/ (accessed 27 October 2021).

Tulip (2021b). Tulip's apps helped Dentsply Sirona cut training times by 75% while reducing errors in a complex kitting process. Tulip. Case Study. https://tulip.co/case-studies/dentsply/ (accessed 27 October 2021).

Tulip (2021c). When demand disappeared overnight, Double H Nurseries stood up a new digital order process in four weeks. Tulip. Case Study. https://tulip.co/case-studies/double-h/ (accessed 27 October 2021).

# PART II

# THE COMING OF AUGMENTED LEAN

# CHAPTER 5

# THE AUGMENTED LEAN FRAMEWORK

I n the next decade, we foresee industry as a whole moving toward mass-customized, digitized, diverse, modular, lean, sustainable, and human-centric principles, aspects that are only found in pockets of industrial activity today. What the organization should demand from its workforce is similarly ambitious: workers need to be ambidextrous, working and training all the time in a combined effort and also resting more effectively and deeply, on work and off. This will amount to a new industrial revolution but not in the way previously construed as Industry 4.0. As should be abundantly clear from the argument we are making throughout this book, the revolutionary change does not lie in the automation of processes but in the augmentation of human intelligence by cautious symbiosis with machines, using data, for the purposes of improving operations. Our argument does not in this case depend on the emergence of some kind of sci-fi hybrid between humans and machines, but rather simply implies clever and seamless machine interfaces that help human workers do what they do best. However, to achieve this, any technology or device present in the workplace or on the shop floor must prove its worth by its augmentation potential, not by its automation effects.

There are striking differences between the way the previous four industrial revolutions were brought about and the way our current revolution will need to unfold. This time, its evolution will be worker-led, or at least led from within the ranks. We have highlighted the role of the operator level on the factory floor. A manufacturing operator is in charge of production equipment before, during, and after manufacturing. This key role is typically filled by someone with a vocational degree or with apprenticeship training. Training is arguably the industry's most pressing challenge. But perhaps we have been thinking about it all wrong. Is it really training when workers are being augmented? It all depends on what augmentation means. If it means being asked to keep learning new technologies that never get any easier to learn, that's perhaps not the solution. Is there another way?

Consider this: at another few levels up in the hierarchy, we find another key set of employees. The unsung heroes of manufacturing are the industrial business process evangelists and engineering product leaders who embrace the augmented lean approach. Traditionally, and for good reason, organizational change requires buy-in from senior management. Augmented lean is similar but different in important ways. The operations managers – many are engineers, others are MBAs in operational roles – who rule our book are Andy Burton at Double H, Marius Schmiedt at DMG MORI, Dan Ron at Dentsply Sirona, Lena Jaentsch at HERMA, Audra Kirkland in Terex, Mark Nash at Outset Medical, and others. You might think of specific figures in your own work context. The striking thing is, they may or may not have global operational responsibility, but their impact tends to far outstrip their formal role. The reason is that they transcend their role. The management literature calls them "boundary spanners" for being willing and able to share knowledge in creative ways across the organization (Keszey 2018).

As for us at Tulip, without these enterprise-wide operations champions, we wouldn't be able to continue to innovate. Our product would not have come as far. We learn every time we interact with them. In any SaaS company, the user feedback sessions are always among the most important interactions to have. These are occasions where the vendor shares new proposed functionality or gets feedback on existing products. Hand in hand with that is the educational platform, which is an extension of the 24/7 product support that differentiates great product companies from traditional businesses. We will explore that platform in Chapter 9. However, this is not only about education. Similar to other companies that bring novelty, the thrust around the product fosters enthusiasm. At times, that enthusiasm becomes a movement. You can usher a movement, but you cannot create it. Now, we want to clarify how the manufacturing industry (and with them sooner or later all of industry) got from classic lean to digital lean. Most importantly, we are witnessing how the most ambitious companies are about to unleash augmented lean.

# CLASSIC LEAN VS. DIGITAL LEAN VS. AUGMENTED LEAN

Today, you can find the terms *lean, digital,* and *augmented* thrown around in various combinations both by academics and by vendors. We think it is useful to bring a bit more precision to the discussion. We have spent considerable energy implementing, productizing, and evangelizing the future of work technologies and approaches. We have done some academically through each of our PhD theses. We have done so in our commercial work through the startups we have co-founded, Formlabs, Tulip, and Yegii. Building on this experience, we feel that the taxonomy in Table 5.1 is warranted.

**Table 5.1   A Juxtaposition of Classic Lean, Digital Lean, and Augmented Lean**

| | Classic lean (1930–1979) | Digital lean (1980–2009) | Augmented lean (2010–2029) |
|---|---|---|---|
| Origin | Toyota Production Systems (TPS) Total Quality Management (TQM) Six Sigma | MES | MIT Media Lab |
| Core value | Shared desire to improve | Control through management alignment and centralized digital tools | Digital yet human centric, distributed, open platforms for collaboration |
| Technique | Eliminating waste Continuous improvement | Aggregating data w/tech Industry 4.0 automation | Democratized digital work in situ Augmenting workers |
| Examples | Toyota Production System (TPS) | Wonderware & World Economic Forum's Lighthouse Network Factories Dassault Systèmes, Siemens, Körber Werum | Tulip (frontline operations) Airtable (productivity) Samsara (fleet management) ServiceTitan (field service) Procore (project management) Vention (manufacturing automation platform) |
| Effect | Productivity | Efficiency | Empowerment |
| Metaphor | Lean as in no "fat" | Lighthouse as in hierarchical "guiding light" | Greenhouse as in distributed "organic growth" |
| Key proponents | Taichii Ohno (Toyota) James P. Womack, Daniel T. Jones, and Daniel Roos (MIT) Fortune 50 | Rick Bullotta (ThingWorx) Enno de Boer (McKinsey) Francisco Betti (World Economic Forum) MES (ABB, AVEVA, Dassault Emerson, GE Digital, Honeywell, iTAC Software, Oracle, Plex, PSI Metals, Rockwell Automation, SAP, Siemens, Körber Werum) | Pattie Maes (MIT) Natan Linder & Rony Kubat (Tulip) Audra Kirkland (Terex), Marc Nash (Outset Medical) |

The time has come for lean to evolve into augmented lean. The transition is not complete by simply adding digital on top of lean. People and processes fail despite digital tools. This is particularly true in industry, where the complexity of the physical environment (factories, supply chains, or customer interfaces) puts constraints on a purely software-based approach where one size fits all. If the first waves of digital business were about empowering office workers, augmented lean is specifically about giving those working in operational environments superpowers.

However, anybody who has been part of a digitization process knows it to be more complex. Why? Because the digital step is simply a fancy way to automate the process. There is not necessarily a feedback loop back to a human being who is now more empowered or more efficient. That's where augmented lean comes in.

# CORE PRINCIPLES OF AUGMENTED LEAN

Augmented lean is in its early stage of evolution (see Figure 5.1). Because it is superior to others in dealing with the complexity of digital transformation, however, it will likely become the dominant approach. As a result, organizations will become more competitive. It is important to recognize, though, that even if you as a leader need a framework to simplify your management strategy by establishing an overarching direction, augmented lean is not all up to you. The approach must emerge not by decree but by virtue of shared values across the organization. Although leadership buy-in is valuable, operators "in the middle" are crucial to spread augmented lean among scores of workers.

Eight principles should rule the era of augmentation. Forgive us the basketball analogy but we call them *Humanizing Organization Operations*

**Humanizing Organization Operations Principles (HOOPs)**

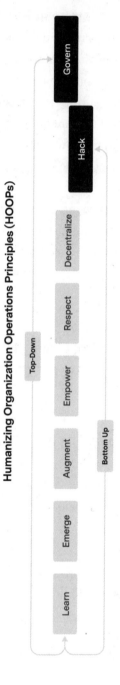

**Figure 5.1** The Augmented Lean Framework.

*Principles (HOOPs)*. They are truly hoops, meaning challenges leaders need to overcome in the pursuit of a better, more efficient organization that works for people, not just for machines. Augmented lean organizations demand something from their humans, too: their full attention.

Beyond pure digitalization, HOOPs put priority on operations managers to enable sustainable change. Once that's in play, HOOPs let workers themselves design their own process, production enhancement techniques, and tracking systems, which ensures less alienation, better user interfaces, and greater work satisfaction. Overall, HOOPs are about a new breed of emergent-governance, which is a combination of leadership and workers interacting with technology to change how a company works. To achieve that, we need to establish principles that value openness to change within certain constraints. Specifically, the eight principles are learn, emerge, augment, decentralize, empower, respect, hack, and govern, which we like to abbreviate as LEADER/HG:

- **Learn.** Every process starts and ends with learning, reflection, and applying what you learn to the next challenge.
- **Emerge.** Industrial organizational changes must emerge bottom-up. They should be human-centric, emphasize self-service over centralized teaching, and be implemented as low-code/no-code apps that don't require software developer skills.
- **Augment.** Build human capability; don't just replace or automate.
- **Decentralize.** Localize responsibility and control; consider operations as a network of people, sites, and systems.
- **Empower.** Each of the workers or managers should be empowered, and so should the plants, factories, locations, and communities that they constitute as a whole.
- **Respect.** Respect all levels of the system, for example, the process, the system itself, the ecosystem, the individual, the workers, and even the boss.

- **Hack.** Ensure all tasks and the overall system remains open, agile, adaptable, lean, and kaizen ("always improving").
- **Govern.** Standardize, clarify, and create a platform for innovation.

Note that these eight principles are only listed *in this order* because they nicely fit the acronym LEADER/HG that, we feel, should become the proud marching order of the frontline operations leaders of tomorrow. The leadership imperative becomes: "Leader: Hack and Govern!" – not because they are process steps that need to be carried out in any particular order. Quite the contrary, we would be incredibly worried about using a waterfall technique to implement *LEADER/HG*. In fact, these are abstract principles that embody an overall approach. However, only implementing three or more of the principles, could potentially yield 80% of the benefits. Each principle is such a major culture shift that getting a handful of them right means setting the foundation for wholesale change. Overall, there is truly only one principle that matters: humans first, automation second. This rule should apply even as the line between humans and machines will further blur as most of us slowly become augmented cyborgs, with more and more essential parts being augmented by technology in some fashion.

Luckily, despite the complexity of doing eight things all at once, augmented lean is not a zero-sum game. The time and attention it takes to become imminently aware of all these activities and embed them into your leadership routine and daily work practices is well spent. Each spills over on other activities and creates doubles and triples in terms of efficiency, especially for larger teams and organizations. Percentages do not do full justice to the concept, since respecting 12.5% of the time or with an eighth of your focus might not be enough to gain trust with a new employee or supervisor. The math is not exact, of course, but try to think of it as a circle of augmentation where each activity augments the other and as a result everyone benefits from it. You can also try to think of a specific digital transformation task and apply the framework to that change process. Eventually, you might find yourself investing more heavily on one aspect one week, in order to master it, and then relax the demands on yourself and focus on another the next week.

Ultimately, any framework is simply an attempt to focus your attention on the most important aspects of your management practice, in a simplified manner that is memorable and shareable. Most conspicuous to many is our omission of Automate, the dictum of most Industry 4.0 digitalization efforts. For us, automation is an interim process, but not a management focus or an end goal in itself. We should only automate to liberate humans to do more creative, value-added, and meaningful work.

The augmented lean framework is not hard to understand intellectually, but it is tricky to execute because one group of persons does not control all the variables. This approach is counterintuitive to classic control theory and how IT leadership typically operates. We offer practical suggestions to overcome that challenge – whether you sit at the top, the middle, or even the bottom. Tables are turned, and the top management will need to rely on well executed actions across the organization – and well beyond its borders. Lastly, even though we describe the framework in this chapter, we have no expectation that it can work as a set of best practices. No framework can do so alone. This is why we have briefly referenced the case studies we use throughout the book and why there are questions at the end of this chapter and all other chapters. Practice is the way to learn, to fail, and to succeed, and the cycle will repeat itself.

---

The uppercase "IT" (as in information technology) is key. Without IT, what you have is Lean + Agile, which is a top-down best practices approach. Digital lean gets you part of the way but is still a top-down approach. Implementing IT, without thinking of empowering operators, simply gives you a digital/agile approach (even if you do it right) and will not answer the complexities of cyber-physical systems management in manufacturing.

---

# Learn IT – Ground Yourself in the Problem

Workplace learning is fundamentally a misunderstood topic. We have traditionally approached it from the perspective of teaching employees new skills needed to operate new equipment as cheaply as possible instead of tackling the intrinsic motivation of the learner. Why would you want to learn? What would you want to learn? How can we assist you? Most teaching and learning moments for adults occur in a practical context, reflecting on a problem they themselves have encountered (Undheim 2020).

We are often impatiently seeking solutions way too early in a process of inquiry. The instinct is understandable. We have a business challenge, so we need a solution. Instead, we should be thinking about what the problem is, what it feels like, when it occurs, and we should describe it deeply from as many angles as possible. Only when we fully understand what the problem is can we truly expect to find solutions. Those earlier solution attempts will not get to the bottom of it, and the problem will keep repeating itself.

Industrial processes, especially operational challenges, might manifest themselves as bottlenecks that would need immediate attention (to get the assembly line moving again, to address supply chain shortages), but they are rarely that simple. The higher-order problems are often to blame. If we don't address those, the problem will yet again reoccur.

Sometimes the problem truly is very simple and should not be over-complicated by explanations. In those cases, there could be extremely easy fixes that address tiny hiccups that occur along the way but that, when compounded, create a problem. Quality is often such a challenge. Work changeover is another.

As we will see in Chapter 7, at Terex, they used augmented lean during COVID-19 to build an access app over a few weeks using extremely basic components (a stand, an off-the-shelf camera, a screen, and a Tulip digital app platform), enabling workers to return to work safely – at a cost of less than $500. At the end of the day, every process starts and ends with learning, reflection, and applying what you learn to the next challenge.

# Emerge IT – Emancipation Through Work

Enabling technology is commonly understood as something of a game changer to a process. It makes new things possible with lesser friction, perhaps at lower cost, at a grander scale. But the emergence principle is not reserved for technology; there are also enabling cultures (much as there are cultures of resistance). Emergence is a freedom principle: do whatever makes what you, the team, or the organization is trying to achieve, easier.

Emergence means acknowledging that change cannot start from the top; it has to emerge from below (Undheim 2008). It is by enabling workers to do things they previously could not, or were not allowed to do, that change happens. Emergence, a favorite principle among those studying complex systems, is human-centric at the core. What we are trying to do is enable human frontline workers, or any employee, to perform at their best, whatever that means. The core of work should be emancipation, making each individual express themselves so as to feel more free than they did before. The emergence principle is therefore an ethical principle, as well. Moreover, it is a self-service concept. Leadership should attempt to foster enabling practices and provide enabling environments, but ultimately, the responsibility for emancipation rests with the individual. Worker – free yourself.

We will see the "emergence principle" at work in Chapter 7 when we describe how Terex deployed industrial apps to train their employees during COVID-19's lockdown phase across the world in 2020. We will see it at play in Chapter 13 as Arun Kumar Bhaskaran-Baba tells us how J&J

enables its lab workers to innovate. However, mandating emergence seldom works, since desirable behavior would typically emerge on its own if the conditions have been right for a while.

# Augment IT – Resist Mindless Automation

Understandably, once invented, machines rapidly made it to the factory floor, making goods more affordable, saving labor cost, and, as a result, raising living standards. At least on paper. The irony is, the quicker they did, the worse the result in terms of overcrowding in cities, pollution, working conditions, and unhealthy work habits (Rafferty 2022). Had we taken the time to reflect, we might have stalled the first few industrial revolutions by a couple of decades, but the workforce would have been better for it. This is why, at this juncture in history, we should not simply continue to add machines, robots, screens, and edge devices without thinking about what it will do to our work process. Each piece of technology, each bit of hardware, each machine will interact with the process in a different way. Is it a wise move? Is it solving a real problem? Is it a long-term solution? Does it benefit the workforce, rather than just the bottom line?

The "augmentation principle" is humanistic; it values humans above all else. It is humans that should be connected workers. It is the machines that should be monitored, not the people. "The augmentation principle is restorative, not substitutive. You should aim to restore balance, dignity, value, sensory function, even foster a sense of belonging through connecting workers more directly to the material world they are working on. This is the opposite of virtualization; you want to create a tangible sense of "engineering," a more concrete sense of the materials being worked on, a more powerful presence on the shop floor. You want to complement human sense making, not obliterate it.

The augmentation principle is personalized. You augment people if and when they themselves agree that added functionality will better human senses (hearing, sight, smell, taste, touch, movement, balance, spatial awareness, and precision), either because it is lost due to accident or age or because superhuman capabilities would be beneficial both to the individual and to the collective.

Importantly, we are not saying that the material and systemic aspects of industrial work are not important – far from it. However, in order to get the orchestration of the parts right, we cannot start with, or always obsess over, what the imperfect machines need to operate better. Instead, or at least in addition to, we need to look at the opposite angle: what do industrial workers need to create better industrial systems? The fact that the "knowledge worker" with a desk is the object of hundreds of thousands of startup innovations and the knowledge worker without a desk only has engendered a few hundred startups is ground for reflection. We should augment information technology with what humans can add to them.

The augmentation principle is best exemplified by the work of Professor Pattie Maes at the MIT Media Lab, featured in Chapter 9, a co-founder of Tulip. At her lab, the Fluid Interfaces research group, all work serves the purpose of enabling humans to be whatever they want to be, augmenting people with increasingly fluid interfaces to technology, despite their mind's or body's shortcomings. With that in mind, together with her students, she has developed prototypes for wearable aroma dispensers (to regulate a user's mood), augmented reality glasses (enhancing cognition), silent speech (enhancing speech), visual helpers (enhancing vision), and much more (NTT Data 2021).

Dr. Maes says:

I realized that computers could augment people. That's what all of my research is really about. Our lives are so busy and there are so many choices to make, so many opportunities to keep track of, and so much accessible information; we end up feeling overwhelmed. If we could make computers smarter and better serve people, we'd be on to something. I think of this as intelligence augmentation – IA rather than AI. (Rifkin 2000)

Future personal digital devices may help us with issues such as attention, motivation, behavior change, memory, and emotional regulation. Many of these devices will serve a purpose in the workplace as well, in which it is particularly important to guard workers against unwanted dependence, poor privacy, or lack of control.

# Decentralize IT – Spread Responsibility to the Edge

Decentralized responsibility is an integral part of most governance paradigms in organizations as diverse as governments and global corporations. We think of it as a key component of augmented lean, because it emphasizes that if you want to foster innovation and have a flexible set of operational practices that cater to individual regions, sites, and regulations, you cannot centralize everything. Specific local challenges might occur in a pattern and time that can be easily monitored centrally. If so, the control of the system cannot only reside within the global leadership. The lean approach is to augment the edge or "bottom-up," so to speak.

Control is always elusive in any complex industrial organization and environment. The amount of X factors that influence demand and production cannot be modeled efficiently with current systems, and perhaps they never will. Given that context, centralized control does not have as many positives as negatives. Standardized interfaces, global governance protocols, and ethical frameworks can and indeed must cross such boundaries but everything else cannot. Even technologies and apps cannot be the same across factories and sites because each context is different. This is one reason why we feel that as useful as the "global lighthouse" approach to best practices might seem, when it comes down to it, nobody should copy another's approach to excellence, even if they could.

Decentralization can be a management strategy to accelerate growth through massively scaled up learning and collaboration. We have seen this principle work with the growth of open source code and community efforts since the late 1990s, now powering enterprise software solutions in most companies worldwide. In manufacturing, the process each company employs is its intellectual property (IP), and companies are thus reluctant to share all aspects of their process. There is no code-sharing repository with version control and collaboration such as GitHub (2008–), there is no tech Q&A site such as Stack Overflow (2008–). However, many software components are already shared and more are shareable, as are best practices. Open manufacturing (Bauwens, 2011) is indeed a new production model in which physical objects are produced in an open, collaborative, and distributed manner.

Emerging open source manufacturing software providers and initiatives include the recent initiative, the Open Manufacturing Platform, a global alliance "helping manufacturing companies accelerate innovation at scale through cross-industry collaboration, knowledge and data sharing, and access to new technologies," founded in 2019 by the Linux Foundation (https://open-manufacturing.org/). There are many ways to go about it, but to catalyze change from the ground up, being organized in communities of practice across companies and concerns is a great way, whether the metric is source code, collaboration, devices, related to specific cyber-physical systems, or industry-wide management approaches. Most successful standardization efforts also emerged this way, so the end result could go beyond sharing and being inspired, evolving into commitment to shared interfaces and platforms. Tulip, as one example, is taking the initiative to build a frontline operations app exchange, taking the cue from

Salesforce, a cloud-based provider in the customer relationship management (CRM) space, who has their enterprise cloud Marketplace where you can "find proven apps and experts to help you solve business challenges" (https://appexchange.salesforce.com/). The degree of openness of such initiatives can vary, but often the mere fact that potential vendors are vetted and organized in one place is a value in itself. Either way, there is no contradiction in the fact that centralizing key insights (through collaboration) can lead to decentralized second-order effects from spreading that same information more widely.

Augmenting humans does not have to mean elevating certain human qualities or leaders to a pedestal so they (from a corporate headquarters) can tread their cookie-cutter solutions down on an unwitting organization. Augmentation means to elevate the cognitive and emotional maturity of the workforce as a whole, and each individual in it, so they each and together, can achieve greater results. Wherever the problem occurred (the shift, the factory, the country, the function) is often where that problem can be best recognized. Having said that, technology does allow greater data to flow to other parts of the organization so that more eyes can be brought on the problem. However, there is always diminishing returns, from the mythical-man-month type of argument (where one found that it doesn't help to add an infinite number of software developers) to get a quicker or better software solution if the problem is sufficiently complex and cannot be compartmentalized, to other business problems where coordination is complex and the full context is not possible to share across distance (Brooks 1982).

As we will see in Chapter 13, J&J has successfully started deploying no-code apps to their smaller factory sites because rolling out full-fledged MES systems would be a waste, given all the license costs, long deployment cycles, complex systems integration (for systems with functionality components far outstripping the local need), and costly annual maintenance fees.

Decentralized responsibility is only one powerful strategy among many. In today's globalized world, coordination across distance(s) has created complex supply chain networks (e.g., in Taiwan or in Shenzhen) that cannot or should not be easily dismissed as too risky or too far away to be efficient. No matter how much supply disruption occurs temporarily, and at unpredictable and sometimes unfortunate timing, such as before holidays, it is not efficient for the world as a whole to reproduce advanced electronics manufacturing in every country or even on every continent. We explored these forces in Chapter 4 where we interviewed Professor Yossi Sheffi at MIT. Each of his six books on the topic are instructive (Sheffi 2020).

Spreading responsibility to the edge to localize responsibility and control is, for the most part, a sustainable path forward.

# Empower IT – Bring Everyone Together

True, *empowerment* is a fancy contemporary term, but it reflects a real desire among workers and leaders alike to gain power for themselves and the collectives they believe in or belong to, based on what they deserve as human beings. That is, empowerment is somewhat distinct from aptitude and performance. The intrinsic idea is that most people not only feel slightly powerless faced with the enormousness of everyday life, work, family, and the challenges that come our way, but also that we would like to be on a path to something greater than ourselves.

Empowerment is perhaps the good side of self-help because it assumes that we gain empowerment through others. It is not simply something we can create for ourselves. For that reason, we quite like the term. It is not introspective but leads to extroversion in ourselves and others. How should this translate to the workplace and to augmenting it? It works itself back to how work is, and nearly always has been throughout the industrial period, key to meaning and belonging.

Empowerment is a necessary component of well-functioning governance bodies, whether we are talking about democracies, public companies regulated by transparency laws and financial regulations and the license to operate, or even a fundamental component of identity itself. Those who don't feel at all empowered lose the desire to live because they lose control over their lives and over their living conditions.

Empowerment is crucial for diversity, equity, and inclusion (DEI) efforts. Workplaces seek to empower their workers because they are starting to recognize humans for who they are. Workers are paid to execute certain tasks, and might (also) be expected to make some adjustments. However does work mean we need to lower our expectations to freedom, autonomy, and (in some cases) respect? Humans are, of course, different—each and every one of us from one another. Yet, the workplace needs to treat everyone equally, fairly, and still find ways to especially encourage excellence. How's that possible? We think the augmented lean workplace manages to both empower the collective and at the same time empower each individual.

Empowerment refers to the shared responsibility for improvements that should be implicit from being part of any organization, but which so rarely is explicitly visible. For that reason, empowerment is seldom the main motivation for going to work and excelling at work performance. Empowerment is a powerful personal motivator, but is also fueled by a sense of collective progress. You could say it brings about both and represents the best of both worlds, the egocentric and the egalitarian.

Large and small companies are leveraging online learning, no-code, and hackathons to empower their workforce to drive the digital transformation of their companies from the bottom up. With the help of no-code application platforms (of which Tulip is a prominent example, but not the only one), these companies are empowering their engineers and operators at scale. You cannot solve industrial challenges without taking into account every social group that would be affected by your suggested change or solution – workers, managers, plants, factories, locations, communities, or ecosystems.

# Respect IT – Don't Change What You Don't Understand

Achieving perfect knowledge of the current state of a company's operations, a factory's inner workings, a team's challenges may not be possible without drastically interfering with those parts of the organization that seem to be the very most delicate and should not be disturbed. This is why nonintrusive ways to gather knowledge are often preferred by most students of management. On the other hand, as the Hawthorne experiments showed back in the 1920s, when conditions were bad, almost any intervention in the workplace, no matter how small or perhaps insignificant in the grander scheme of things (switching lights on or off, in their case), might make a difference and actually increase productivity because people feel listened to (Mayo 2004).

If contemporary technologies, including data analytics from machines, sensors, and advanced machine learning algorithms have taught us anything at this early stage, it is perhaps that we don't (yet) have perfect knowledge of all that is happening. In fact, knowledge has ballooned just in the past few years – at least the amount of information has. New sources of information pop up all the time (not all equally credible), whether from machine monitoring of traditional industrial equipment, mass survey data from aggregated surveys across industries, or even visual observation data from AI-enhanced vision systems. An increased ability to process that information is only available for the wealthiest, most knowledgeable individuals, teams, and organizations who find themselves centrally located in those information flows in the first place.

Even if information flow has increased toward those in power (managers, executives, governments, big tech companies), that does not mean that the workforce necessarily has benefited from the same. And, if they haven't, your company has not optimized its learning and is not getting the maximum effects out of its investments in industrial technology. Dashboards that only flow up the hierarchy are significantly less useful than those that flow both ways. Transparency only enhances productivity if it is complete; otherwise, the bits that are missing could mean the context to interpret the information is lacking.

Most organizations are blind to their operating performance. At best, some data is collected but remains in its original context where it was collected (inside of a machine's memory, in a spreadsheet, on a whiteboard, or even on a piece of paper). Deep understanding of where it is produced and what it means is often not done. If we are lucky, the data is translated to the next level as a digest. For example, Splunk Infrastructure Monitoring, founded in 2003, is the market-leading service for monitoring and observability of modern cloud environments. We do not question the need for such a service anymore. However, production visibility in manufacturing is hard. Augmented lean tools make it easier, as they generate tons of real-time data that has context. Executives need to fully understand their own organizational levers as well as how the outside world is working and changing. Workers need to fully understand the impact of their own efforts so they can adjust (and improve) their efforts accordingly. Operators need to deeply understand both executive functions and workforce realities on the shop floor; otherwise, the management principles they enshrine into operating procedures will risk being counterproductive. In contrast, the point of augmented sensemaking is to expand human senses, collectively and individually, to see further, listen more intently, and achieve a better understanding of the domain of frontline operations, based on both empathetic and cognitive mastery. Those are the kinds of industrial companies that should build the future.

# Hack IT – Fostering the Factory Hacker

Hackers were early on heralded as the heroes of the IT revolution (Levy 1984). How is it then that industrial IT became so stale? We think the explanation is that the hacker mentality never quite seeped into the thick industrial walls of traditional factories. The culture was already one of control at all costs, which is counter to the experimental, research, and data-led mentality of hackers. What would be the value of resurrecting the hacker mentality and applying it full force to industry? We think considerable benefits are waiting to materialize. As outlined in Chapters 6–9, the open source movement is slowly seeping into manufacturing. However, in addition to adding open source software and the mentality that creates and sustains it into the mix, we would suggest that hacking in industry means something different than it did in academia and in the software industry.

What the "factory hacker" should feel entitled to do is not take any process for granted. If things are done a certain way, and experienced workers or novices who see things in new ways, question them, this should be taken seriously. Very likely, there is no best way. Observation of factory life has repeatedly shown that what we think is a standardized set of activities is in reality occurring quite differently from plant to plant, even from team to team. In classic lean this was an anomaly. In digital lean, one tried to smooth it out by using analytics to show what the efficient way is. In augmented lean, any process needs to start with this consideration: does it empower human beings individually and collectively to perform better as a team? For example, if we are concerned about throughput, we have to ensure that human workers gain and do not lose from efficiency efforts. All humans, regardless of where they operate in the hierarchy of things, should control their own work process. Having agile tools that simplify the digital environment greatly facilitates this quest. Having accountability to the data you produce bottom-up means changes can be well governed without elaborate monitoring schemes.

The "Hack it" principle is not reserved for a specific layer in the organization (e.g., workers, operators, senior managers, directors, or executives). You can and should hack any process at any time. In fact, anybody in the organization should be incentivized to propose such changes and should be allowed to test the best suggestions. The "Hack it" principle does not mean that all standards are bad. There could be a very good reason to keep a few factors stable while you innovate on top of those agreed standards. That has proven fruitful across many domains. The important thing is that unless most stakeholders buy into the standard, it isn't really a standard (Undheim 2021).

The "Hack it" principle ultimately means that one needs to ensure all tasks, and the overall system remains agile, adaptable, and lean. Not only do all workers, operators, managers, and executives need to strive to change for the better, one typically should measure continuous improvement in various ways. However, getting too stuck up in the key performance indicators (KPIs) is also a trap. The kaizen methodology's ideal of gradual productivity improvements must not blind the organization to where discontinuous improvement potential exists. In most organizations, democratizing IT must also mean democratizing OT, operations technology. Forgetting that is often why digital lean efforts fail despite good intentions, expensive tech, and decent tech talent in the IT department. Contrary to what some executives who read too many business books think, you cannot really plan much for innovation. What you can do is adapt, throw everything in, and catch the wave if you are made aware that it is in front of you. Any process, no matter how efficient it seems, will ultimately become a barrier to positive change because better alternatives have emerged. Spotting those opportunities is the job of the scout, but acting on it is the job of the factory hacker.

Adopting the hacking mentality means one must accept that any governance ordinance, management principle, or organizational structure must be thrown out wholesale if/when it, again, becomes a barrier to positive change. To know when that happens, not only should principles be regularly reviewed, they should be regularly and unceremoniously broken. We saw the "Hack it" principle at work in Chapter 8 when we discussed cobots in the industrial workplace, and particularly when we studied how Ready Robotics efficiently trained older-generation mining workers to operate robots.

# Govern IT – Clarify Principles and Standardize the Approach

Governance is a meta-principle of the HOOPs framework and the LEADER/HG principles, because, as a leader, you need to jump through hoops. You cannot force through some idealized changes without adapting to what's in front of you. Obstacles will always materialize, often on short notice. Without governance, no sustainable innovation becomes possible. Doubling down on governance is comforting to larger organizations because this is an approach many are familiar with. However, there is an old way to govern, which is top-down at the detail level at the detriment of local initiatives, and there is a new way to govern, which is rarely top down, but has decisions that need to be made on frameworks within which everything else must operate.

How one gets to those decisions can be fairly democratic, can take into account ample feedback, and does not have to be an executive decision (it would probably be better to put it to a vote). Also, the thing to remember is that governance is the last resort. Only set such rules if absolutely necessary. The reason is that most people do not appreciate governance. The only exception would be if they directly benefit from it, which is rarely the case. Governance is mostly a coordinating function to ensure there is a wide enough pipe, a standardized set of interfaces, or that parts of the organization (or technology) integrate well with other parts, even if they do not necessarily interact in the present moment. Governance is insurance for the future. At best, it creates a platform for innovation.

Lastly, we need to take privacy seriously, not just as a legal imperative, following the letter of the law wherever our factory is operating. Rather, we need to take the eternal view: Is what we are doing conducive to improving the human race and its ability to survive on this planet (or elsewhere)?

# CONCLUSION

Ever simpler production enhancement techniques and tracking systems should ensure less worker alienation, better user interfaces, and greater work satisfaction. We think of augmented lean as a framework of a few elements that include a set of distinct human traits (a hacking mentality), organizational enablement (tools, techniques, technologies), leadership mindset (augment, decentralize, and empower), and systemic awareness (understanding – and respecting – all levels of the system). We offer practical suggestions to overcome that challenge – whether you sit at the top, the middle, or even the bottom – but you have to experience it yourself. In many ways, tables are turned, and even if you are at the very top of the management chain, you will need to rely on well-executed actions across the organization, and well beyond its borders.

Augmented lean is not just a continuation of classic lean, or simply a hybrid of lean and digital (digital lean). Rather, it is a perspective that is highly critical of mindless automation agnostic to the use of technology (unless it makes a critical difference), and that allows a richness of inspiration and creativity in the workplace. What we need in this world is for the majority of people to have jobs that give dignity, a solid wage, interesting challenges every day, and which is as far from dirty, dull, or dangerous as you can get. However, it is not as simple as reproducing the Human Relations school of management (Bolman and Deal 1991), since a lot of technology has happened since those early days of management theory.

Augmented lean is often supported by digital tools, but those would be no-code tools that don't take specialist skills to learn to use. You do not need to go to a university to take part in an augmented lean process, workplace, or team. You simply need to show up with the right attitude and a willingness to explore, listen, learn, and improve with feedback. We should note that augmented lean is not usually a workplace without leaders. Process engineers would still tend to design the broad strokes of your work process, but there would be tremendous liberty in the way you could implement it and ample opportunities to provide positive and negative feedback about how you think it works.

Adopting an augmented lean approach does not mean a workplace without conflicts. Such a workplace might not exist or if it does, we have not seen it. Sometimes you will disagree with the manager, protest the way a peer carries out a process, or lament aspects of the system that are not yet adjusted. No system can be perfect, and since conditions change, even a process highly attuned to system dynamics will never be fully optimized to any and all circumstances.

Lastly, augmented lean is not a place where you do not need skills, it simply is a process where you can learn the skills on the job. The demands to coordinate with others tends to get accentuated. The interdependency on others, even on machines, is quite pronounced. But you are not a mindless part of the network; you work with intention, spirit, and pride.

In the upcoming chapter, we will discuss how to roll out industrial technology according to AL principles. That discussion, for us, is a juxtaposition of two management approaches, one top-down and the other bottom-up. Incidentally, the next chapter serves as a reminder about how hard it is to transfer best practices. We do not pretend that just reading a framework will enable you to put it in place. For that, you need to experiment on your own, and if and when given the right tools, you can make it happen.

# REFERENCES

Bauwens, M. (2011). The Emergence of Open Design and Open Manufacturing. *WE_Magazine.*https://snuproject.wordpress.com/2011/12/17/the-emergence-of-open-design-and-open-manufacturing-we_magazine/ (accessed 9 March 2022).

Bolman, L. G., & Deal, T. E. (1991). *Bolman, L. G., & Deal, T. E. (1991). Reframing organizations: Artistry, choice, and leadership. Jossey-Bass.* San Francisco: Jossey-Bass.

Brooks, Frederick P., Jr. (1982). *The Mythical Man-Month: Essays on Software Engineering.* Reading, Mass.: Addison-Wesley Pub. Co.

Keszey, T. (2018), Boundary spanners' knowledge sharing for innovation success in turbulent times," *Journal of Knowledge Management,* Vol. 22 No. 5, pp. 1061–1081. https://doi.org/10.1108/JKM-01-2017-0033

Levy, S. (1984). *Hackers: The Heroes of the Computer Revolution.* Sebastopol: O'Reilly Media.

Mayo, E. (*2004*). *The Human Problems of an Industrial Civilization.* London: Routledge. [1933]

NTT Data (2021). Machines will expand our capabilities and help us better understand our internal state. NTT Data. Research Projects. (March 15). https://www.nttdata.com/global/en/foresight/academic-collaborations/mit-media-lab-pattie-maes (accessed 20 November 2021).

Rafferty, J.R. (2022). The Rise of the Machines: Pros and Cons of the Industrial Revolution. *Britannica.com* (accessed 20 January 2022).

Rifkin, G. (2000). Pattie Maes and Her Agents Provocateurs. Thought Leaders. *Strategy+Business.* Third Quarter 2000. Issue 20 (July 1). https://www.strategy-business.com/article/19707 (accessed 20 November 2021).

Undheim, T.A. (2008). *Leadership From Below.* Morrisville, NC: Lulu Press.

Undheim, T.A. (2020). *Disruption Games.* Austin, TX: Atmosphere Press.

Undheim, T.A. (2021). *Future Tech.* London: Kogan Page.

# CHAPTER 6

# HOW TO ROLL OUT INDUSTRIAL TECHNOLOGY THE RIGHT WAY

Enno De Boer, the well-groomed and enthusiastic Global Head of Manufacturing at McKinsey & Company, approached the World Economic Forum about the Global Lighthouse Network back in 2018, a best practice initiative for factory automation and productivity. Growing up in Germany, his dad was an engineer, and young Enno first got stimulated to get into the steel industry, but wanted something more sophisticated. Initially, he worked in the automotive industry, for BMW, and got really excited about it. He ended up getting his master's and doctorate in mechanical engineering. Eventually, De Boer got even more excited by the shop floor. "That's where the real music is," he said. His passion became to make products better.

De Boer is a poster child for innovation in his field and could seemingly even convince a rock to get engaged. "I think it's one of the most exciting spots to be for all young people. I just say, go into manufacturing. That's where all the fun technologies come to bear. Is it augmented reality, virtual reality? Are they digital twins? Is it AI? Is it digitalization? Is it 3D printing? All of that is coming to manufacturing." De Boer feels there's an impending renaissance in manufacturing, although, to him, it's been an evolution, "because in the manufacturing sector, you cannot change overnight" (Augmented 2021, ep. 4).

To a sailor, the lighthouse metaphor is easily explained: "When I'm coming to the coast and the first thing is I see this light and it's gone up and it's leading the way." What that means in manufacturing is that:

> First of all, we want to see impact at scale. Second, we want to see that unleashed by several use cases, several technologies that enable that like really innovation there. And then we want to see that this is sustainable, that there are the measures and the enablers below that it's not only sustainable, but also scalable [...] a lighthouse [is] something that excites people. They say I want to have a lighthouse in my organization. How do I do this? That's exactly what we wanted to create. We wanted to [ensure] that everyone gets a feeling of what this really is, Industry 4.0. (Augmented 2021, ep. 4)

But even though De Boer and his team at McKinsey, together with the World Economic Forum, initially surveyed some 1000 facilities to get to their first 20 "lighthouses," the difficulty is not in recognizing excellence. The complexity is in recreating it, which De Boer is the first to admit. To our question of how to innovate in manufacturing:

The first question I have is: what business impact do you need to drive? That determines everything because a lighthouse is not a lighthouse. First of all, I need to know whether you want to drive growth, whether you want to drive agility, mass customization, sustainability, productivity, or speed to market. Let me know. That's already a hard question because a lot of [the people I meet] say: "I haven't thought about it." Then, let's go backwards and say, what are Lighthouse [use cases] that will really help you? Typically it's 20 to 30, maybe 40 use cases that immediately will drive fundamental value. Let's take them. And then, the most important thing is let's figure out: how do we scale this? Because that's what has been the biggest challenge. I would say that is what differentiates the 1% of the lighthouses and the rest of the 99%. It's called pilot purgatory. We have seen thousand-flowers-bloom-approaches, pilot after pilot, and they are not scaling. [...] The other part, I think, is culturally, Lean has taught us to desegregate, to democratize, and to spread literally every-thing across all our production network and let everyone do a little bit of something. (Augmented 2021, ep. 4; see Interview 6.1)

**Interview 6.1**  A Renaissance in Manufacturing. Episode 4. Interview with Enno De Boer, Partner, Digital Manufacturing Lead, McKinsey. Augmented podcast.

As we see it, you have two choices when it comes to learning best prac-tices and rolling out industrial technology: the lighthouse approach or the greenhouse approach. A lighthouse is a tower designed to emit light from a system of lamps and lenses serving as a navigational aid for maritime pilots at sea. A greenhouse is a structure made chiefly of transparent material, in which plants requiring regulated climatic conditions are grown. Even if greenhouses now are part of precision agriculture with digital parameter control, a greenhouse is still an organic growth vessel where each plant is allowed to bloom in its own individual way, as opposed to the lighthouse, which steers ships into a cleared path.

What are the duties of an industrial best practices "lighthouse keeper" compared to an industrial tech "gardener"? How different are these two approaches when you apply them as metaphors for contemporary industrial operations? What are the realities on the ground? How do you implement each approach well? Which one is more inspirational? Which is leaner? Which is more scalable? Which is more sustainable? Can they be combined, and if so, what would this mean for manufacturing leaders?

With the lighthouse approach, which is top down, you follow the world's best factories according to the World Economic Forum, and attempt to copy the blueprint approach. This is, needless to say, the McKinsey approach (and the project is led by none other). With the greenhouse approach, which is bottom up, you experiment on your own, letting your own resources and workforce grow in the most efficient way, yet still according to their own direction and desires. This is Tulip's approach. Do both methods have merit? Can they be combined?

# THE GLOBAL LIGHTHOUSE NETWORK: TOP-DOWN SYNTHESIZED BEST PRACTICES

The Global Lighthouse Network, a World Economic Forum project in collaboration with McKinsey & Company, has collected best practices from 90 factories that represent the best of advanced manufacturing from big industrial companies around the world (accompanied by a few notable smaller companies), arguably with outsized performance improvements such as 250% productivity increase, 89% faster to market, and 97% $CO_2$ emissions reductions (McKinsey & Co. 2021a, WEF 2021). As Marc Nash at Outset Medical says: "One of the things within the Lighthouse Network that I find very compelling is some of the cash flow improvements that they've shown through modeling working with McKinsey" (Augmented 2022, ep. 70). Of the 90 and growing in the network, there were 9 in the original cohort in September 2018 (WEF 2018), 7 were added in January 2019 (WEF 2019), 10 were added in July 2019, 18 added in January 2020 (WEF 2020), 10 added in September 2020 (Whiting 2020), and 21 new sites were added in September 2021(WEF 2021). Only two are greenfields, and only two are small-and-medium size companies, which arguably means there is a slight selection bias against smaller companies, facilities, and factories. See the Appendix for the full list of factories, their industries, locations, mother companies, and what they were awarded for.

To judge by the lighthouses, the most digitally advanced manufacturing facilities are in China by a large margin (see Table 6.1). However, both the US and Germany have a few excellent factories. Regionally, Asia dominates Europe and North America. All of this was generally known, but the lack of US excellence in manufacturing is perhaps shocking to policy makers in the US – and we would indeed hope it is, given its automotive legacy. Germany's five lighthouses is also not an impressive number considering their reliance on manufacturing. In terms of technologies, it would seem that China dominates manufacturing AI and digital supply chains. Similarly, European lighthouses are overweight in digital twin technologies. Surprisingly, perhaps, China comes out strong in the new sustainability metrics. There is not enough data to say something meaningful about other countries given that the numbers are so low (not that any of these differences are statistically significant, apart from the China dominance). Lastly, only two of the 90 factories, Arçelik (2018, Ulmi, Romania) and Tata Steel (2016, Kalinganagar, India), are greenfields.

Table 6.1    Broad Typology of Lighthouses

| Country (# of factories) | Technology | Sector | Impact |
|---|---|---|---|
| China (27) | AI, Analytics (15) Mass-customization Supply chain | Automotive (1) Compressors Electrical equipment Sensors | Mass-customization (2) Productivity Sustainability (5) |
| USA (10) | Bioengineering (1) Robotics (2) | Consumer products (1) Electronics (1) Pharma (1) | Customer conversion rate (1) Labor cost (1) Speed-to-market (1) |
| Germany (5) | Chemical (1) Digital twins (1), Industrial tech IoT Robotics (1) | Automotive (1) | Agility (1) Customization (1) |
| Asia (45) | AI Analytics (20) Mass-customization Supply chain Sustainability | Automotive (1) Sensors (1) Steel (5) | Efficiency Productivity Sustainability |
| Europe (22) | Digital twins (5) Robotics (2) Smart factory | Consumer products (1) Digital twins (5) Pharma (1) | Agility (1), Customization (2) |

Now, are all of these things true? They are certainly truths with modifications. For example, there are hundreds, perhaps thousands of excellent small factories all around the world that are not (yet) part of the Lighthouse Network. We know this, because we have worked with some of them, and they cannot all be outliers. Does that matter, you say? We think it does, because the lighthouse methodology (so far) invites big brands, companies that are members of the World Economic Forum, to apply, and the rigorous assessment criteria favor large factories and staff that have the time (and incentive) to answer such questions. As a result, if you only look at lighthouses, you get a skewed impression of what digital excellence takes. Perhaps it doesn't involve big budgets? Perhaps leadership buy-in is less important than it seems so far? Perhaps the technologies assessed here skew toward the fancy (5G, AI, drones, robotics) versus the everyday efficiency challenges of the shop floor, which still involve going paperless, or conflate the value of simple, inexpensive sensors? We will leave these questions for now, and explore the lighthouse effort in much more depth, which it deserves.

The goal of the Lighthouse Network is to help the more than 70% of companies that are still stuck in "pilot purgatory" through top-down inspiration. At the same time, the movement of software-driven manufacturing largely driven by tech startups is arguably proceeding in an opposite direction. New tools have given subject area experts technical capabilities outside of their area of specialization, allowing them to proceed bottom-up with some governance criteria.

Broadly speaking, one might say that industrial frontrunners excel at the three key drivers of the fourth industrial revolution – connectivity, flexible automation, and intelligence (deBoer, Leurent and Widmer 2019). A 2019 report on the insights derived from Global Lighthouse factories found that the designated forerunners in their network were scaling Industry 4.0 transitions faster than its peers because they operated differently on six dimensions:

1. Practiced agile working modes, failing fast and learning continuously in two-week sprints not one-year pilots
2. Partnered with an outside ecosystem of suppliers, customers, and universities, exchanging data and solutions across tech platforms
3. Deployed effective learning methods through gamification, digital learning, and experimenting with augmented reality
4. Committed to often costly scale-up efforts to upgrade their IIoT infrastructure
5. Co-located multidisciplinary transformation teams (engineers, data scientists, product managers, and agile coaches)
6. Established clear governance models including a centralized transformation office across the enterprise (WEF 2019)

Common among all lighthouses seems to be a strong focus on upskilling their workforce. The De'Longhi plant in Treviso, Italy, which makes bean-to-cup automatic coffee machines, went from a relatively uncompetitive site into a manufacturing lighthouse, where its labor productivity rose by 33%. Similarly, US-based manufacturer Flex's site in Althofen, Austria, raised revenue by 50% within the same physical footprint by "building a future-ready workforce" (de Boer, Giraud and Swan 2021).

Technology is clearly front and center of lighthouses, too, even if it's not their most striking feature. One example is BMW, which has standardized on a new technology recently unveiled by graphics chip maker Nvidia, the Omniverse, to simulate every aspect of its manufacturing operation, reducing production planning time by 30%. The shift must be understood in the context of the increasingly customized high-end car market where BMW now gives customers 2100 ways to configure their car. Having production systems (CADs, PLMs, ERPs, MESs, QMs, and CRMs) "synchronized around a single source of data everyone could understand," and simulating and testing model configurations at scale, is essential to achieving speed and accuracy once BMW goes live in production (Columbus 2021).

# Critique of Best Practice Approaches

Having run two major best practice frameworks (ePractice.eu and MIT Startup Exchange), Trond can say with some confidence that the advantages in such approaches lies in the aligned interests of the organizers and the awardees in promoting the scheme. That part tends to produce positive externalities and inspiration where inductees pat themselves on the back (which is good and, at times, well deserved).

Internally in an organization, creating a lighthouse can have unintended consequences and could actually contribute to the "pilot purgatory" it attempts to bypass (Littlefield 2021). If the lighthouses are too visible, for example, they might lead to a mindset that focuses on technology testing rather than on solving business problems. Lighthouses also add strength to strengths rather than emphasizing moving the bottom half of plants to higher efficiencies, less waste, and lower downtimes. Alternatively, one can also simply deploy incremental approaches that focus on low-hanging fruit that lead to small wins without huge investments. Arguably, a lighthouse is not scalable, is often an expensive endeavor (upwards of $10 million per plant), and makes use of highly specialized, external resources (e.g., the likes of McKinsey & Co or other top tier industrial strategy consultants such as Bain, BCG, or Arthur D. Little).

A major issue we see with the Lighthouse approach is the false implication that creating a lighthouse entails hiring strategy consultants, quality coaches, or third party implementers. Whilst, again, we see nothing wrong with taking advice from others, there is a distinct advantage to making the best use of an organization's in-house capabilities (which we also cover in the upcoming Chapter 7).

Either way, a most interesting type of analysis would be to revisit the lighthouses three to five years after their designation to see what happened. For example, synthetic biomanufacturing darling Zymergen (Emeryville, USA), founded in 2014, has highly automated labs for materials discovery and microbe engineering as well as facilities for scale-up and manufacturing (Bomgardner 2021), which became a lighthouse factory in July 2019, "having realized a 40% increase in our production yield and a 50% reduction in lead time, all while lowering our operating costs by 42% – simply by optimizing our capacity, inventory and teams" (Hoffman 2020). The World Economic Forum description of its factory said: "A digital native, this bio-engineering site is using robotics and artificial intelligence on processes that have traditionally been highly manual, resulting in a doubling of its innovation rate" (WEF 2019).

Zymergen did a spectacular IPO where it raised $500 million, yet is letting go 120 workers after its first product failed and its CEO departed. The reason seems to be manufacturing-related, too, given that several major customers were encountering challenges with the implementation of Hyaline, a high-quality flexible polymer film used for electronic displays, into their manufacturing systems (Levine 2021). The question then becomes: What good does it serve to be efficient in the use of Industry 4.0 if quality suffers? Also, what went wrong at this world top-90 factory? Clearly, even external scrutiny cannot always detect flaws. Either way, the scale-up of Hyaline reportedly will be moved to a contract manufacturing facility in Japan (Bomgardner 2021).

# What the Lighthouse Approach Gets Right

What does the lighthouse approach get right? We agree that digital technologies are ready to scale in the world's biggest industrial factories and companies. We also agree that in order to scale it is often best to plan for scale (and this is an essential part of the recipe to escape pilot purgatory) but also remember to iterate and adjust to new circumstances. Lighthouses also demonstrate that the necessary commitment is both to emerging technologies, to management approaches, and to the workforce. All of these aspects have to work in unison in cross-disciplinary efforts. Finally, sustainability, a focus of current World Economic Forum lighthouses, is good for the bottom line because eco-efficiency implies good economics and reduced waste, key aspects of lean (Klaess 2020).

Favoring greenhouse, bottom-up experimentation, tech startups like Tulip and others are sending out "factory kits" for engineers who Gartner calls "citizen developers" who try out solutions on their own, and solve problems without coding expertise. When equipped with 24/7 online support as well as training videos, they build IoT-enabled apps that spread across their organization organically. We cover this approach in Chapter 7. For example, an operations manager from a medical device company bought a Tulip factory kit and started experimenting on his own, given the company's issues with having machine data and production data in separate systems, production managed by paper, and only local performance transparency despite the multi-site reality of running a big-scale manufacturing operation. He started small but soon found support within the company and scaled to hundreds of stations across five sites, enabling facility management to make better staffing, work routing, and operational decisions with ~7% capacity improvement and one-month ROI per facility.

Tech needs to be packaged up so people can quickly get the value themselves and show results, teach other people, and scale it. This is the answer for how to avoid being stuck in pilot purgatory. Greenhousing also avoids misusing ROI too early and before you know which direction the process is going.

*The Phoenix Project: A Novel About IT, DevOps, and Helping Your Business Win* (2013) by Gene Kim tells the story of IT manager Bill Palmer, who has 90 days to rescue an overbudget and late IT initiative for an auto parts company, code-named The Phoenix Project. DevOps is a portmanteau of the words *development* (creative chaos) and *operations* (order), two business functions that may have opposite goals but that increasingly must work together seamlessly to succeed in contemporary business. In the *DevOps Handbook* (2016), the argument is extended toward the agility of technology organizations in general, claiming the approach leads to increased reliability and security, as well, because if followed, "regardless of where someone performs work, they do so with the cumulative and collective experience of everyone in the organization" (Kim et al. 2016:13). Sounds like a pipe dream, but when it comes to life, it likely is the ideal scenario for any manufacturing organization that is about to get transformed by the opportunity of empowering operators through letting them use powerful no-code platforms. In such a scenario, the identity of the IT department must change but its mandate does not go away because additional complexity elsewhere in the stack (cybersecurity comes to mind but also because IT must empower nearly every other business function it should not matter to IT departments that they become less of a control function and more of a coordination function) keeps them occupied and essential.

Either way, DevOps focuses on *three ways* to practice agile: (1) the software engineering version of lean flow (technical flow), (2) creating practical ways to enable feedback from both peers, operators, and customers (technical feedback), and (3) enabling learning (technical experimentation), which seems to be their interpretation of Peter Senge's *The Fifth Discipline* (1990). We find the most valuable contribution of DevOps to be that it shows how technology must be seen as a value stream, not as a goal in itself. When that's the idea, no tech can be developed without taking into account end users, and that's a good design principle. It also changes the dynamics between IT and Ops functions as they become peers in a new quest, not antagonists in another quest for dominance. Having said that, as the recent books *Inspired* (2017) and *Empowered* (2020) by product guru Marty Cagan have shown forcefully, productization is hard work that cannot be subsumed to taking in feedback. Creativity is also about making decisions that interpret findings and feedback and consolidate it into product offerings that manage to delight and surprise customers, as well.

## Digital Transformations by Combining Lighthousing and Greenhousing

Throughout this book we have spoken as if industrial tech transformation were one thing. We were simplifying. In reality, there are distinct elements that go into any transformation process and they are not always the same and certainly don't occur in the same order. Companies are at different stages, have different legacy technology, different levels of workforce readiness, and different wallet sizes, needs, and appetite for change.

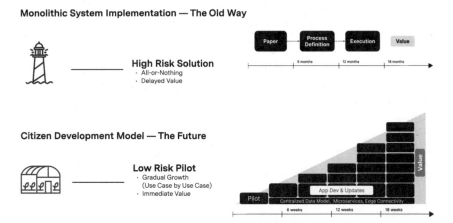

**Figure 6.1** Guided Greenhousing: combining "lighthouse" inspiration with "greenhouse" workforce initiatives.

The fact that we recommend taking an organic approach to rolling out industrial transformation efforts does not mean that we don't seek order in the process. To prove that, we will now cover the organizational elements that most typically can be transformed by a no-code enhanced frontline operations platform. Merely reading a long list of discrete operational processes and tasks that others have accomplished might not be sufficient. For sure, its ROI may convince an executive or senior digitization manager. It might reassure board members that changes are congruent with the organization's core business challenges at any given time. But it will rarely be conducive to building the necessary enthusiasm to enact, at times, painful changes among the workforce or its line operators. Many of these line items are pervasive throughout the operations function, too. This easily becomes overwhelming.

The broad stroke is that there are a few key reasons why operations change more rapidly than ever before. The specific issue of retiring experts can cause a particularly difficult to handle loss of integral production knowledge on the factory floor. Thin profit margins can keep complex operations from scaling successfully, and can lead to conservative approaches and risk-averse behaviors in sectors that exhibit this characteristic. In whichever dynamic environment, industry, or sector we might have in mind, monolithic systems tend to fail. The problems could be complex deployment, systems hard to use by operators, systems that invite an all-or-nothing approach, predefined usage patterns, poor interoperability and many lock-in features, the lack of understanding between operators and the IT department (or even the business leaders), and a strong reliance on vendors and third parties.

A frontline operations platform unlocks value because of its ability to maintain flexibility yet allow for governance protocols that make it work in regulated environments. Cloud-based systems defy the limitations of traditional on-premise installations. Off-the-shelf apps are more flexible than monolithic systems where a host of features are preconfigured but cannot be adapted without great effort. However, it is important to point out that an "app" in this case does not just mean digital visibility of basic information. It would imply the functionality of building logic into workflows where the app either measures the workflow itself or (even better) is connected with tables of information that change something in the real world (takes inventory, ships product, alters machine settings). Such a platform should be able to accommodate a plethora of plug-and-play edge devices (cameras, monitors, sensors, etc.). The interface should be intuitive and allow self-service so you don't have to wait for the IT department to address a service ticket. Finally, the time-to-value should be almost immediate, and should occur before major commitment to a long-term rollout and systems integration is made.

As Table 6.2 shows, the major distinguishing feature of a frontline operations platform is that all the opportunities it captures are available simultaneously to the frontline workforce directly and to management.

**Table 6.2    Critical Capabilities of a Frontline Operations Platform**

| Opportunities | Description | Use cases |
|---|---|---|
| Augment | Enabling workflows with dynamic (digital) work instructions and edge connectors (machines, systems, cameras, devices), enhancing human capabilities (physical or cognitive) | Modular capability, no-code interface, digitized work instructions, guided workflows, training apps, quality detection apps, real-time knowledge apps |
| Digitize | Tracking work orders, jobs, products, skill sets, BOMs, and more with embedded logic where apps are connected with tables and inventory | Work-order tracking, dynamic work instructions, modular app platform with flexible logic |
| Capture | Providing e-compliance, visibility, standardization by collecting data from people, machines, and devices | Audit checklists, weight & dispense, safety & quality checks, GxP, logbooks, and line clearances |
| Monitor | Connecting devices, new and legacy machines, cameras, and sensors to monitor statuses and track KPI | OEE, machine monitoring (both analog and modern machines), machine utilization |
| Visualize | Visualizing everything of relevance on a factory floor, in a facility, and across operations | Production visibility, real-time dashboards, vision capability (camera-tracking of execution steps) |
| Integrate | Ensuring systems are accurate and up-to-date by connecting apps to external systems | Manufacturing control, connecting to systems of record (ERP, MES, IoT platforms, etc.) |
| Improve | Implementing lean practices without disrupting operations, enabling industrial engineers to solve problems without waiting for IT or acquiring software skills | Digital lean manufacturing, kaizen funnel, Andon lights, enabling workers, empowering engineers as creative problem solvers at software scale |

The app-based approach to frontline operations moves whiteboard-and-magnet efforts as well as most paper-based tracking to digital dashboards, smoothes workflows, and fosters tracking with little effort, increasing shop floor visibility, operator efficiency, and management control in the process. All efficiency concerns can be addressed and often a fix that was put in place for one end of the process creates efficiencies in other parts of the process because the benefits of transparency spread across the network. Overall, there are five areas where the frontline operations platform excels: efficiency, quality, analytics and machine monitoring, compliance, and bottom-up enablement.

Throughout the book, we have given examples of how industrial organizations struggle with maintaining the best balance between simplicity and complexity in their operations. Too simple, and you are not able to produce customized products making optimal use of the global supply chain or your own workforce. Too complex, and you clog down your organization in cumbersome processes that end up existing only because the IT system demands it.

# The Best-of-Breed Tech Stack in Manufacturing

A technology stack is a list of all the technology services used to build and run an application, in this case the manufacturing sector as a whole. The emerging tech stack in manufacturing is evolving fast. On-premise solutions will be phased in the near future, but legacy issues prevail in complex factory environments or in smaller sites. Most of the time, the existing, older machines, processes, and databases still determine the flexibility of vendor choice and new efficiencies, unless one is prepared to break with legacy and take the pain of full digital conversions.

It is clear that we are living through a time where the industrial tech stack is changing. The number of software applications is increasing dramatically, and the characteristics of those applications are changing as well. Across the board, user interfaces are becoming more visual and easier to operate for nonspecialists. Specifically, the creation or at least the setting up

## Table 6.3 The Emerging Manufacturing Tech Stack

| STACK -><br>BUSINESS<br>FUNCTIONS<br>\|<br>V | Legacy<br>(1980–) | Transitional<br>(2006–) | Experimental<br>(e.g. state-of-the-art)<br>(2010–) |
|---|---|---|---|
| INFRA-<br>STRUCTURE | The communication backbone went from analog to digital. | Cloud services entered the scene. | Hybrid clouds and industry-specific clouds start to appear. 5G allows no latency in wireless communications. |
| SERVICES | Systems integrators become dominant operations technology consultants. | IT consultants capture territory. | Strategy consultants attempt to bridge the OT/IT divide. |
| OPERATIONS, HR & WORKERS | Paper-based tracking prevails. | On-premise solutions are partially converted to cloud-solutions, allowing some remote operations. | Frontline operations platforms emerge, empowering operators (giving flexibility and freedom from IT-departments or systems integrators). |
| SUSTAINABILITY | Corporate social responsibility (CSR) is born, but no tools, only cumbersome annual reporting. | Eco-efficiency emerges as a concept, a mix that allows for economics within sustainability. | Carbon monitoring emerges as a strong priority, given climate change reality. |
| FINANCE | The first ERP and BI systems emerge. | Accounting moves to the cloud. | Native cloud-based systems change the game. |
| CUSTOMERS | Paper-based tracking and spreadsheets prevail. | On-premise databases with customer data. | Cloud-based CRMs and industry specific ones drastically increase the grasp of the customer. |
| SUPPLIERS | Paper-based tracking and spreadsheets prevail. | On-premise databases with supplier data. | Startups emerge with a new mindset and AI/ML. |

*(Continued)*

## Table 6.3 (Continued)

| STACK -> BUSINESS FUNCTIONS ↓ | Legacy (1980–) | Transitional (2006–) | Experimental (e.g. state-of-the-art) (2010–) |
|---|---|---|---|
| PRODUCTION | Clunky systems emerge. | On-premise solutions (partially) are converted to cloud. | Cloud-native or successfully converted solutions emerge. |
| FACTORY AUTOMATION | On-premise control systems, SCADA, emerge. | Industry specific SCADA emerge. | Factories gradually move to the cloud and greenfields are cloud native. |
| R&D | Little digitization apart from statistics using computers. | The first lab information systems emerge. | Cloud & AI/ML systems begin to change the game. |
| HARDWARE | Basic, bulky, dangerous industrial robots. | One-trick ponies and prototypes of things to come in robotics and wearables. | Edge devices, microlocation, and autonomous capabilities emerge, RPA becomes viable, AR infancy, VR is still embryonic. |
| QUALITY | Statistics, certification, standardization, and lean methodology emerge. | Life science QMS mature. | AI/AR enabled life science QMS began to change the game, but tech still fails to capture operational realities. |
| CODE & LOGIC | Office suites prevail. | The web changes nearly everything, but industry lags behind. | Low-code and no-code software enter industry and prove transformative. |

of applications is becoming possible for engineers and operators who are not software engineers. Given where cyber-physical integration is at, with machines, sensors, and e-commerce systems potentially connected, these applications have the potential to streamline frontline operations. Previously developed applications within a factory or even in a different company, can at times be shared because the processes can often be described without giving away company-sensitive information. Along with that, the quantity and quality of data is increasing, because data can be harvested from nearly all hardware and software sources.

The promise is great. According to Chief Economic Strategist Michael Mandel of the Progressive Policy Institute: "The new manufacturing stack could unlock as much creativity and growth in the industrial sector as the TCP/IP stack did for the internet – not just in the advanced countries but around the world" (Mandel 2019). We would tend to agree, unless the technocrats who don't see the need to integrate humans and technologies the right way prevail and value streams get stumped.

# FOUR DISTINCT WAYS TO DIGITALLY TRANSFORM AN INDUSTRIAL ORGANIZATION

Based on client experiences from hundreds of clients, from multinational corporations to small-and medium sized businesses, we have defined four equally good ways to digitally transform an industrial organization. Which one to choose would depend on the urgency, the organizational culture in place, having identified early champions, and the risk profile of each organization (as well as a host of other factors, but we are simplifying to illustrate four ideal typical ways to go about it). Also, it might be more appropriate to say that the approach will choose you, since one seldom can plan how a transformation occurs.

Table 6.4 is a 4 × 4 table with Tulip clients embedded showing the different models we see, each of which could work well, depending on context. Again, note how we take issue with best practice approaches that prefer distinct implementation modes.

**Table 6.4   Typology of Industrial Transformation Approaches**

|  | Emergent | Planned |
|---|---|---|
| Agile rollout | **A** Outset Medical (medical device) Stanley Black & Decker (industrial) AstraZeneca (pharma) | **B** DMG MORI (industrial) Lærdal (medical device) |
| Incremental rollout | **C** Dentsply (medical device) Pharma company | **D** J&J (pharma/ consumer) |

The four ideal typical ways in which industrial companies successfully approach digital transformation appear to be either: (A) Agile rollout with emergent use cases as they make sense over time and prove out (or upon) need either strategically or based on site-specific demand, (B) Agile rollout planned out from the beginning in great detail to avoid surprises and ensure enterprisewide adoption, standardization, and orderly process, (C) Incremental rollout with emergent use cases as they make sense over time and prove out (or upon) need either strategically or based on site-specific demand, or (D) Incremental rollout but where each element is planned before executing. We will now explain each of the four approaches in more detail.

# Agile and Emergent

Speedy rollout with emergent use cases as they make sense over time and prove out (or upon need either strategically or based on site-specific demand).

# Outset Medical

Marc Nash, vice president of Manufacturing at Outset Medical, Inc., downloaded the Tulip player (the digital platform in which operators can create applications that simplify their shop floor workflow by adding analytics and automatic process steps) and spent several hours using it in trial mode. He was able to make a minimal viable product easily and thought it offered a lot of promise. He said: "My process engineers who work on the floor every single day would definitely be able to manage and thrive in this space more so than I could even thrive" (Augmented 2021, ep. 70).

Nash wanted to make sure that they thought of digitalization from day one, with data collected in real time and displayed throughout the factory to provide both an indication to leadership of "where we are" and to allow for collaboration.

They also wanted ease and flexibility and a tool that didn't take years to learn. Nash said:

Tulip provides a platform that is very flexible, very modular, and is no-code. One of the things that I found very compelling and different in working with Tulip is when we invited them onsite at our headquarters in San Jose, they didn't show up in their traditional suit and ties and leather bound notebooks. They showed up with a Pelican case and said, "Hey, let's get to work," we're not going to actually take anything that has been polished. We're going to actually just build an app together. We're going to learn, and we're going to take your process and do it together in front of you. That was really refreshing. We had brought other large vendors in such as Camstar and some of the other traditional MES platforms. But the conversation was much more of a, let us show you what is possible. (Augmented 2021, ep. 70)

Once Outset Medical had set up the agreement with Tulip, they started a two-month wireframe exercise. "Our thought in how we run our business outside is we go slow to go fast. That is a really key pillar and concept or mantra, if you will, that we use," Nash said. Once they had that framing done, which took about two months, they spent the next four months converting 2,700 pieces of paper and 7,000 steps into over 90 applications. They used a team of three process engineers with zero experience with Tulip:

> The machine that we're talking about is Tablo, which is our console. We're talking almost a hundred hours to build and test the machine. There's over 2,000 components that go into that machine. Each app is going to tell or guide the operator on how to put the machine together. It's going to provide instructions, pictures, and videos we're working on. [It took] two months building one app, getting the framework done, getting it all right. Then within four months we generated 89 other apps. Just imagine the speed and only three people working on it, 60 days roughly of working time between three people, so 180 days, and you have to build 89 apps. Almost every other day an app has to be created. We have about 148 apps on our floor and the additional apps are incremental process improvement steps. They might be a process for spare part inventory or even people operations from an HR time and attendance perspective. [...] It is a vital part of our business to be able to go quickly. If you're in some of these larger monolithic systems if we change our processes, if we change deep changes of how we have some connectivity that [means] tens to hundreds of thousands of dollars of additional incremental consulting work. It could take months to get done. (Augmented 2021, ep. 70)

This empowered the employees and team members, because they felt they could change something that was wrong or could be improved. "I really believe in the empowerment of our employees. If we empower our employees to go leverage the technology, to go learn about the technology, they will surprise us on what they can accomplish. For example, our Mexican quality manager built a tool that aggregates 10 different quality metrics in one dashboard – having only spent three weeks using the Tulip app platform" (Augmented 2021, ep. 70).

What are the impact figures Outset looks at? The areas that they continually look at are quality and the metric is "defects per console." Nothing leaves their factory with a defect. Any defects found during their test process increases over-processing or reprocessing time. They use "first pass yield" as a similar metric, and look at "line capacity," "productivity," or even "consoles per person per day" (or per month). Onset has seen significant improvements in each through controlling the test process upstream, software simulations, or monitoring how the machine is put together. "We're really looking at how we digitize our processes and connect systems, not just in manufacturing, but throughout the entire business from an end to end supply chain perspective," says Nash (Augmented 2021, ep. 70). All in all, Outset Medical created, grew, and scaled a facility in nine months. Already at the six-month mark, it had ramped up capacity 6x.

**Interview 6.2** Disrupting Dialysis by Digital Operations. Episode 70. Interview with Marc Nash, Vice President of Manufacturing at Outset Medical, Inc Augmented podcast.

Outset Medical thinks of manufacturing as another example of innovation within Outset. Their new facility now incorporates a state-of-the-art cloud-based manufacturing and documentation system, according to Outset CEO, Leslie Triggs, naming Tulip on a NASDAQ earnings call in 2021 (Reuters 2021):

> Our integration of manufacturing 4.0 technology allows our facility to run paperless with the ability to perform material, personnel, and equipment traceability inquiries in minutes, not days or weeks. With digital work constructions and process control tracking, we collect manufacturing process performance data continuously, and we can identify trends and anomalies in real time. We are very proud of the forward-thinking approach our team in Mexico has taken to ensure the production behind the product is just as cutting edge.

# Agile and Planned

Speedy rollout planned out from the beginning in great detail to avoid surprises and ensure enterprisewide adoption, standardization, and orderly process.

## DMG MORI

DMG MORI's method is highly structured, linearly focused on return on investment, yet awards individual performance. They recognized that implementing digital apps should be handled through a mix of clear governance and bottom-up initiative. They kicked off the enterprisewide implementation of Tulip with a two-week train-the-trainer event that resulted in trained champions, production apps being deployed, and new use cases live on manufacturing stations.

DMG MORI chose this approach to combine their legacy of precision with the opportunity to leverage contemporary technology's flexibility. What we can learn from this approach is that digitization is not one size fits all. Your organizational culture, your core capabilities, should determine the right approach for you (also see Chapter 3).

# Lærdal

Lærdal Medical is a world-leading provider of training, educational, and therapy products for lifesaving and emergency medical care. Lærdal, the mother company, began in 1940 as a toy company dedicated to "bringing children joy" but discovered its soft plastic dolls could be used to produce the world's first mannequin for resuscitation. The company created *Resusci Anne* in 1960, which is estimated to have saved 2 million lives. Says Wolfgang Dohrn, director of digitalization for supply chain and manufacturing at Lærdal, an enthusiastic and experienced operations manager with a background from Siemens and an MBA in production logistics:

> We are experts in CPR, which is cardiopulmonary recovery. And we have an ambitious goal: we want to save 1 million more lives by 2030, each year. So how are we going to do this? For us, quality [is key]. We are a high mix, low volume company, so we have many different assembly lines. This brought us to Tulip. We started an initiative in 2019 which we called the digital factory. All the facilities are quite familiar with Lean, but [are now] going the next step embracing Industry 4.0. (Tulip 2020)

The company's approach is to start small but go very fast, and it chose Tulip because they could digitize processes themselves. The no-code app editing capability was the main selection point. Dohrn says:

> Three elements make it attractive and successful. The first thing is that we got real-time feedback within a week, quality-wise and productivity-wise. The quality feedback comes from the shop floor people, and they

are now able to influence [operations]. The second element of empowerment is the manufacturing engineering team who can digitize any process. This was not possible before. If they needed to change a process, we would have to talk to our ERP system. [This would be] long-term change, a lot of money and not really give us what we wanted. Number three is connecting the manufacturing engineering team to the shop floor people. This created a new team spirit, which we were not imagining. We get engineering teams [who] say they get daily feedback on how to improve the app and how to improve the process. What Tulip is showing on the PowerPoint [display], is realizing as we speak. (Tulip 2020)

How does a frontline operations platform complement MES and ERP solutions and capabilities? Wolfgang Dohrn: "Most of the big ERP systems lack granularity on the ground. It gives insight into manufacturing, like on a golf course when you hit the ball and then, you don't see the ball for some time. Then all of a sudden it plops down on the other side of the ground" (Tulip 2020).

Dohrn says:

Tulip is lowering the entrance barrier to all IoT stuff, automatically digitizing processes. Purely by this, I can immediately see ROI coming for us. [In fact], we already have ROI, [because] now we are taking pictures of our failures in the early stage. For example, we have a molding process in Mexico and we mold silicone skins, which are then put on our mannequins and then they are delivered to Texas. In Texas, we rejected these and we had to ship them back. With on-time feedback, the Mexican colleagues create a skin and take a picture. It's visible for the quality guy on the other side in Texas. He can immediately give quality feedback—no back and forth. This happened in a week. We were all super fascinated. Another element is, now we will be able to check our routings. Before, we measured once or twice a year, and then we updated this in our ERP system and measured productivity against it. Now, if you apply it line by line, then you will have your own online routings. The ROI options are massive and it's going into productivity, quality, et cetera.

Lærdal has decided to just have two or three engineers to build the apps, because the organization prefers focus and planning, but also because those that specialize on it tend to get really good. This is somewhat counter to the no-code vision Tulip has, but it seems to work for them. "At the beginning, we started with a larger group, but [. . .] the more you create the apps, the better you get. [. . .] I [recommend that you] stay focused so you can speed up your capability of building these apps" (Tulip 2020).

How does Lærdal manage the app development process? Dohrn says

I think the interesting thing about this is that at the beginning, we didn't need the IT department. This was fascinating for them because they were saying, "Okay, do you need any help?" And then we said: "no, we're fine. We are good at the moment. So we don't need you." Of course, we will need them when we start connecting our Tulip [apps] to our ERP system [...]. [At Lærdal], we have one person who is Mr. Connection, I call him Mr. Spiderman. He connects all our IT systems in the company. I let him look at Tulip and he said, "Hey, work on this looks nice." So this is easy from that perspective. It's not so easy from the ERP system perspective because the architecture is from the eighties. To make a long story short, building the apps, you don't need the IT department, but connecting the apps, you need the IT department and [for us] this dynamic starts now. But I'm confident that we can solve [and will] get the leverage out of the full connectivity. [...] Our CEO, he has the dashboard, he wanted it, and now he can see in real time what's happening in Mexico at this moment on the shop floor, in cell X, and this is "wow," so we are very excited about it (Tulip 2020).

# Incremental and Emergent

Slow but gradually picking up speed and learning along the way, being able to innovate through change.

## *Dentsply Sirona*

As we mentioned in Chapter 3, the digital lean journey of Dentsply Sirona, the world's largest manufacturer of dental solutions, was facilitated by Tulip's no-code frontline operations platform. Dentsply Sirona's approach is incremental and based on site-specific demand. It chose this approach because the company had already achieved an 80/20 effect from previous digitization attempts. For that reason, there was less urgency to fly fast, some understandable reluctance to throw out recently established (although not ideal) digital workflow, yet a clear understanding of the value of simplification through apps that operators actually understand how to use. Mass personalization is not an atypical challenge facing many sides of the manufacturing industry, yet error proofing, cost, and transparency still matter. What we might learn from this approach is that any organization

**Interview 6.3** Digitizing Medical Device Operations. Episode 63. Interview with Dan Ron, Lead Engineer, Dentsply. Augmented podcast.

with previously established standards of practice might face similar challenges, and will have to balance the innovative no-code experimentation with the governance concerns of those already happy with 80/20 muddling through, as opposed to aiming for perfection. The only way Densply made headway with enhancing its digital operations was through Dan Ron's work as a champion for change. The good news is that, if done right, it often does not take more than a single champion in an organization to start seeding change. The bad news is that executive decision makers who are looking for such a champion might be left wanting, as they don't always exist. The long-term solution, therefore, is for organizations to encourage intrapreneurship within its ranks as an insurance policy for future innovation needs.

# Incremental and Planned

---

Incremental rollout but where each element is planned before executing.

---

## J&J

J&J is a complex organization. It operates in a regulated industry with many governments watching over its back, dealing with important health and safety issues. Digitizing J&J needed to happen stepwise and planned. However, there are many aspects of the organization that are unregulated. In those areas, change can happen much quicker. Also, there's great diversity in the size and situation of each manufacturing facility.

In many ways, J&J's mission, and its organizational culture, shapes its approach. Culturally, J&J is a "family" of companies that have retained their own identities, brands, and ways of working. So what's the glue? J&J puts operators at the center of its strategy. Operators are the key to the next phase of industrial evolution, one that involves the deep digitalization of manufacturing, its supply chain, production capacity, personalization, and with that, the reinvention of factory production itself. The solution J&J found is to have a robust, consistent architecture and break monolithic software into smaller, nimble apps. Piloting is organized by a central unit. Rollout happens after proven success on similar sites, and global rollout (organized by each site) happens with executive go-ahead once the confidence level is high. Simultaneously, it maintains a strong focus on training the rest of the organization so that such changes can happen smoothly. J&J is being challenged even by its own customers who, for the most part, are digitally savvy. Altogether, a complex organization might need to evolve more carefully yet cannot afford to ignore the opportunities brought by new technologies.

# CONCLUSION

There is room for both top-down inspiration (lighthouses) and bottom-up experimentation and growth (greenhouses) in order to roll out industrial tech. Discovery of best practices, however, is only one component. The problem is how to make that best practice understood by the whole company and get them motivated and able to implement it. This is where greenhouses have an automatic implementation step from day one, which saves time and energy both in case of success and failure. Successful change needs to address inertia, deal with pilot purgatory – and avoid misuse of ROI too early.

Looking to lighthouses or other best practices – such as consulting frameworks, peer sites in your organization, books, academic experts, or making good use of senior leadership experience – is a common starting point for change. Once you start implementing, there are four distinct ways to digitally transform an industrial organization: agile and emergent (quick, risky, innovative), agile and planned, incremental and emergent, or incremental and planned. What's your style? Which approach fits with company culture? Also, is there urgency? Clearly, if you are unprofitable and about to shut down (the famous factory scenario in Goldratt's (1984) fictionalized *The Goal*), you need to act fast. On the other hand, if you work for a greenfield factory or site and have a fresh budget and new staff, you may be able to make a choice between all four. You may even be able to combine them. However, strategy choice only takes you so far, then reality sets in. That's why any framework had better work with flexible components wherever possible: enter no-code platforms.

In the upcoming chapter, we look at democratizing operational technology using the dynamic capabilities of the firm, meaning its internal resources. With no-code platforms, this is an enticing new way to avoid dependency on third-party implementations and consultants.

# REFERENCES

Augmented (2021, ep. 4). A Renaissance in Manufacturing. Episode 4. Interview with Enno De Boer, Partner, Digital Manufacturing Lead, McKinsey. *Augmented podcast.* (Feb 23) https://www.augmentedpodcast.co/a-renaissance-in-manufacturing/ (accessed 21 November 2021).

Augmented (2021, ep. 70). Disrupting Dialysis by Digital Operations. Episode 70. Interview with Marc Nash, Vice President of Manufacturing at Outset Medical, Inc. *Augmented podcast.* (December 15) https://www.augmentedpodcast.co/70

Bomgardner, M.M. (2021). Synthetic biology firm Zymergen raises $500 million in IPO. *Chemical & Engineering News (April 22).* https://cen.acs.org/business/finance/Synthetic-biology-firm-Zymergen-raises/99/web/2021/04 (accessed 8 December 2021).

Cagan, M. (2017). *Inspired: How to Create Tech Products Customers Love.* New York: Wiley

Cagan, M. (2020). *Empowered: Ordinary People, Extraordinary Products.* New York: Wiley.

Columbus, L. (2021). BMW uses Nvidia's Omniverse to build state-of-the-art factories. *Venture Beat* (November 16). https://venturebeat.com/2021/11/16/bmw-uses-nvidias-omniverse-to-build-state-of-the-art-factories/ (accessed 23 November 2021).

de Boer, E., Leurent, H. and Widmer, A. (2019). 'Lighthouse' manufacturers lead the way—can the rest of the world keep up? McKinsey & Company. https://www.mckinsey.com/business-functions/operations/our-insights/lighthouse-manufacturers-lead-the-way (accessed 23 November 2021).

de Boer, E. and Giraud, Y. and Swan, D. (2021). CEO dialogue: Perspectives on productivity and sustainability. McKinsey. (November 3) https://www.mckinsey.com/business-functions/operations/our-insights/ceo-dialogue-perspectives-on-productivity-and-sustainability (accessed 23 November 2021).

Goldratt, E. (1984). *The Goal*. Great Barrington, MA: North River Press.

Hoffman, J. (2020). Growing Zymergen's opportunity to drive the fourth industrial revolution through biology. Blog. Zymergen *(March 9)*. https://www.zymergen.com/blog/company/growing-zymergens-opportunity-to-drive-the-fourth-industrial-revolution-through-biology/ (accessed 8 December 2021).

Kim, G. (2018). *The Phoenix Project: A Novel about IT, DevOps, and Helping Your Business Win*. Portland, OR: IT Revolution Press.

Kim, G., Humble, J., Debois, P., and Willis, J. (2016). *The DevOps Handbook*. Portland, OR: IT Revolution Press.

Klaess, J. (2020). 10 Things Lighthouses Are Getting Right. Tulip.co [blog]. https://tulip.co/blog/10-things-lighthouses-are-getting-right/ (accessed 7 December 2021).

Levine, S. (2021). Why shares of Zymergen plunged 62% in August. *The Motley Fool*. (Sept 8). https://www.fool.com/investing/2021/09/08/why-shares-of-zymergen-plunged-62-in-august/ (accessed 7 December 2021).

Littlefield, M. (2021). Do lighthouse plants drive industrial transformation – or just an exercise in excess, ego, and marketing? Industrial Transformation Blog. *LNS Research*. https://blog.lnsresearch.com/do-lighthouse-plants-drive-industrial-transformation-or-are-they-just-an-exercise-in-excess-ego-and-marketing (accessed 8 December 2021).

Mandel, M. (2019). Building the new manufacturing stack. *Forbes*. [contributor] (Aug 20). https://www.forbes.com/sites/michaelmandel1/2019/08/20/building-the-new-manufacturing-stack/?sh=1bc51d63561f (accessed 9 December 2021).

McKinsey & Co. (2021a). The global lighthouse network. *McKinsey & Co.* https://www.mckinsey.com/featured-insights/world-economic-forum/knowledge-collaborations/the-future-of-production (accessed 6 December 2021).

McKinsey & Co. (2021b). Lighthouses live. *McKinsey & Co.* (Sept 29). https:// solutions.mckinsey.com/csd/events/lighthouses-live (accessed 8 December 2021).

Reuters (2021). Edited Transcript of OM.OQ earnings conference call or presentation 9-Mar-21 10:00pm GMT. *Reuters.* (March 9). https://www.yahoo.com/now/ edited-transcript-om-oq-earnings-220000684.html (accessed 24 November 2021).

The Digital Edge (2022). The Digital Edge (25): Anders Romare, CIO for Novo Nordisk. [podcast]. https://podcasts.apple.com/us/podcast/the-digital-edge-25-anders-romare-cio-for-novo-nordisk/id1455778733?i=1000532237519 (accessed 20 January 2022).

Tulip (2020). Session Highlight: How to get started: adopting a digital culture roundtable. *Agile Manufacturing 101 Series.* Tulip (Oct 14). [YouTube] https:// www.youtube.com/watch?v=8dm_2-X6aDQ (accessed 24 November 2021).

WEF (2018). Europe, Asia Lead the Way to the Factories of the Future. *World Economic Forum.* (7 September). https://www.weforum.org/press/2018/09/ europe-asia-lead-the-way-to-the-factories-of-the-future/ (accessed 8 December 2021).

WEF (2019). From steel to smartphones, meet the forum's new factories of the future. *World Economic Forum* (Jan 10). https://www.weforum.org/ press/2019/01/from-steel-to-smartphones-meet-the-forum-s-new-factories-of-the-future/ (accessed 8 December 2021).

WEF (2019). Global lighthouse network: Insights from the forefront of the fourth industrial revolution. *World Economic Forum.* White Paper. (December). https://www3.weforum.org/docs/WEF_Global_Lighthouse_Network.pdf (accessed 23 November 2021).

WEF (2019). Global lighthouse network: Unlocking sustainability through fourth industrial revolution technologies. *World Economic Forum.* Impact Paper. (September). https://www3.weforum.org/docs/WEF_Global_Lighthouse_ Network_Unlocking_Sustainability_Through_4IR.pdf (accessed 23 November 2021).

WEF (2020). Sustainability at scale: 18 new factories of the future drive impact in the fourth industrial revolution. *World Economic Forum.* https://www .weforum.org/press/2020/01/sustainability-at-scale-18-new-factories-of-the-future-drive-impact-in-the-fourth-industrial-revolution/ (accessed 7 December 2021).

WEF (2021). 90 manufacturing sites are scaling innovation on our learning network. *World Economic Forum.* https://www.weforum.org/impact/advanced-manufacturing-factories-light-the-way-as-learning-beacons/ (accessed 13 March 2022).

WEF (2022) Augmented workforce: harnessing Industry 4.0 technologies for workforce empowerment in advanced manufacturing and value chains. White Paper in Collaboration with University of Cambridge. *World Economic Forum.* (January 2022). https://www3.weforum.org/docs/WEF_Augmented_Workforce_2022.pdf (accessed 13 March 2022).

Whiting, K. (2020). These 10 new "lighthouse" factories show the future of manufacturing is here. *World Economic Forum.* https://www.weforum .org/agenda/2020/09/manufacturing-lighthouse-factories-innovation-4ir/ (accessed 7 December 2021).

# CHAPTER 7

# DEMOCRATIZING OPERATIONAL TECHNOLOGY USING THE DYNAMIC CAPABILITIES OF THE ORGANIZATION

In a July 14, 2011, press release, Gartner analyst Ian Finley stated that citizen developers – folks outside of the IT group, including employees with no particular software experience – will build at least 25% of new business applications by 2014. Finley spent the next three years as an analyst covering application development outside of the traditional IT group. It would take more than five years before industry adoption of citizen development reached any kind of significant percentage. The reason is historical IT is complicated, and big enterprise systems often fail, are subject to major implementation delays, or become more expensive than planned. You never hear "success by IT" just "death by IT." In this chapter, we explain what developing dynamic no-code capabilities within your company would mean and who will need to be involved (see Figure 7.1). We then will show you examples of how to go about it. In turn, we also show how this will refocus the IT department as a strategic asset instead of a control function.

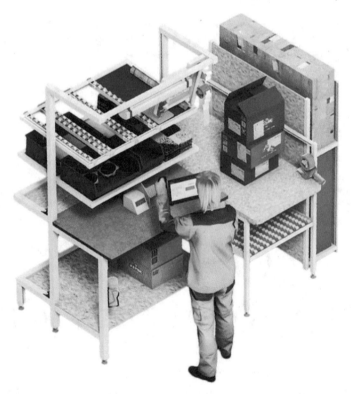

**Figure 7.1** The Liberated Operator Thinks and Acts on Data.

# NO-CODE AND LOW-CODE

The history of no-code starts with developing software coding languages that start to resemble human language. This process began in the postwar era. A coder (a person) would write English-like code, and a compiler (a program) would turn code into binary language (zeros and ones), which is what computers understand.

Throughout the next 30 years, the evolution of graphical user interfaces fueled by so-called object-oriented programming slowly percolated into software development circles and products. However, it wasn't until 2014 that the term *low code* was coined by industry analyst Forrester (Richardson and Rymer 2014), as platforms that "enable rapid delivery of business applications with a minimum of hand-coding and minimal upfront investment in setup, training, and deployment." Today, Gartner's Magic Quadrant for Enterprise Low-Code Application Platforms (LCAP) includes manufacturing applications such as Power Apps and Service Now by Microsoft, Mendix, Salesforce, Oracle Application Express (APEX), Appian, Kissflow, Webcon, and Pega Platform. These platforms are accessible to any user who has a minimum amount of coding experience.

The slightly more ambitious term *no-code* (from the perspective of the company making it) refers to platforms that are accessible to any business user. The learning curve will vary but would be near plug-and-play. Tool onboarding to get familiar with the capabilities of the platform might still be needed, but it will be quick and painless. You might also need to know how it interacts with the rest of your tech stack and other associated tools and applications used by the business. No-code is instantly recognizable to most office workers because most productivity tools (email, messaging, word processing) belong to that category.

Engineers on the front lines don't need a perfect software solution that forces adherence to an idealized optimal state. Instead, they need an agile set of tools that enable them to embrace change and manage complexity in a decentralized way. Here's how it typically works. Engineers begin by analyzing their process and identifying a problem that needs to be solved. Perhaps shop floor associates need guidance on a complex custom assembly, or they want to measure the overall effectiveness of a machine. Maybe they're looking to track the root cause of defects on a new line. Other times, there are more generic process needs. One might be looking for increased production visibility, better machine monitoring tools, leaner processes, or more interactive work instructions for their operators.

The engineers responsible for these operations build apps with custom logic and content. This entails that these apps do not just document what is happening on the shop floor but will also drive the operations forward by executing actions (e.g., inventory, staffing, purchases, supply chain instructions, work orders) and process steps (place, deliver, ship) that impact the work conducted by people or machines. These apps can then be connected to and incorporate data from machines, sensors, and back-end systems found on the shop floor. The result is that manufacturing engineers have the ability to quickly implement process improvements, see the impact, and adapt their solution based on hard data. These apps can then be deployed as a single point solution, or in parallel by tens of engineers all working on different problems.

Despite the recent popularity and progress of low-code, IT departments still question whether low-code platforms are suitable for mission-critical enterprise applications. The most worrisome aspect appears to be shadow IT (e.g., systems that get downloaded or implemented without explicit IT department approval). The claim is that an increase in applications built by shadow IT means they tend to be unsupported (by themselves, at least) and as a result, will cause problems later.

Shadow IT is clearly a governance issue. Any organization should have clear guidelines for what type of software or hardware interfaces are allowed on computers used to carry out their business. However, the fact that some no-code software is so easy to operate that the operations tech perceives that the IT department is not needed and for that reason not consulted, is not a reason to dismiss it. That is a communication issue. Good practice would be to let the IT department review the no-code platform and set general guidelines. Once that has been clarified, many no-code systems can help engineers build locally needed or requested solutions that do not necessarily need to be shared or adopted globally. They are able to do so faster and cheaper than before.

In contemporary industrial organizations, there tends to be a fight for resources and influence between those from the information technology (IT) department and those who run or advocate for operational technology (OT) systems. As counterproductive as it is, better to address it head on. Clearly, the IT department still has a key role as the arbiter of viable no-code systems. Their role is less of an implementer, which frees up resources to take on other important tasks (e.g., notably innovation, cybersecurity, interoperability, coordination, and governance). Properly conceived, no-code systems represent an opportunity for the whole organization to become more effective. We will spend the rest of this chapter discussing how no-code can help democratize technology.

# The Key Coordinating Role Played by IT Departments

What no-code systems do is unshackle the development of software from traditional software developers and IT executives in such departments. Information technology refers to all of the hardware and software components necessary for processing and storing information. IT includes hardware like laptops and servers, software, as well as enterprise systems software like ERPs, inventory management programs, and other business-related tools. The challenge is both the perception that IT are the "plumbers," who "will come to fix it," and the reality of this function, which is that they have limited visibility across the organization even if they have a strategic mandate.

Instead, contemporary IT departments should tackle radical innovation, for example how to move to declarative systems. As Brian Mathews,

CTO of Bright Machines says, a software-first approach is where you layer on the entire workflow of low-code/no-code environments. Declarative programming doesn't entail saying "Do step one, step two, step three." That's procedural programming. That's the way we program robots today:

> If you think ahead, you can be goal-oriented. I want to pick the screw up from the screw presenter, and I want to put it in the heat sink. Why am I telling [the robot] the XYZ coordinate when the CAD file knows where the coordinate is and the answer to that as well? What the CAD file says and what the robot has in front of it are always two different things. That's where computer vision comes in. If you [...] put them all together, I shouldn't be programming robots in the first place. Things should just be doing the stuff on their own. (Augmented 2021, ep. 29)

Interoperability, coordination, and governance make up a third set of responsibilities that any forward-thinking IT department must handle well. With no-code systems, there's a lot of trust. Trust in machines. Trust in the workforce. Trust in distributed solutions that are not all necessarily globally shared. The only way this approach can work is if there are clear guidelines, a set of rules of the road. However, once in place, productivity is unleashed. Lastly, the IT department has to be at the forefront of making analytics available to everyone. It is not enough to collect data; it must be shared real-time, and the organization must be able to act upon it to make processes more efficient. This is a tall order. It does not happen overnight regardless what IT platform you put in place.

# The Increasingly Mission-Critical Role of Operational Technology (OT)

The operations function refers to all the activities that focus on producing goods and services for the customers. In a manufacturing firm, operations are where key supply chain and other organizational delivery processes are defined, planned, and monitored. Increasingly, the operations function monitors and controls industrial equipment through technology. Thereby we get the expression operational technology (OT).

Operations deploys hardware and software to control industrial equipment (recall Chapter 3's discussion of industrial tech software). This is not a small challenge. As Lior Zadicareo from Visual Factories says: "Some of the machines that manufacturers are using today have been produced, in the eighties, the seventies, sometimes even the forties and fifties. Manufacturers are actually using machines, which are quite old, and they're still very much effective" (Augmented 2021, ep. 32). The job of those managing industrial machinery has become more efficient through the use of various IT tools. Culturally, they tend to count every cent, which is a mindset designed for reducing cost of goods sold (COGS) and making sure their company hits its growth margin goals. With the digitization of older machinery and newer fully digitized machines the job has evolved.

In the last decade, the previously separate domains of operational technology (OT) and information technology (IT) have grown interconnected. Analysts have called this the IT/OT convergence. The IT/OT convergence is the integration of manufacturing systems controlling physical events and processes with back-end hardware and software for conveying and processing information (Klaess 2021).

The first attempts to provide machine monitoring are examples of how IT and OT converge. Machine monitoring seems pretty advanced to the outside observer. It is at least easy to be swayed by a sales pitch for such a thing if one provides convenient metrics. However, in many cases, the mere fact that an increased amount of data from machines can now be processed by IT dashboards does not immediately make this data useful and actionable. For that, advanced business process awareness is needed. Are you capturing the right type of data? What can be done with it? There's great variability in the ability of machine monitoring vendors to capture valuable data that is actionable by operators or managers. The bottom line is that being able to capture or generate an abundance of data is not impressive in and of itself.

Historically, OT has included systems like MES, SCADA, PLCs, and CNCs. Given the breadth of OT in manufacturing, and the different concerns at any given moment of time, the modern factory often includes many machines, devices, and control mechanisms operating in relative isolation, having been acquired for different purposes to solve specific issues, and communicating using a variety of proprietary protocols that provide little or no interoperability. This has created silos, communication difficulties, and blindspots in processes that not only harm efficiency, but that tend to throw realism into any attempt to make processes leaner.

# Using Operational Technology to Foster Worker Empowerment

Big tech firms have understood the gravity of the challenge of making operational technology more efficient, useful, and simple to use. As an example, Çağlayan Arkan, Vice President of Manufacturing Industry at Microsoft, is passionate about democratizing operational technology. Arkan, a Turkish-born ex-Siemens executive, bicyclist, back-country skier, sailor, and windsurfer, is mindful of the need to more deeply understand the manufacturing sector, starting at the executive level. In the old days, the CIO was from "Mars," meaning they were not a mainstream executive in the company and did stuff that nobody really understood. Now, it's different, feels Arkan, because technology *is* the business (Augmented 2021, ep. 21).

And the impact is also felt on the shop floor: "First line workers, your shop floor, the very people who get the job done, they typically did not use any technology. They used very antique equipment [such as] blue screens [...] and anyone who's close to manufacturers will know that they use a lot of paper. Today's frontline worker is actually acting on data, acting on predictions, double clicking on a modern interface and responding to traffic lights, responding to alerts" (Augmented 2021, ep. 21).

Startups are part of the transformation picture. Big corporations that work well with startups, and disruptive startups that learn to work within the boundaries of larger players can co-innovate and obtain the trinity of quality, scale and speed. That's what Microsoft and Tulip do together, for example. We have a good partnership with Microsoft. Big players and disruptive startups can work together. Startups leverage resources and industry relationships at scale and big companies get to position themselves to learn from and benefit from the disruption, not get cut down by it. Speed is no longer dictated by size alone. Arkan says (see Interview 7.1):

What startups do is they teach you the new normal. They teach you [what] is possible. Then, they go on and do it. This is how you carry from years of implementation time, to two weeks. This is how you go from hundreds of millions of dollars to pennies and cents. [...] Let's take the Tulip example. They go into the shop floor and they look at the local no-code citizen developers, and then they bring it to life in the context of manufacturing operations. And suddenly the human machine interfaces get modernized, the legacy heavy applications that do not necessarily connect the enterprise change and there's a new workflow in place. And people just act on data and intelligence. The job is much easier to do, et cetera, and then you can build on it. And so what they do is just extremely important, actually much bigger than the number of people that they employ." (Augmented 2021, ep. 21)

**Interview 7.1** The Future of Digital in Manufacturing. Episode 21. Çağlayan Arkan, VP of Manufacturing Industry at Microsoft. Augmented podcast.

What would that mean for the future? Arkan feels it's going to be a combination of "vision and aspiration," with "augmented society" as the first priority because of the importance of achieving diversity and inclusion" (Augmented 2021, ep. 21). According to Arkan, a whopping 95% of Fortune 500 and 70% of World Economic Forum Lighthouse factories (see Chapter 6) are running on the Microsoft Azure cloud platform (2010–). Microsoft products for manufacturing also include Dynamics 365, Holo-Lens2, 365, Teams, Power, and Autonomous systems with AI.

# LEVERAGING ORGANIZATIONAL CAPABILITIES

These days external innovation is so fashionable that we at times forget a powerful perspective in management theory developed by Berkeley-professor David Teece in 1997, which calls for leveraging internal dynamic capabilities instead of always looking for insight or expertise from third parties (Wong 2016). Third parties would typically be consultants, partners, or suppliers.

Dynamic capabilities are unique to each organization and build on its own strengths. They also reflect what the company does, the functions it carries out, and its business models. What that looks like from a technology perspective is very clear. If you leverage the knowledge that is already within your company, not only do you save on consultants or software integration costs, you are also making your own workers feel empowered. If operational technology also can be developed and implemented by folks whose primary function is not IT related, there are more of them, and they are dispersed across the organization.

This means fewer potential bottlenecks. Moreover, you get closer to the problem at hand.

Process engineers, machine operators, designers, maintenance engineers, plant operators, all of these employees are deeply embedded in the business. Often, they feel like they cannot afford to see the business from an outside-in perspective. Either way, they are always in it because their function cannot rest. On the plus side, they have years of knowledge on how your production lines work (Lamarre 2020). The "democratizing" potential of empowering your own employees does not so much lie in letting them get the vote (this also matters, of course). However, the intangible benefits of giving them operational freedom are far greater. If you think about it, that is the extensive ideal that democracy aspires to and, at times, delivers. It is often by capitalizing on the tension between degrees of freedom and global standardization that the innovative potential can be reached.

Digital transformation expert and Tulip's Industry Practice Lead Gilad Langer, who has a PhD in industrial engineering (Langer 1999), was already back in 1999 envisioning an "agile shop floor control system" to satisfy the needs of the future manufacturing business. Back then, he wrote: "Existing manufacturing control systems are mainly based on deterministic algorithms operating in a predictable and stable environment, the future manufacturing systems will be increasingly more dynamic" (Langer 1999). Today, he works at Tulip and has found much of what he is looking for: a distributed, cloud-enabled frontline operations platform communicating with both machines and people. Still, there's room for future enhancements, and in truly agile systems, those can be provided by a system that is made up of components that integrate software, equipment, and users in a collaborative network. He writes: "The future digital factory will be supported by a network of [...] software components that will have been put together from the bottom up. They will develop and mature over time through emergence rather than a top-down design and development process" (Langer 2021).

# Visualizing, Tracking, and Training at Terex

Classic lean states that quality is everyone's job. The story of distributed quality apps has brought this notion into the digital sphere and has drastically empowered individuals' ability to customize their job content and manage and track their own quality improvement. However, what does that mean in practice? We will draw your attention to industrial equipment manufacturer Terex, because its augmented lean journey is simply mind blowing, and it was not easy. It still isn't easy.

Terex Corporation is a $4.3 billion revenue (2017) global manufacturer of lifting and material handling equipment used in industries as varied as construction, energy, mining, shipping, transportation, refining, and utilities. According to John L. Garrison, chairman, president, and CEO, Terex is currently undergoing a transformation from an acquisition-driven company to a process-driven company by focusing the portfolio on aerial work platforms, cranes, and materials processing; simplifying the company structure, both in complexity and cost; and executing to win by optimizing the supply chain (Terex 2021). How that translates to digital lean is expressed by CIO Andrew Campbell: "Our IT organization was 250 people, but we had 183 different titles," says Campbell. "Often, the title didn't represent the work the person was actually doing." He decided to try to turn the global manufacturer's IT "generalists" into "specialists" who are "true partners with the business." Three years later, Terex IT has 30 titles, shifted from digital "plumbers" to strategy "co-creators," and the workforce shifted into roles that made more sense to them, resulting in high employee engagement scores, although "it is always the middle of the organization that is the hardest to change" (Heller 2019).

Audra Kirkland is the director of Digital Manufacturing at Terex Corporation; she is responsible for supply chain and warehouse quality as well as for executing digital tools. Her 21 years of experience includes working for GE Power, having spent over half of her career developing and implementing applications for factory team members. Audra, a self-declared rebel, wants employees to hack, and is escaping pilot purgatory through inspiring her co-workers to find their own solutions to any problem. She found the move to remote work had a productive influence on some parts of her operations. This was particularly true for training. "We normally have peer training," Kirkland stated. But now Terex is testing digital training applications that can be practiced remotely. "We're moving through a guided work approach where we're having people learn on the job as they're doing the work, but through a guided process without a human having to be right next to them. It's been eye opening how we can use technology in order to limit exposure in the future now that we know what the future may hold." Terex adopted Tulip for production ops, due to its ability to rapidly get up and running and because it allowed them to be on AWS, which they had already installed, Kirkland said (Tulip 2021d).

How did Terex end up deciding which processes to streamline through digitized apps? Augmented lean brings tools that previously only software engineers and product managers were using. Now they are deployed to get operations work done. Kirkland gathered user stories from each of their manufacturing sites to see what they were looking for. The main things turned out to be digital work instructions, quality management, visual Andon (a management tool that highlights the status of operations in an area at a single glance and that signals whenever an abnormality occurs), and lean line performance management (a tool to monitor waste in production by monitoring employees). She quickly learned that her factories didn't have the kind of data and processes you need for a standard MES system to get started." Kirkland said: "It is quite telling that MES systems need organizations to be set up a certain way. It should be the other way around. The system should adapt to the organization."

On the other hand, Terex did have experience with Lean. Kirkland says:

[We] blended the manufacturing engineers with the digital IT teams and built a collaboration group. I'm a big promoter of citizen developers. If you have business team members who have a very good understanding of what problem they are trying to solve in a Lean trained organization that is very good at problem solving, and you marry that with putting a digital toolset in their hands, you have agile and lean together [...].

Recall that *augmented lean* has a governance element, which Kirkland understands well. Although she is tied in with the supply chain side, she is from the IT side herself. That leads her to try to put in place a level of structure and some guard rails. What does this entail? A global cloud structure for our database with replicas provided for everybody. Global reporting capability for global shared needs. Equally, each site has their own local Tulip instances where they can go and develop for local needs as well. "We don't want to hinder anybody from getting something solved at their plant. The management team gets standardized metrics and reporting and local teams can build to their needs and don't have to roll up to metrics globally," says Kirkland (Tulip 2021d). It is this combination of governance and local empowerment that constitutes the core of augmented lean.

Enabling workers through technology can be very powerful and effective at every skill level, Kirkland says. She strongly believes technology is an enabler for the frontline worker. The frontline worker is the level in the organization where small changes can have a large impact. "Those guys have skills we value. I shouldn't be trying to make a welder into a typist [stuck to a screen]. It is my job as a technologist to help get that information that the organization needs without putting the burden on making a welder into a typist." Kirkland evokes Gemba, or management by walking around, because frontline workers will tell you what they need, as long as you are willing to partner (Tulip 2021d). In fact, Kirkland is a big believer in enhancing worker experience: "I'm not trying to replace the worker, I'm trying to enhance their ability to make their job better, faster, easier, safer. I'm trying to make it a more livable job. Make their job be the best, most productive job they can have. And I want them to go home to their families the way they came to work that day" (Tulip 2021d).

When COVID-19 hit and facilities shut down, Audra contacted Tulip, who facilitated initial training 100% remotely. Terex citizen developers were able to rapidly build a suite of apps to help facilities open safely. The process was one of agile adoption, with rapidly evolving requirements around safety, and having to respect privacy in the process. There were multiple stakeholders, but in the end, the digital apps built were stunning, surprising, and swiftly implemented.

Alan Madorin, manufacturing engineer at Terex and a leader of Industry 4.0 initiatives such as MES development and the quest to digitize all paper processes, shared with the Tulip Community (and on YouTube):

Since returning to work in April, Terex AWP Rock Hill, South Carolina, team members have participated in a daily COVID-19 screening process similar to procedures implemented at Terex facilities around the globe. However, recently, the Rock Hill team developed a new, touchless, fully automated COVID-19 temperature scanner, improving the efficiency of the screening process while also enhancing safety by reducing face-to-face interactions. The new temperature scanning system comprises a tablet and thermal scanner that are powered by a rechargeable battery pack and a gateway and application powered by Tulip, the digital manufacturing solution being implemented across AWP. This allows the station to be entirely wireless and placed anywhere in the facility. Now, when a team member arrives at the Rock Hill facility, he or she scans a QR code on their badge – an enhancement implemented in preparation for the new touchless system – and steps into position for a temperature check. Team members whose temperatures read higher than 100.4

degrees are allowed a rescan in the event of a faulty reading. HR and HSE receive text messages to alert them to any repeat high temperatures so that, if necessary, team members can be asked to remain home for the appropriate length of time under the Terex COVID-19 return-to-work protocols. The new system took only two weeks to build and cost just over $500, including the cost of the tablet and scanner. (Tulip Community, 2021)

If necessary, employees can be asked to remain home for the appropriate length of time under the Terex COVID-19 return-to-work protocols.

Alan is a versatile multilateral thinker who creates parts, assembly, and drawings of designs in SolidWorks (a company we mentioned in Chapter 3), and also spent two years in Micronesia, where he picked up five native languages. He received a Tulip Groundbreaker "Golden Shovel" Award for his efforts to innovate on the frontlines of operational industries. The award program gathers content and resources crafted for the evolving community of engineers, systems-thinkers, and technologists. Alan is an active member of the Tulip Community (www.community.tulip.co), a global community of thousands of engineers and problem-solvers who want to share their passion for building apps to solve complex problems with others. Mechanical Engineer Giovanni Carrara, head of Tulip Community, says:

This is, to our knowledge, the first online community for forward-looking manufacturers looking to connect, learn and advance agile manufacturing together. The community is meant for anyone working in manufacturing or looking to get into the field. You can find resources to gain the skills you need to be a digital manufacturer, identify use cases, as well connect to a community of other practitioners eager to share their experiences from the trenches. Finally, this is the place for practical Tulip support and troubleshooting, both from Tulip staff and from the incredibly crafty user community of Tulipians.

**Video 7.1** Terex – Rock Hill, SC – Tulip COVID Scanning Station.

To build this scanning station, the hardware Terex deployed included a consumer off-the-shelf Android tablet, a rechargeable battery pack, a generic tablet stand, and an Arduino microcontroller with temperature and proximity sensors connected to an edge machine (Tulip Edge MC, a low-cost, currently $150, low-profile device that enables computing at the edge, accessible and wireless USB connectivity, and machine monitoring). Edge MC connects to Tulip-supported IoT devices with USB. It can connect to machines and sensors with built-in support for Node-RED. Edge MC enables you to monitor and translate machine data, connect non-Tulip supported devices and sensors with Node-RED, and wirelessly transmit data to Tulip.

Kirkland explains: "We were looking for a fast, cost-effective way to build solutions that leverage sensor and machine data for a variety of applications. Edge MC has allowed us to wirelessly transmit data to Tulip for interaction with the human interface so that we could collect information and use it to guide the team member's next actions" (Tulip Testimonial 2021).

Jacob Dahlgren is an industrial process development leader focused on lean manufacturing concepts, but he is not a software engineer. Rather, he has a bachelor of science degree in mechanical engineering technology, which means his expertise lies in materials, thermodynamics, machinery, fluid dynamics, and mechanical design, although he is certified in SolidWorks. When handed the right no-code digital tools, however, he turned creative. We strongly feel that augmented lean processes should empower industrial workers, not constrain them to cater to machines or cumbersome digital procedures.

The Terex Genie operations team, based in their Redmond headquarters, built the future of the shadow board, a device for organizing a set of tools, augmenting the worker as opposed to merely introducing a tool to be self-managed. As tools are picked from where they're hanging, at arm's reach behind the assembly station, three processes happen simultaneously in the background: First, Tulip ensures the tool that was picked was the correct one for the next assembly task. If not, the assembly technician is alerted and the process is halted. Second, Tulip displays the relevant assembly process on an auxiliary screen that the assembly technician can reference for assembly instructions and warnings. Third, events are tracked via backend databases and sent to their programmable logic controller (PLC) (e.g., an industrial computer ruggedized and adapted for the control of manufacturing processes, such as assembly lines, machines, edge, or robotic devices). The solution relies on markers that an engineer created with Tulip, printed and attached to the surface behind the tools on the shadow board that the camera picks up once the tools are grabbed by the assembly technician. Once the camera picks up the unique markers, information is processed through Tulip Vision and sent to Node-RED, the open source flow-based visual programming tool for wiring together hardware devices, APIs, and online services. This enables two processes to be triggered simultaneously: first, interactive and media-rich procedural information is displayed on an app running at the station, and second, information is sent to Node-RED for other machines to trigger events based on the tool that's grabbed.

The digital shadow board app enables assembly technicians to focus on the task at hand, rather than flipping through pages and pages of documentation. Computer vision ensures that technicians follow the correct procedures and pick the correct tools from their shadow board. Through collecting information at each step, the solution with Tulip provides insightful reporting, detailed automatic time studies, and key assembly metrics for the operations team to drive improvements. The solution was built by a team at a site in Washington, where it's currently undergoing testing in a production setting. Upon completion of the testing, global sites will have access to the app (and accompanying documentation) to enable sites to start using the solution self-sufficiently. We think that this is a great example of how powerful tools in the hands of capable engineers can be deployed to build groundbreaking solutions that fit the needs of specific operations, shop floors, or factories.

# CONCLUSION

Democratizing operational technology is currently driving change in industrial organizations. For the first time in history, we now have the potential to make technology do right by the workforce. Not just automate them away, as we did in the first or second industrial revolution. Not merely provide statistics to management, as we did in the third industrial revolution. Not just attempt to digitize "everything," as is still attempted during the ongoing fourth industrial revolution. However, technology is always a double-edged sword that can hurt or heal. To succeed, organizations and people need to work closer together: startups and corporations, operators and executives, or clients and vendors.

What "democratization" looks like is different in each workplace, because it depends on dynamic capabilities that are unique to companies, cultures, and teams. What executives need to do is pick the right technology platforms that are flexible enough to handle such a charge. What managers must do is allow control to pass on to the level closest to the shop floor. What workers need to do is upskill tremendously fast so they are ready to take on the next challenge.

With no-code applications, engineers with no particular software training can aggregate data from multiple machines, departments, or processes into a single dashboard for real-time process visibility. That alone is not enough but can, when implemented well, contribute to closing the IT/OT divide that hampers innovation in factories.

In the next chapter, we explore how even though engineers are becoming increasingly digitally literate, the demand for operational IT skills must extend far beyond professional industrial engineers.

# REFERENCES

Augmented (2021, ep. 21). The Future of Digital in Manufacturing. Episode 21. Çağlayan Arkan, VP of Manufacturing Industry at Microsoft. *Augmented podcast.* (June 9) https://www.augmentedpodcast.co/the-future-of-digital-in-manufacturing/ (accessed 15 November 2021).

Cottyn, J. and Van Landeghem, H. and K. Stockman, K. and Derammelaere, S. (2011). A method to align a manufacturing execution system with Lean objectives, *International Journal of Production Research*, 49:14, 4397-4413, DOI: 10.1080/00207543.2010.548409 (accessed 15 November 2021).

de Ugarte, B. Saenz, Artiba, A, and Pellerin, R. (2009). Manufacturing execution system – a literature review, *Production Planning & Control*, 20:6, 525–539, DOI: 10.1080/09537280902938613 (accessed 15 November 2021).

Klaess, J. (2021). IT/OT convergence – tips for gaining visibility in your connected factory. Tulip.co. Blog (Sept 14). https://tulip.co/blog/it-ot-convergence-tips-for-gaining-visibility-in-your-connected-factory/ (accessed 15 November 2021).

Lamarre, C. (2020). The rise of the citizen developer in manufacturing. *Tulip. co.* Blog (Jan 25). https://tulip.co/blog/the-rise-of-the-citizen-developer-in-manufacturing/ (accessed 12 November 2021).

Langer, G. (2021). The return of custom built manufacturing software. MFG.works. *The Industrializer* (February 8). https://mfg.works/2021/02/08/the-return-of-custom-built-manufacturing-software/ (accessed 16 November 2021).

Langer, G. (1999). HoMuCS. A methodology and architecture for holonic multi-cell control systems. DTU. [PhD thesis] https://orbit.dtu.dk/en/publications/homucs-a-methodology-and-architecture-for-holonic-multi-cell-cont (accessed 24 March 2022).

Mohammed, W.M., and Borja Ramis Ferrer, B.R. and Iarovyi, S. and Negri, E. and Fumagalli, L. and Andrei Lobov, A. and Martinez Lastra, J.L. (2018). Generic platform for manufacturing execution system functions in knowledge-driven manufacturing systems, *International Journal of Computer Integrated Manufacturing*, 31:3, 262–274, DOI: 10.1080/0951192X.2017.1407874 (accessed 15 November 2021).

Richardson, C. and Rymer, J. (2014). New development platforms emerge for customer-facing applications: firms choose low-code alternatives for fast, continuous, and test-and-learn delivery, *Forrester* (June 9). https://www.forrester.com/report/New-Development-Platforms-Emerge-For-CustomerFacing-Applications/RES113411 (accessed 15 November 2021).

Terex (2021). Why Invest? Investor Relations. *Terex* (corporate website). https://investors.terex.com/investor-relations/home/default.aspx (accessed 29 October 2021).

Tulip (2021d). Tulip + Terex: Automate away human errors with augmentation for safer, more productive operations. YouTube video. *Tulip* (August 1) https://www.youtube.com/watch?v=EbLrC4Qa5yY&t=904s (accessed 2 November 2021).

Tulip Testimonial (2021). Testimonial from Audra Kirkland, Terex. Approved for Tulip media use.

Tulip Community (2021). Terex, Rock Hill, SC – Automated COVID-19 scanning station. *Tulip.co* https://community.tulip.co/t/terex-rock-hill-sc-automated-covid-19-scanning-station/676 (accessed 28 October 2021).

Wong, A. (2016). The Key to Keeping Up: Dynamic Capabilities, *California Management Review*. (August 22). https://cmr.berkeley.edu/2016/08/dynamic-capabilities/ (accessed 15 November 2021).

Woo Jeon, B., and Um, J. and Yoon, S.C. and Suk-Hwan, S. (2017). An architecture design for smart manufacturing execution system, *Computer-Aided Design and Applications*, 14:4, 472–485, DOI: 10.1080/16864360.2016.1257189 (accessed 15 November 2021).

# PART III

# ENGINEERING, TECH, AND SKILLS

# CHAPTER 8

# THE EMERGENCE OF THE DIGITALLY LITERATE INDUSTRIAL ENGINEER

Pete Hartnett is a recent bachelor's degree graduate in industrial technology from Iowa State University. He says the learning curve for almost all the current software tools that are used is high and that few digital tools were being taught at school. Those that were available were all electives. "What they're teaching is traditional manufacturing, where you learn the specific software to write CAM [Computer-aided manufacturing software] for the CNC mill [milling machine], but you don't learn how that connects to your operations or connects to your business. But, you need to learn how to build an app to do a basic quality check, right? Because that's fundamental to what you're doing as a manufacturing engineer."

Hartnett had an interest in programming and ended up leveraging his skill set at various internships. He now works as an industrial engineer at Tulip, although he also has experience from digital manufacturing service provider Protolabs. He is the engineer of the future, but he had to be self-made (see Figure 8.1). How's that possible?

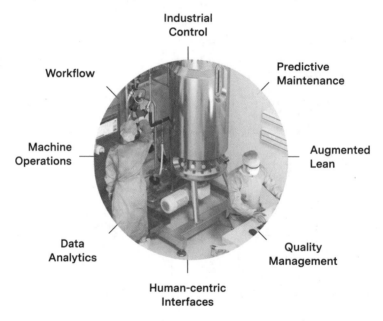

**Figure 8.1** The Disciplines of Digital Industrial Engineering.

There are currently an estimated 292,000 industrial engineers in the United States (US Bureau of Labor Statistics 2022). Despite that the manufacturing industry is rapidly digitizing, few industrial engineers have software as their primary, or even secondary, expertise. Instead, they are experts in systems-thinking, on discrete manufacturing techniques, and discrete statistical methods. Is this lack of software experience a problem? How are leading manufacturers and educational institutions addressing this skills gap? Can the industrial engineer operate fully digitized operations without being software literate?

We live in a time where the entire manufacturing process is morphing into a technologically infused process where digital literacy, competence working alongside machines, and leadership skills are in almost equal demand. We believe that freely accessible knowledge and training will transform manufacturing. We see encouraging developments across the professional lifecycle of the industrial engineer, from their formal training, to on-the-job reskilling programs, all the way to less formal methods like peer group exchanges and e-learning.

# THE EVOLUTION OF THE INDUSTRIAL ENGINEERING FIELD

We would put the evolution of engineering into five historical phases: perennial (generic and military uses), the Renaissance (mechanical), the eighteenth century (civil and electrical engineering), the nineteenth century (chemical engineering, materials science, operations research), and the twentieth and twenty-first century (systems engineering, aerospace, computers, biomedical, and energy systems) (Jackson 2016).

Perennial engineering is characterized by the gradual growth of awareness around the engineering needed to build basic habitats, extending to the advanced structures we know from historical civilizations (temples, monuments, pyramids, religious shrines, bridges, dwellings). Military engineering has also been present from humanity's cradle, and has ebbed and flowed throughout history in response to specific application contexts such as conquest, survival, and becoming bigger, better and more powerful than the enemy, etc.

The Renaissance brought a second phase, characterized by massive progress in calculations about material strength, a boldness surrounding architecture, a willingness to invest, and a curiosity about science. It also brought Leonardo da Vinci, arguably the defining engineer of the period. The eighteenth century also brought a growing institutionalization of engineering and, after electricity was discovered, eventually a massive growth in electrical engineering in the late nineteenth century, which was needed to build the grid. The nineteenth century brought chemical engineering. The twentieth century brought materials science. With that came an increased fascination for metallurgy. New materials such as silicon emerged. The ability to manipulate materials at the micro level and eventually at the nano level became possible. Systems engineering also evolved, with the capability to build and maintain more complex systems (the electricity grid, missile defense systems, telecommunications infrastructures, etc.).

Though industrial engineering evolved as a science and as a profession throughout the first and second industrial revolutions, it only came into its modern form in the early twentieth century. In *Principles of Scientific Management* (1911), Frederick Taylor (1856–1915) laid out a mandate and process that is highly focused on standardization, specialization, and process measurement. This led to the formalization of such sub-disciplines as production planning, scheduling, and inventory control (Moynihan 2021). In *The Engineering Magazine* in 1901, James Gunn suggested that a profession and curriculum of industrial engineering be established and organized similarly to that of electrical and mechanical engineering. By 1908, Pennsylvania State University offered industrial engineering as an elective.

The industrial engineer rapidly became a profession in high esteem with the help of Henry Ford's assembly lines (1913), an innovation that reduced the time it took to make a car from more than 700 hours to 1.5 hours.

We see the professionalization of industrial engineering as a response to ambitious production goals, which are themselves a response to growing leisure class purchasing power and consumer demand for affordable automobiles. The changes we're seeing in engineering today are a response to consumer demand for a wider variety of products, delivered instantly, and customized to their liking.

The American Institute of Industrial Engineers was founded in 1948. The engineering discipline of computer science began to be established as a distinct academic discipline in the 1950s and early 1960s, and the University of Cambridge's degree program was established in 1953. Starting in the 1960s, computers became decision-support systems. However, they did not yet play a key part in assembly lines. In fact, the Israeli scientist Eliyahu M. Goldratt (1990) introduced the Theory of Constraints in his immensely popular industry novel *The Goal* (Goldratt and Cox 1984). Goldratt showed that systems typically are limited by a small number of constraints, where the "weakest link" can adversely affect the outcome, most detrimentally by stopping the assembly line. Machines, when running, make an assembly line far more efficient, but can also be such a constraint, especially if only a few employees are trained to operate it. By the mid-twentieth century, the traditional factory-centric perspective in manufacturing applications shifted outward to the analysis and improvement of the entire supply chain.

Fast forward to the early 2000s, and the notion of operational technology as applied to industrial control systems was first published by Gartner in 2006, and already, it was noted that "IT and operational technology differences are resulting in suboptimal corporate performance and more costly technology deployment across enterprises. Breaking down the barriers is essential" (Williams et al. 2006). Data analytics in engineering evolved significantly throughout the 1990s but only in 2005 did Roger Mougalas from O'Reilly Media coin the term *Big Data*. By that time, IT and OT were set well apart in two different professional engineering disciplines, computer science and mechanical engineering. That fact put in motion a set of path-dependent problems related to tribalism (artificially opposing the values of digital vs. physical) and led to a lack of shared expertise crucial to efficient operation in the evolving industrial workplace.

Today, industrial engineers in the manufacturing industry are responsible for quality control, statistical process control, and increasing productivity through management of people and methods of business organization. Consider the job descriptions commonly found in job postings: they will ask for experience with business process frameworks (e.g., Six Sigma, Lean). They might ask for project management skills, including requesting experience leading cost savings and cycle time reduction projects. Financial analysis is also part of the picture. Risk management is rising in importance. Data analysis such as having worked with value streams, KPIs, and ROI is part of the newer skill set required. Operating knowledge of systems such as warehouse management systems or manufacturing execution systems is also assumed. Some exposure to supply chain issues, including facility layouts, logistics, or capacity analysis, is expected. However, industrial engineers got insufficient IT training. IT engineers, on the contrary, were for far too long educated on a path that contained far less of these foundational industrial skills.

Industrial engineers traditionally deal almost exclusively with systems of discrete components, optimizing production systems by sequencing orders, scheduling batches, determining the number of materials handling units, arranging factory layouts, and so on. The task is often to integrate workers, machines, materials, information, and energy to make a product. More than any other engineer, the industrial engineer is dealing with people, and depends on a workforce in a factory setting.

Not more than a few decades ago, industrial engineers were not required to have any particular knowledge of software. Many other mechanical technologies, as well as their industrial specialization, took center stage. Not so anymore. The future of industry belongs to the fusion of three things: operations + data + software. Mastering all three is no easy feat. Success depends on having practical knowledge derived from real work – by faculty and industry mentors, a type of learning program engineering and management schools variously describe as experiential learning or action learning (Marquardt 2011).

Gradually, throughout the 1990s, computer engineering broke out of its home in electrical engineering, although some taxonomies still have it as a sub-discipline. When a field breaks out it means that scientists find it important and usually that there is demand from employers. Will the current engineering disciplines evolve? Definitely. Thirty years from now it would be surprising if there were not a few notable additions to the list we have described above, and some fields might be completely gone or subsumed. Computer engineering is a candidate for drastic change, as what it means to study a computer will change as those evolve, and the entire concept of what a computer is will change. Not only will computers be much more efficient but also they might be smaller, more distributed, and perhaps connected to us by neural link, which would remove the need for a clunky keyboard or screen. The issues to study then would be largely derived from the neuropsychology of cognition.

As manufacturing engineering changes to encompass 3D printing within the transformational paradigm of additive manufacturing (in essence: manufacturing in layers instead of as separate components), it is also not evident that the skillset is the same for each of the quite distinct manufacturing processes that will ensue. The following are the emerging fields of engineering:

| Computational engineering | Nuclear engineering | Virtual reality; augmented reality |
|---|---|---|
| Information science | Neuroengineering | Green technology; clean technology; sustainable technology |
| Nanoscience; Nanotechnology | Automation | $CO_2$ capture; $CO_2$ conversion |
| Nanobio applications | Additive manufacturing | Biodynamics |

In order to show this evolution a bit more clearly, let's examine mechanical engineering specifically. Consider the following taxonomy, where we've added the emerging fields within it in italics:

| Mechanical engineering | Energy systems | Energy systems |
|---|---|---|
| Acoustics | Computer-aided engineering | Heat transfer |
| Dynamics | Computer-aided design (CAD) | Ocean engineering |
| Controls | Electro-mechanical systems | Manufacturing |
| Applied mechanics | Piezoelectric materials | Combustion |
| *Biomechanical engineering* | Tribology | |
| *Smart materials* | *Nanoscale fabrication* | *Digital fabrication* |
| *Green composites* | *Emerging materials* | *Nanotechnology* |

If we now only pick one of those emerging fields, they, of course, have their own taxonomy. For quick illustration's sake, let's take digital fabrication.

| **Digital fabrication** | Materials beyond silicon | Plasmonics |
|---|---|---|
| Oxide semiconductors | High K dialectrics | Spintronics |
| 3D integration | Low K dielectrics | Multiferroics |

Each of those terms also has its own nomenclature that changes fast. What we can clearly see from this type of analysis is that the specificity needed to operate as an efficient student of emerging science and technology fields is astounding. Needless to say, it rapidly becomes so complex that even recently graduated engineers in one of these subdisciplines could get lost, depending on how much time they spent reviewing the adjacent fields versus simply developing one narrow expertise. The time it takes to become "outdated" as an engineer were you to simply not read publications or follow the field at all by going to industry events or talking to colleagues in the field, or by some other information source, is likely *less than a year* at this point. For the rest, the degree largely serves as a course in how to learn and a piece of paper certifying that you might be good at learning something. Additionally, one would hope schooling helps to develop the "engineering mindset."

# ENGINEERING: THE HYBRID OF SCIENCE, TECH, AND INNOVATION

We cannot speak about technology or engineering without considering the ties between technology and engineering. The terms are fairly overlapping. To our understanding, engineering is a theoretical discipline arising from a practical challenge in the real world, whereas technology is one of its most prevalent solutions. In fact, new technologies continually improve engineering. You could also see it the other way around, as engineering approaches often are a way to scale emerging technologies that might otherwise be more experimental.

For instance, digitization has improved many, if not all, fields of engineering at this point, spanning concept, design, development, management, implementation, rollout, and follow-up phases of an engineering project. In fact, most of the disruptive technologies we have considered so far, and certainly augmented reality (AR), virtual reality (VR), artificial intelligence (AI), and additive manufacturing (AM) are improving engineering as we speak.

The benefits of new technology to engineering even have the ability to change the underlying methodologies used by engineers. Indeed, new technology is hastening the adoption of agile methods (meaning rapid iterations instead of stepwise planning) within industrial engineering. Agile is itself a software development derived process for managing a project that refers to working in teams that quickly iterate, test, and gather feedback on a product, often in small loops of time called *sprints*. In agile mode, where you rely on informal collaboration in autonomous teams, coordination, and learning from technology's intended users early on, there are no big projects, only sets of small ones (Dybå et al. 2014). If technology provides new manufacturing tools for engineers, it also changes the underlying project management frameworks they use to bring their products into being.

Being an engineer is an identity nearly as strong as being a lawyer or a doctor. Strong organizations exist to perpetuate each of these traditional professions. The same is historically not the case with technology, although technologist is becoming a more commonly used term. However, unlike engineering, the term *technologist* means different things to different people. Technologist doesn't necessarily imply that you have the skill to engineer something yourself but is a management term implying a project team expertise or topical mastery. One might envision technologists, for example, whose main education was in the social sciences but who specializes in studying technology. You might also imagine engineers who specialize in studying an array of technologies relevant to their profession's future. Writes Bertoline (2011), a former dean of the Purdue Polytechnic Institute and a professor of computer and information technology as well as a senior vice president for Purdue Online & Learning Innovation:

> The technologist is a highly skilled professional that is positioned in the "sweet spot" between the engineer and the technician and skilled craftsmen. Technologists serve an important and unique role as the "integrators" in business and industry. Technologists have a deep understanding of the human-made world and use a problem solving methodology that can lead to innovation through the development of new and improved artifacts, systems, and processes.

# THE SLOW EVOLUTION OF CONTEMPORARY INDUSTRIAL ENGINEERING

Despite the realization among top levels of manufacturing management and even in engineering schools of the need to educate a new generation of industrial engineers, it is not happening fast enough. According to *The Global State of the Art in Engineering Education* by MIT, only a few schools, Aalborg in Denmark, Delft in The Netherlands, UCL in the UK, as well as Charles Sturt University in Australia, are truly known for having embraced change toward project-based learning and simultaneously becoming pioneers in online learning (Graham 2018). Making any significant changes in learning is hard and typically requires fundamental overhaul and rethinking of nearly every aspect of teaching, learning, and accompanying infrastructure. As a result, it is a costly, risky, as well as innovative endeavor.

This is even realized by top schools such as MIT, which is now revamping its educational program to address the new realities calling for polymathic competences both of theoretical and practical nature. Babi Mitra, founding executive director of the New Engineering Education Transformation (NEET) initiative at MIT, is in charge of one key initiative there. This kind of initiative is complex and doesn't happen by chance. You have to engage stakeholders, industry, students, and faculty to change learning. "At MIT, we are aware of the urgent need to update the way we educate our engineers, which is an effort happening at engineering schools worldwide, including at the top schools. The stakes on re-imagining education just got higher because of COVID-19. [...] "for remote student projects, we ended up sourcing sensors directly from the manufacturer and it'll get shipped directly to the student" (Futurized 2020, ep. 22; see Interview 8.1).

**Interview 8.1** The Future of Engineering Education. Episode 22. Interview with Babi Mitra, Founding Executive Director of the New Engineering Education Transformation (NEET) Initiative at MIT. Futurized podcast.

If you have studied the history of industry and even if you have not, you might think that the concept of a machine is quite straightforward. We often think of an apparatus consisting of mechanical parts. That's unfortunately far too limiting. Instead, simply put, a machine is a thing that is created by people to make work easier. At MIT, the emphasis is on building new types of machines. Mitra lists some of them: "advanced materials machines, living machines, and renewable energy machines." To teach students about those, MIT uses project-based learning. Bringing engineering education back to real-life challenges is the clear objective here. The approach keeps evolving. Because many MIT students create their own company, if you build your own company in a domain, you can swap that out for an on-campus project. The machine metaphor is even confusing to MIT students: "We added 'systems' to the word 'machine'," says Mitra, "because we found that there were a lot of students for whom machines still (only) meant mechanical things and they could not visualize anything beyond" (Augmented 2020, ep. 22).

Specific manufacturing engineering degrees also exist. For example, Northeastern's Department of Mechanical and Industrial Engineering offers the Master of Science in Advanced and Intelligent Manufacturing to "meet the growing demand for engineers, researchers, and scientists trained in advanced manufacturing and Industry 4.0 technologies." Their three key curriculum components of the MS in Advanced and Intelligent

Manufacturing program are advanced, smart, and digital. The median annual salary for industrial engineers (US Bureau of Labor Statistics 2020) is $89,000. Northeastern University (2021) combines academics with experiential learning to "prepare students for real-world engineering challenges" through their co-op program. Past industrial partners include GE, IBM, Raytheon, Dell EMC, Flex, Northrop Grumman, Analog Devices, Tesla, Bose, Mathworks, Wayfair, and Dana Farber Cancer Institute.

# THE NEED TO RAMP UP CHANGE

Programs for engineers and those carrying out lower-level tasks similar to engineers and operators are too few and far between. They are also not a clear package. The result of scattered industrial engineering education experiments and programs is that the contemporary workplace has a massive shortage of engineers with what it takes to perform well in the industrial world we are in now. Such an engineer would (a) be competent in industrial systems thinking, (b) have a clear notion of the constraints of industrial practice, and (c) have full awareness of the impact of IT and OT and the related legacy constraints.

One reason for this might be that information technology (IT) rose rapidly as its own branch of engineering. IT's own graduates are well versed in a particular type of software systems that has become known as enterprise IT. These systems are typically monolithic and require specialty knowledge to develop and operate. Their most detrimental feature is to create separation between functions that need to work closely together for things to work out. Each has different incentives. Those who create the system (a set of vendors) are external to the problem and have incentives to sell, not to improve a process. Those who procure and often implement the systems (the IT department) have a control motive and an incentive to be up-to-date on the latest and greatest, but in the end, they are rewarded for buying the cheapest and the most reliable (e.g., the industry catchphrase "Nobody ever got fired for buying IBM"). Those who attempt to tweak the systems and analyze their output on a regular basis (process engineers) or operate it (the IT specialist on the team) are incented to get the best analytics out of the data but might not see the impacts beyond their own turf. Those who use the system on a daily basis (shop floor managers) have daily productivity goals and can typically care about little else.

Typically IT professionals are trained and driven to perform a task: They work on a box, a virtual machine, a storage area network, or a firewall. They might not be impressed by technologies on the shop floor. Dealing with older-generation tech is not that fun – and they might not understand why these machines or operating terminals are still around. In reality, there could be many reasons why: cost, legacy, training, license agreements, or other reasons. Perhaps nobody knows there is a better alternative at a reasonable cost. They might not realize that they are a part of a larger control system operation. In a real factory setting, the things engineers do can impact others very directly.

Operations engineers, in contrast, are not so concerned if the tech is old as long as it works and solves the problem at hand (Welander 2013). The cultural divide between OT and IT as it, arguably, exists in academia is crucial to overcome, and is ideally first embraced as an educational challenge so the conflict does not translate into the workplace.

Traditionally, shop floor technologies, machines, and approaches have not evolved as fast as software technology has in the office worker environment. However, even as this is now starting to happen, an ability to engage in life-long learning and an understanding of the need to keep current of the developments in the specific field of specialization is more important than ever. The systems you are taught in school may not be in operation by the time you get to the workplace.

The no-code systems that are only very recently being rolled out on shop floors simplify everything by essentially only needing to engage two groups: process engineers and shop floor employees. Because the interface is simplified, those two can work effortlessly together. Each has access to data and evidence in real time and can have input on how the system should improve.

# Relying on the Community College System in the US Is Not Enough

With a shortage of trained workers in the manufacturing industry, community colleges are "stepping up to provide the necessary education to get more prepared workers into the industry as quickly as possible" (Chen 2019). That's perhaps not surprising, given that community colleges play a critical role in workforce development across the nation and were designed to do so.

The idea has also been to support the success of low-income students by more effectively linking training to work opportunities and employment. Appropriately, for example, the Massachusetts Advanced Manufacturing workforce plan includes a recommendation to assess the alignment and system capacity in a "comprehensive regional approach" that includes "community college certificate and degree programs and not-for-credit training programs," pointing to the top 10 technical skills mentioned in entry and mid-level advanced manufacturing job ads, including quality assurance, CAD, and process controls.

Their reasoning is that "the advanced manufacturing workforce has changed dramatically in recent years and this evolution will continue to accelerate as new technologies, materials, and processes transform the nature of Massachusetts made products" (DHE 2015). Why do community colleges believe they can deliver on upskilling at scale? Training is not just about new talent, it is about maintaining talent, retraining, and reskilling, which is not addressed in the workforce plan.

# Can Free and Flexible Industrial Engineering Curricula Be a Solution?

At MFG.works, we mapped industrial operations courses and found a plethora of online courses relevant to industrial engineering, Industry 4.0, and manufacturing, from providers such as Coursera, edX, MESA International, Titans, and Udemy. However, the pricing was all over the place, from free to quite expensive (up to $450 per course). Many corporate actors have their own course platforms, mostly with product-related courses, but also a few providing technology skills. Industrial tech startups such as Bright Machines, Fictiv, Tulip, Vention, and more were notable for their extensive course offerings.

The concept of MIT OpenCourseWare (www.ocw.mit.edu/) grew out of the MIT Council on Education Technology, which was charged by MIT provost Robert Brown in 1999 with determining how MIT should position itself in the distance learning environment. By September 2004, 900 MIT courses were available online. Today, 2,500 courses are available, representing nearly all MIT course content, although courses are often older versions of the courses. The site has had over 500 million visits. The most popular industrial courses are undergraduate courses such as Introduction to Computer Science, Classical Mechanics, Quantum Physics, and Principles of Microeconomics, as well as one notable graduate course, Blockchain and Money.

Today, the edX consortium offers 2,000 free online courses from 140 leading institutions worldwide, has engaged 160 partner institutions, reached more than 39 million learners, and exceeded 110 million course enrollments. In the summer of 2021, MIT and Harvard University sold their online platform to ed-tech firm 2U for $800 million, effectively turning edX into a public benefit company. The Open edX open-source software platform would still be owned by MIT. Under 2U, edX will be an aggregator of university-level courses, whilst the nonprofit instead will focus on the development of more personalized and responsive learning experiences that can be applied across the educational spectrum (MIT News 2021).

Even with the onset of the global pandemic and the accompanying surge in remote learning, with publicly traded ed-tech firms attracting major investment, it would be fair to say that industrial learning online is still in its infancy, with a quite limited and unattractive offering even compared to other fields. One of the reasons why is undoubtedly that teaching engineering is hard work and has tended to require props like labs as well as hands-on mentoring with detailed hand-holding. Can these shortcomings be remedied short term by online means or hybrid offerings? Time will tell. Newer techniques such as designing interactive learning through 360° videos or immersive virtual reality (VR) or viewing video renderings in 3D environments show some promise, and the role of public and academic libraries in facilitating such efforts seems pivotal, especially in areas where broadband access or other limitations could stop learners from getting full value of remote offerings (Abumandour 2021).

Currently, there are massive amounts of individual e-courses covering almost every engineering topic provided by well-known educational organizations as formal education or informal education (Abumandour 2021). Several colleges and universities, such as Keiser University and Morehouse College, offer online engineering degree programs. *U.S. News and World Report* (2021) ranks Columbia University, UCLA, and Purdue University as the top three online engineering degrees. However, some online engineering schools feature in-person requirements, such as engineering labs, fieldwork, or internships. Top three engineering schools MIT, Stanford, and UC Berkeley don't appear on the list.

Thus, we can observe that top engineering schools are more than willing to experiment with online learning, but are not yet willing to take the full dive by providing online degrees for their core programs, very likely because they fear for the survival of their highly lucrative campus-based model of teaching and learning. MBA programs at those same types of schools have been more willing to do so, perhaps because those programs were already in trouble because of mushrooming online learning offerings and some very real question marks as regards the value of their campus based offerings (Abumandour 2021).

In the world of acronyms, one might ask: does Industry 4.0 need Education 4.0? If so, Education 4.0 characteristics might include introducing *e-learning* to enable flexibility in time and place of learning, make personalization cost-effective, and allow greater choice of learning style. One might want to make learning *project based*, including a planned field experience focused on data interpretation and on testing knowledge during practical application not via exams. Taking it a step further, *letting students be responsible for their own learning* by setting their own learning goals and curricula would be an ingredient. Stronger emphasis on *mentoring*, or bringing in an *interdisciplinary perspective*, also seems key. Due to massive availability of online information, and an enhanced learning setting through social enabling spaces, faculty is no longer (always) the subject matter experts (Das et al. 2020). In fact, one might argue that libraries can take the role of educational institutions and might be more fundamental to learning than any community college or high school. However, just reading books or stuff online is not interactive, so it is important to focus on physical space and infrastructure for experiential learning where the digital and physical meet.

The maker movement of independent inventors, designers, and tinkerers has converged computer hackers and artisans around the common goal of taking the future into their own hands to make (almost) anything. The MIT version, which we know best, is MIT Professor Neil Gershenfeld's FabLab concept. FabLab stands for "fabrication laboratory." The Fab Lab program was started in the Media Lab at Massachusetts Institute of Technology (MIT) in 2001, and explores how a community can be powered by technology at the grassroots level. The initial goal was to make an accessible and affordable maker space, a "human based design platform." The concept took off and there are now 1,750 such spaces across the world (FabLabs.io 2022). A FabLab might contain anything from an electronics workbench with CNC routers, to hand tools, WiFi, computers, software, rapid prototypers (3D scanners and printers), cutters (laser, vinyl, plasma, water jet, knife cutter), a sewing machine, and various materials.

However, none of the above touch the main issue required for teaching Industry 4.0, or better, teaching Augmented Lean. The reason is that it is hard to teach cyber-physical systems, precisely because they are tightly related to the thing you are physically producing. In that context, a *digital only* environment only goes so far. To get around this, with Tulip University, charged with teaching our clients how to use no-code apps for frontline operations, we ship them factory kits with a pre-configured "factory in a box" consisting of our Edge IO hub for devices, sensors, machines and equipment, light strips and a light stack (for Andon lights), a barcode scanner, a break beam for motion detection, temperature and humidity sensors, and a foot pedal to make your apps hands-free. We also suggest they order an industrial workbench on wheels from our partner, Vention, where all the equipment can be attached, organized, and mobilized in an ergonomically sound way. At this point, coupled with digital courses and 24/7 online support, it is possible to augment shop floor operations in days, without preexisting digital skills. We are currently involved in a host of experiments with polytechnical institutes as well as community colleges to see if we can provide support for Augmented Lean at scale. If we succeed, it will revolutionize contemporary industry.

We realize it is a tall order to deliver quickly, at scale, and without re-training teaching faculty and rejiggering educational institutions quite extensively. Who knows if it's even possible to design such a process at scale, and at low cost, across the educational landscape. Who knows how long it would remain state of the art before new changes awash, which is why we advocate more modest learning experiments before we get there. One reason why we know this is because one of us (Natan) has a degree from the MIT Media Lab, and another has worked across MIT (Trond), probably the learning institution closest to this vision. That lab was established in 1985 and the model has not changed much, but the brand is peerless, its resources are immense, the scale is modest (25 faculty, 50 students/year, 163,000 square feet of lab, office and meeting space), and the faculty and students are world class. Could the same happen on more modest resources and skills, and without significant industry backing? Part of the reason we are writing this book is to help shift the mindset in industry, in educational institutions, and among government decision makers and funders of major manufacturing initiatives. There's urgency, and resources are needed, but the overall approach that has been in place for 30 years has to dramatically change.

# CONCLUSION

Even top engineering schools, such as MIT, are revamping their educational approaches, curricula, and tools to become ever-more relevant to their students and to society. The longstanding engineering profession is changing faster than in earlier eras. After eras of increased specialization, engineers are again becoming generalists and trained in interdisciplinary ways. With that engineers are becoming increasingly digitally literate, regardless of their subfield. Given the way contemporary industrial technology startups are slowly embracing the cyber-physical systems challenge, the artificial divide between operations technologies (OT) and information technologies (IT) should dissipate. No company, education track, or government funding vehicle should be *either* engineering, hardware, or software-focused. Rather, such initiatives need to integrate all of them. Shepherding that process along is crucial if we expect step-change innovation in the manufacturing sector. Ushering frontline operations with industrial momentum at internet speed is possible, but not with today's tools and past-era mindsets.

We feel that the future of industrial engineering does not only depend on what happens with engineering degree programs at elite universities and colleges or even the actions of the engineering societies and associations. Professional programs can only do so much. In a world where engineering is practiced everywhere that industry exists, by people who either have an outdated engineering degree (say more than five years old) or never had the time to go to school for that long, engineering is becoming a core requirement for effective operations much like language skills are key to communication. Engineering tasks are prevalent, and the tasks won't wait for educated engineers. Instead, companies will have to educate their employees as best they can and workers will have to learn on the job – increasingly, on their own. Given that prospect, we better ensure that the freely available curricula, the training opportunities, and the mentorship programs that exist are top notch. Certification programs and formalization at the scale of continuously educating 20% of the workforce will come, but we cannot wait for it to emerge. That challenge is quite different from the entirely institutionalized imperatives of the past decades, but not entirely different from the challenges of past industrial revolutions. When factories emerged en masse, and cities became filled with former farmers who now had to clock in and carry out meticulous manufacturing tasks, schooling had to change, too.

The emergence of a new type of industrial engineer is therefore a process not controllable by any single entity. Having said that, in the next chapter, we turn to the true challenge of training the process engineers of the future, which is to be found in workforce development spearheaded by industry. We say process engineering because once in the workplace, it doesn't matter if you trained in mechanical, electrical, or computer engineering; the job to be done is an industrial process and there can be any number of legitimate, nonacademic shortcuts to get there.

# REFERENCES

Abumandour, E.-S.T. (2021). Applying e-learning system for engineering education – challenges and obstacles. *Journal of Research in Innovative Teaching & Learning.* (ahead-of-print) https://doi.org/10.1108/JRIT-06-2021-0048

Futurized (2020, ep. 22). The Future of Engineering Education. Episode 22. Interview with Babi Mitra, founding Executive Director of the New Engineering Education Transformation (NEET) initiative at MIT. *Futurized podcast.* (August 27) https://www.futurized.org/the-future-of-engineering-education/ (accessed 2 November 2021).

Augmented (2021, ep. 62). Manufacturing in Michigan. Episode 62. Interview with Jon Sobel, CEO, Sight Machine.) *Augmented podcast.* (February 23). https://www.augmentedpodcast.co/62 (accessed 28 November 2021).

Bertoline, G. (2011). What is a technologist? *Purdue University Polytechnic Institute Blog.* https://polytechnic.purdue.edu/blog/what-technologist (accessed 9 March 2022).

CESMII (2022) Smart Manufacturing Innovation Platform. *CESMII.* https://www.cesmii.org/technology-smip/ (accessed 28 November 2021).

Chen, G. (2019) Manufacturing Training Expanding at Community Colleges Nationwide. Community College Review (December 28). https://www.communitycollegereview.com/blog/manufacturing-training-expanding-at-community-colleges-nationwide (accessed 28 November 2021).

Das, S., and Kleinke, D., and Pistrui, D. (2020). Reimagining Engineering Education: Does Industry 4.0 Need Education 4.0? 127th ASEE Annual Conference, Montreal, Canada. 10.18260/1-2--35136. https://www.researchgate.net/publication/339983822_Reimagining_Engineering_Education_Does_Industry_40_Need_Education_40 (accessed 28 November 2021).

DHE (2015) Advanced Manufacturing Workforce Plan. Massachusetts Department of Higher Education. https://www.mass.edu/strategic/documents/16a_AttachmentAdvancedManufacturingWorkforcePlan_Spring2015.pdf (accessed 28 November 2021).

Dybå, T., & Dingsøyr, T., and Moe, N. (2014). Agile Project Management. 10.1007/978-3-642-55035-5_11.

FabLabs.io (2022). FabLabs.io. https://fablabs.io/ (accessed 13 March 2022).

Giffi, C., Wellener, P., Dollar, B., Manolian, H.A., Monck, L., and Moutray, C. (2018). 2018 Deloitte and The Manufacturing Institute skills gap and future of work study. https://www.themanufacturinginstitute.org/wp-content/uploads/2020/03/MI-Deloitte-skills-gap-Future-of-Workforce-study-2018.pdf (accessed 28 November 2021).

Goldratt, E.M., and Cox, J. (1984). *The Goal*. Croton-on-Hudson, NY: North River Press.

Goldratt, E.M. (1990). *The Theory of Constraints*. Croton-on-Hudson, NY: North River Press.

Graham, R. (2018) The Global State of the Art in Engineering Education. *MIT New Engineering Education Transformation (NEET)*. https://jwel.mit.edu/assets/document/global-state-art-engineering-education (accessed 27 November 2021).

Jackson, T., ed. (2016). *Engineering. An Illustrated History from Ancient Craft to Modern Technology*. New York: Shelter Harbor Press.

Marquardt, M. (2011) *Optimizing the Power of Action Learning: Real-Time Strategies for Developing Leaders, Building Teams and Transforming Organizations*. Boston: Nicholas Brealey.

MIT News (2021) MIT and Harvard agree to transfer edX to ed-tech firm 2U. *MIT News*. (June 29). https://news.mit.edu/2021/mit-harvard-transfer-edx-2u-0629 (accessed 28 November 2021).

Moynihan, G.P. (2021). Introductory chapter: Background and current trends in industrial engineering, concepts, applications and emerging opportunities in industrial engineering, Gary Moynihan, *IntechOpen*, DOI: 10.5772/intechopen.94606. (Jan 7). https://www.intechopen.com/chapters/74074 (accessed 28 November 2021).

National Research Council (2003). *Assessing Research-Doctorate Programs: A Methodology Study*. Washington, DC: The National Academies Press. https://doi.org/10.17226/10859.

Northeastern University (2021). Master of Science in Advanced and Intelligent Manufacturing. https://mie.northeastern.edu/academics/graduate-studies/ms-aim/ (accessed 28 November 2021).

Williams, B., Spiers, J., Sumic, Z. and Steenstrup, K. (2006). IT and OT interaction: Why conflict resolution is important. *Gartner* (Sept 15). https://www.gartner.com/en/documents/496363/it-and-ot-interaction-why-conflict-resolution-is-importan (accessed 28 November 2021).

Taylor, F. W. (1911). *Principles of Scientific Management.* London: Harper & Brothers.

U.S. Bureau of Labor Statistics (2022). Industrial engineers. https://www.bls.gov/ooh/architecture-and-engineering/industrial-engineers.htm (accessed 9 March 2022).

U.S. News and World Report (2021). Best online engineering programs. https://www.usnews.com/education/online-education/engineering (accessed 28 November 2021).

Welander, P. (2013). IT vs. OT: Bridging the divide. *Control Engineering.* (August 16). https://www.controleng.com/articles/it-vs-ot-bridging-the-divide/ (accessed 2 November 2021).

# CHAPTER 9

# TRAINING THE PROCESS ENGINEERS OF THE FUTURE

According to the young German industrial researcher Elisa Roth, currently working at Cambridge University's Institute for Manufacturing, augmented worker technologies are becoming increasingly intelligent, interactive, and supportive. Roth is committed to improving the state of the manufacturing industry, the future of which is arguably increasing in "complexity, efficiency, and sustainability." Roth explores novel forms of technology-augmented upskilling and assistance in industry. One of her particular interests is integrating human factors into technology development, implementation, and evaluation. As complexity increases, and manual tasks get taken over by robots (or robotic process automation), cognitive support systems for operators would likely become better and more intuitive. Her research shows that assistive technology will benefit from early stakeholder engagement across the hierarchy – from executives to operators – and points out that co-bots are still perceived as unfeasible on most shop floors (Roth and Moencks 2021).

If cobots are still seen as unfeasible, what does augmentation mean? To Roth it is about augmenting natural human abilities, not only replacing or supplementing human abilities but even exceeding natural human abilities to help humans to do their work better by augmenting sensors on [the] information collection side. It can also be about augmenting analytics skills or information processing skills. "Beyond that, we have opportunities to augment knowledge management," she says. "Other things are more sophisticated, like decision-making support, machine learning and AI capabilities, [and] reaching further into the communication and collaboration side [...], actually augmenting the interaction between humans themselves" (Augmented 2021, ep. 2; see Interview 9.1).

**Interview 9.1** How to Train Augmented Workers. Interview with Elisa Roth, Doctoral Student at the Institute for Manufacturing at the University of Cambridge. Episode 2. Augmented podcast.

Augmentation challenges teaching, training, and learning in manufacturing, at all stages of the employee lifecycle including onboarding, to on-the-job training, retraining, and offboarding. As Roth says, the traditional way of teaching and manufacturing was to do formal education such as a three-year apprenticeship and then university, which she says is a very rigid system that provides you with skills that are expected to be useful for a couple of decades. Then there is on-the-job training, which is the non-formal side, consisting of learning from colleagues, talking to colleagues, observing colleagues, and digging through work instructions and operations manuals. But, as Roth says, we have reached the boundaries of that set of tools. "We see complexity is rising, new customization increases. We have a lot more product variants than we used to have. In addition to that, the workforce is aging. So all the experts we used to have are now retiring and the manufacturing industry's really struggling to attract new talent" (Augmented 2021, ep. 2). To Roth, what this means is that we have to build a culture of life-long learning as well as designing amazing learning paths with amazing content.

Each day, in the US, 10,000 baby boomers retire (Kessler 2014). Additionally, as if baby boomers retiring was not enough, millennials and Generation Z tend to switch jobs more frequently. What this means is that upskilling for new workers needs to be immediate, because ramp-ups of months is not feasible if the employee is likely to switch jobs or employer within a year or two. It is not an exaggeration to say that the companies that figure out how to instantly train and retrain their employees will win in the long term. Moreover, motivated employees are less likely to switch jobs, so empowering the workforce equally helps. Also, the complexity of jobs is not a competitive advantage. Rather, manageable jobs that are reasonably compensated, and regularly give workers (at all levels) the experience of having a meaningful workday, are likely to be more desirable than jobs where escalating complexity of (failing) technology and processes create perennial challenges and frustrations.

A convenient argument in many cultures and political traditions would be to point to individual responsibility. But even though learning is largely individual, if it's not supported by the organization, it usually won't get off the ground. Employees need allowances to "set aside time every day to learn new things, even if it takes away from productive operations time. For that to work, however, we need to embed learning into daily work life." Roth says that in the future, employees will need problem-solving and critical thinking skills because they will frequently be assigned to a new workstation or a new product, and they will have to use new tools. This entails, according to Roth, "analyzing the situation, identifying what resources you might need to fulfill your task and what information you need to fulfill your task" (Augmented 2021, ep. 2).

For Roth: "The whole lean philosophy builds on having empowered workers that take ownership of their process. So we need to keep in mind that there is no successful digitalization without lean." Beyond that, "People are different and [we need to adapt] the content of technologies to different skill levels, and to the individual."

# THE PROCESS ENGINEER: TODAY AND TOMORROW

Process engineers are responsible for the design, implementation, control, and optimization of industrial processes (Black 2018). Although it is possible to earn an associate engineering degree in just two years, to get this job, they typically have a bachelor's degree in chemical, manufacturing, or industrial engineering. To do the job, however, requires rapidly gaining experience in a specific industry, such as agriculture, automotive, biotechnical, chemical, food, material development, mining, nuclear, petrochemical, pharmaceutical, or software development. Process engineers may be charged with considering product design improvements, changes to the materials used, and often have a hand in revising or tweaking the manufacturing process or technology used. Ultimately, great process engineers become specialized industrial engineers who either know their industry's processes particularly well or get to know particular industrial processes within their industry. Either way, they tend to become responsible for the equipment, system, and methods used in a manufacturing facility to transform raw ingredients to their final product form.

The process engineer of the future would ideally come prepared from some type of college training, but even if not, tomorrow's training is likely to more often than not take place on the job. Given the gargantuan upskilling needs of the future of the industrial workplace, the best way to train engineers (or any employee) is likely to be through a community approach, not formal training, or not even apprenticeships. Industry, as we saw from the case study of DMG MORI in Chapter 4, and from academics such as Roth (quoted above), envisions enabling integrated life-long learning within production systems. Even though training is still a business for many large industrial firms such as ABB, small attempts are already being made. ABB Robotics Academy Online Learning has been open to the public since 2020 as long as you register on their site and have a basic level of knowledge. The five courses currently under offer are built on the same materials used in its popular classroom-based courses normally run at ABB's Robot Training Centre in Milton Keynes, UK. The training only requires a microphone, a computer, and downloading ABB's simulation and offline programming software (Edwards 2021). RobotStudio allows robot programming to be done on a PC in the office without shutting down production. The program is an exact copy of the real software that runs your robots in production and offers virtual meetings using a VR headset, digital twin capability, which simulates the production system, and visualization of robot solutions using augmented reality (AR).

Specific training is still done live, working directly with industrial robots, but the company is also offering more training online. However, even though ABB did launch a new training website in 2021, it offers many choices: training onsite at ABB training facilities, locally at your plant site, or online, given that usage training on robots tends to require a physical environment to be realistic (ABB University 2022). Training can generate goodwill and business leads and is also often a way to educate the supplier ecosystem.

This is also the way Stanley Black & Decker thinks about it. Based in New Britain, CT, Stanley Blacker & Decker operates and maintains approximately 30 manufacturing facilities across the US, and more than 100 facilities worldwide. Says Carl March, director of Industry 4.0, the 23,000 square-foot "Manufactory 4.0" facility located in downtown Hartford, CT, is not just a showcase and an attempt at making Hartford the central innovation hub for New England but, more importantly, a training center for the company's "smart factory" initiatives. They want the public to experience it, allow their technology partners to showcase it, and train and upskill their own supplier network to get an "experiential sense of what the technology can accomplish." March says, "we're trying to uplift the entire system" by filtering through the noise for SMEs and providing a consolidated technology map against a framework (Augmented 2021, ep. 27). A recent MIT study found "technological change may be proceeding too slowly within manufacturing SMEs compared with firms of a larger scale" (Helper et al. 2021).

# HOW TO AVOID TRAINING THE WORKFORCE FOR YESTERDAY'S CHALLENGES

The history of workforce training is complex. Historically, middle-skills jobs, "those that require more education and training than a high school diploma but less than a four-year college degree," served as the springboard into the middle class (Burrowes et al. 2014). The reasons behind this stagnation are complex, but basically, industrial complexity means nearly any job (even shop floor jobs) requires more than basic skills and a set of "middle skills" that cannot typically be acquired the traditional way. Middle skills is a confusing term but might imply soft skills, technical job skills, machine operation, production-relevant skills, training on proprietary systems, or context-specific troubleshooting that are part of a job. Many of these types of skills, by the way, are rendered unnecessarily complex by outdated manufacturing processes, old proprietary equipment, and nonexistent training protocols and procedures.

To take a US example, the promise is to go from being a manufacturing technician making $16–20 an hour or so to an advanced technologist role starting at $30–$40 an hour, effectively doubling your salary. Taking it one step further, according to the Bureau of Labor Statistics, the median annual wage for chemical/process engineers was $108,540 ($52/hr) in May 2020 with projected job growth of 8% from 2019 to 2029. Right now, very few programs around the world are able to provide this training reliably. The million-dollar question is, what, beyond an advanced four-year university degree, will? To make matters worse, the bachelor's degree is also in crisis. Fewer than half of Asian-American students, just one-third of white students, less than one-quarter of Latino students, and less than one-fifth of black students attain their STEM degree within five years, according to the Higher Education Research Institute (DegreeQuery 2021).

Today's decentralized workforce education, where schools have become disconnected from workplaces, is perhaps disappointing to many (workers, policy makers) and certainly has its shortcomings, including low completion rates at community colleges (at around 30%). If the goal is to rebuild America's working class and tackle inequality, not only do we need a pipeline of skilled workers for future jobs, we need to give workers the skills they need now, and we need to train more workers more quickly (Bonvillian and Sarma 2021). Ways to get there can be many: short, intensive courses that offer college-level certification, embedding industry-recognized credentials into educational programs, building a new model for apprenticeships. More ambitiously, it also entails reviewing the roles of community colleges, employers, governments, and universities in workforce education. Finally, it means embracing new education technologies (including online) that can deliver training to workers. However, as Bonvillian and Sarma argue, online education cannot replace effective instructors or hands-on work with actual equipment.

In 2020, the Commonwealth of Massachusetts was awarded a $3.2 million grant from the US Department of Defense's Manufacturing Technology Program (DoD ManTech) for a manufacturing technician training program that will serve as a national model. The effort, MassBridge (www .cam.masstech.org/massbridge), aims to provide a state-based training curriculum and a career pathway model deployed through vocational and academic high schools and across six community colleges across Massachusetts. Says one of the MIT scientists involved, George Westerman, a senior lecturer at the MIT Sloan School of Management and a principal research scientist at J-WEL Workforce Learning: "Working with Industry 4.0 requires [...] systems level thinking, more ability to troubleshoot rather than just follow instructions" (Augmented 2021, ep. 30). Westerman claims there are "uniquely human skills that will be immune from machine replacement for the longest."

At MIT, Westerman's team has developed the Human Skills Matrix (HSX) to capture the nontechnical skills – thinking, interacting, managing ourselves, and leading – that make rapid learning and adaptability possible across all industries (J-Wel 2022). And how to learn? His research identified a new model of corporate learning and development called The Transformer CLO (chief learning officer) where corporate training officers not only put on skills-based and compliance-oriented courses, perhaps sprinkling in some leadership development training for a lucky few, but "embrace a role where they reshape capabilities and organizational culture" in the process. They do so by "transforming their organizations' learning methods, making them more experiential and immediate, and atomizing content for delivery when and where it's needed. And they're transforming their organizations' learning departments, making them leaner, more agile, and more strategic" (Lundberg and Westerman 2020). The use of peer teaching makes such efforts easier to scale. Finding the right balance between face-to-face and digital learning is also crucial, since soft skills, complex, ad-hoc, or ever-changing content is still best taught in person.

# MIT Study on the Industrial Work of the Future

According to the authors of the book from a recent MIT study *The Work of The Future: Building Better Jobs in an Age of Intelligent Machines* (Autor, Mindell, and Reynolds 2022), the United States lags behind other industrialized countries in sharing the benefits of innovation with workers and has too many low-quality, low-wage jobs, often without benefits. Why? Europe's labor laws are much stronger, which translates into higher concern for workers. Says Elisabeth Reynolds: "If you're paying a lot for your work, you are going to invest in them because you want higher productivity." But, despite the hype about automation dystopia, technology is neither the problem nor the solution. Says Reynolds: "Technology absolutely eliminates work, but we can't forget that it also creates work. And so our challenge going forward will not be the end of work. [...] The challenge, I think, will be the quality of that work." Reynolds argues that revamping and rethinking an organization's production system around data-driven decision-making is a cultural change. "It's not just about these machines over in this cell" (Augmented 2021, ep. 7; see Interview 9.2).

**Interview 9.2** Work of the Future. Interview with Elisabeth Reynolds, Executive Director, MIT Task Force on the Work of the Future. Episode 7. Augmented podcast.

In fact, the MIT study finds we can build better jobs if we create institutions that leverage technological innovation and also support workers through long cycles of technological transformation. Skills programs that emphasize work-based and hybrid learning (in person and online), for example, empower workers to become and remain productive in a continuously evolving workplace. Fueled by new technology that augments workers (rather than automate them into oblivion), good jobs can be created, and federal investment in R&D can help make these industries worker-friendly. However, as Reynolds says: "it's pretty simple to calculate ROI when you replace a worker with a robot [in terms of the] bottom line; it's less obvious how you calculate the ROI on a collaborative robot that's assisting and augmenting a worker in the process" (Augmented 2021, ep. 7).

# How Fast Can You Learn to Operate a Robot?

Robotics is often thought of as a complex subject. There is no justification for that today, unless you refer to making robots. Operating them should be easy. When robotic control systems are done well, the complexity is hidden.

Says Kel Guerin, co-founder of Ready Robotics: "The people who've been deploying automation for the last 20 years have been experts. Therefore, there was no need for any robot manufacturer to make their software easy to use. They just focused on making a better, faster robot." Over time, to scale deployment, that's not sustainable. In other industries, there are software development kits. "What it really means is that the tool set, the tools are available and well-documented for you to build something on top of that platform. The example is Android." Similarly, at Ready, they wanted to build a robotic SDK (see Resource 9.1). Now, with a conversational, drag-and-drop programming interface, their clients can deploy that robot to the factory floor themselves in a matter of hours or days, instead of weeks or months. Guerin cites the example of a machinist operating one CNC Lathe, a machine tool, who didn't have any robotics experience nor any higher education in the technology space. As a result, there were four other machines that were not seeing a lot of use because any time he spent programming them, he wasn't making the parts on the first machine. With a little training, he was able to leverage his knowledge about the product, which was profound, and use the easy-to-use technology to actually get the robot to make the product in the right way. Now, he runs five CNC Lathe machines and is freed up to do what he is really good at, and focus on where his key value is, which is programming machines. This also works at scale.

**Resource 9.1** Ready Academy - a free online training resource in robotics automation for manufacturing professionals, teaching the skills needed to design, deploy, manage and troubleshoot robotic automation.

In a Ready Robotics pilot, they had former coal miners learn robotics:

We taught a robotics course using our software and on top of that a two-week training course. The goal of that training course was to take their CNC skills and give them robotics on top of that. What we found was, when you're learning robotic technology, you're going to spend two to four weeks learning the basics of using the robot; making it move around, maybe grab objects, but really the basics. And then you're going to spend a huge amount of time learning about automation.

This course pilot was carried out at Academy, a training center in Kentucky whose goal is to retrain people who have been displaced by the decline of the mining industry in that region.

"By making the automation tool much more accessible, you can very quickly get to learning about the industry, the process, the task that you're going to have to learn." This is especially important for people coming from a different industry and up-skilling into the manufacturing space. Guerin points out that in other industries, that's not even a thing: "When you go and learn to be a carpenter, you don't spend two months learning how to swing a hammer. You spend five minutes learning how to swing a hammer, and then you learn about how to be a carpenter."

In fact, once robotic operators have the basics of how to do *audit* robotic automation, they can walk into a factory setting prepared to do far more than that specific task that they may be tasked to do. They can also look around and ask themselves where else they can use this technology. "They start looking at the entire factory floor through this lens of what's possible," says Guerin. He has seen that with not only newcomers into the industry but also incumbents." It's theirs. They own it. And they're motivated to keep it running. To put in *more* robots, which is striking, given the rhetoric that people are supposedly fearful robots will take their jobs. All of this because they feel empowered (Augmented 2021, ep. 6; see Interview 9.3).

**Interview 9.3** Human-Robot Interaction Challenges. Interview with Kel Guerin, Co-founder, Ready Robotics. Episode 6. Augmented podcast.

Even if the user interfaces become simpler, that doesn't take away from the need to be skilled to invent those interfaces. Says Etienne Lacroix, co-founder of Canadian startup Vention, a new breed of modular factory automation: "If you're a young teenager or have your own kids that are considering to go into manufacturing, my first [suggestion] would be, you need to learn how to code and you need to learn data." Lacroix says a lot of complexity takes place behind the scenes to make technology look easy.

Upskilling is a multifaceted challenge. At Vention, he says: "We maintain this through internal employees that are just there to make sure we spread the knowledge right and help others. But the community also has to play a role, talking to one another, exchanging use cases with one another to go deeper into what's possible to democratize" (Augmented 2021). Vention provides a cloud CAD e-commerce web interface where anyone can customize and order modular parts (e.g., made-to-order industrial work benches) that ship the next day. Compare that with ordering a one-size-fits-all metal workbench that might show up after a three-month delay. Vention's product offering democratizes machine building by engineers on the shop floor because they no longer suffer from dependency on generic parts, long supply chain delays, and an inability to structure their own physical workstations and shop floors.

# REIMAGINING TRAINING

Sarah Boisvert, founder and CEO of Fab Lab Hub and the nonprofit New Collar Network, is deeply engaged in reimagining workforce training. Her own background stems from having manufactured and sold the LASIK eye surgery back in 1999. Nowadays, her focus is on new-collar jobs, that is, blue-collar jobs that have become digital. "I spoke to 200 manufacturing companies who said, we're getting all these new technologies and you haven't got some guy in the back of the machine shop who has done this before, and we're getting machines that are being built that have never been built before." She continues, "I was looking at operators and technicians, but people I spoke with were also looking for technical skills, CNC machining, CAD design, and AI. In fact, predictive analytics was probably the number one skill that the international manufacturer CEOs were looking for" (Augmented 2021, ep. 3).

A FabLab, or a small-scale digital fabrication laboratory, is a place to play, to create, to mentor, and to invent: a place for learning and innovation. Boisvert says that FabLabs are workshops and studios that incorporate many different kinds of digital applications, utilizing technologies like 3D printing, laser cutting, and CNC machining. "Yet, the power of digital fabrication is social, not technical," says Boisvert (Augmented 2021, ep. 3; see Interview 9.4). There are now 1,750 fab labs around the world. Having been engaged there, and seeing the accelerated learning curves with that approach, Boisvert realized that there was no need for a two-year curriculum. In fact, it seemed like "digital badges were the fastest, easiest, most affordable way to certify folks to work with a particular skill set." Boisvert has now contributed to training some 400 people with her approach. Learners range from people who have not finished high school to PhDs.

**Interview 9.4** Reimagine Training. Episode 3. Interview with Sarah Boisvert, Founder and CEO, Fab Lab Hub, LLC and the Nonprofit New Collar Network. Augmented podcast.

But is it that easy? Boisvert is realistic:

In one course or one digital badge it is possible to get some jobs. But it probably takes a combination of courses in order to have the right skillset, because it's typically not one skill you need, it's typically a combination of skills. So to run the 3D printers, for example, you need CAD design. You need to understand the design for 3D printing, and then you have to understand how to run the machines and fix them when they break. You could do our master batch, which comprises five or six badges and get a job in six months for about $2,000. However, even with one class you could get a job part-time and continue the other badges and be paying for school while you're working in a field that is paying a substantial increase over working at McDonald's. (Augmented 2021, ep. 3)

# OPEN-SOURCE MANUFACTURING

Today, it is common to develop proprietary industrial edge programs and software platforms. However, arguably, the best way to share techniques faster than ever is through open-source manufacturing. According to

Tulip's co-founder Rony Kubat, open source has the potential to revolutionize the way manufacturers train their workforce, and how workers develop their skills as individuals. In fact, he says Tulip was started with the idea of open-source software in mind. The co-founders wanted to create a platform that would bring the creativity and innovation of open source software to operations. The parts where open source could contribute would be in creating a community for sharing ideas and collaborating on common goals, fighting information silos on the shop floor, as well as between engineers at different organizations.

Manufacturing could also benefit from an open-source style application exchange. Engineers would share their digital apps (created to improve the transparency of a business process). Others could purchase, download, fork, or version them to fit their own processes. Why should every factory have to reinvent the wheel? Open source taught us that sharing tricks and best practices helps codify them (see Figure 9.1).

**Figure 9.1** Application areas that benefit from open source manufacturing approaches.

The collaborative nature of open source enables companies and individuals alike to turn their visions into reality and keep up with established players such as Siemens, Microsoft, and Rockwell, even without a large number of programmers and engineers. The United Manufacturing Hub is an open-source industrial IoT and manufacturing data platform enabling users to connect all IT – OT devices to a secure infrastructure. Currently establishing an Industry 4.0 community, this hub already provides a robust and scalable architecture to connect, store, and access all relevant data sources in industrial manufacturing sites. "Manufacturing and Industrial IoT is not about developing new software at the drop of a hat. It is more about solving individual problems and challenges," according to The United Manufacturing Hub's Documentation (2021).

# Frontline Operations Platforms Train the Frontline Workforce

Tulip University (2022) is an example of reimagining corporate training. Similar to several other cloud-based IT or manufacturing start-ups (e.g., Autodesk, Bright Machines, Bubble, Fictiv, Hubspot, Ready

**Interview 9.5** What Is Tulip University? Interview with John Klaess, Product Education, Tulip. Episode 72. Augmented podcast.

Robotics, or Vention), Tulip provides ample free, online training to the world. Some are certification courses on its products, other courses represent broader industry topics such as the no-code approach and agile for manufacturing. The focus is on a specific challenge key to its mission: "Learn how to build operations apps in hours." Tulip University, operational since 2020, has a plethora of courses on topics such as: app building, design and methodology, product feature deep dives, machine monitoring, and digital manufacturing best practices (see Resource 9.2).

**Resource 9.2** Tulip University.

What is the intent behind these courses? Tulip is a generative platform that allows people to create new software quickly and without the overhead that comes from traditional software development processes. Its visual programming language abstracts away all of the stuff that you're doing in code and allows you to move things around the screen to quickly come out with sophisticated software products.

What Tulip University attempts to do is help the industrial engineers. John Klaess, Product Education Lead, Tulip, says, "You're not just learning to think computationally and to write functions and deal with databases and data models, but you're learning how to transfer what's happening in one domain, the domain of software and solutions, to your domain, which is physical products, operations, and people" (Augmented 2021, ep. 72; see Interview 9.5).

"We're teaching people a couple of things. I would put them into three distinct buckets. One I would call feature type courses, how you use Tulip features, functionality, product things. They're very straightforward tutorials on 'This is how you create a database in Tulip, this is how you write trigger logic. This is how you create specific types of applications'." The second he calls context courses: "This is how you create this particular use case with our tools," so work constructions, quality machine monitoring, production visibility, all of our sort of bread-and-butter use cases. In that scenario, an instructor provides the sort of a model scenario. "So you're a production manager at this plant. You need to figure out what your work orders are doing at any given time, create an application to do that. All of the sort of design decisions you need to make at any given point to produce an application that successfully does that. And then finally you would have methodology courses."

Tulip is taking on the industry-wide challenge of teaching no-code to operators and teaching underlying concepts along the way (see Table 9.1). Klaess says, "It's great for us when more people can use Tulip, but it's [even better] if people are looking to learn transferable skills. It's critical not to teach particular technologies, but to teach enabling frameworks, mindsets, and concepts that underlie many technologies, [such as] computational logic, working with functions, variables, and using those variables."

**Table 9.1   Types of Corporate Customer Education Courses**

| Types of courses | |
| --- | --- |
| Feature | Explaining products so clients can best use its features |
| Context | A broader view of what the product aims to help the client achieve |
| Methodology | The steps involved in progressing with the product to achieve value |

Tulip sees people start to be proficient in terms of being able to do very basic things after a couple hours, so they can become proficient in three to four hours, assuming someone with no prior experience, no coding experience. After putting in 20 hours into the platform, they're able to write fairly complex software applications. After a couple of months, they're moving into the territory of power users. Klaess is inspired by specific corporate learning approaches: "I like the companies that are making e-learning role-based and contextual and relevant to what these folks are doing in their work life and supplementing that, or leading that with instructor-led interactions."

You do not need to have a manufacturing background to train on no-code systems:

> The thing that I keep getting excited about is seeing people who have, not necessarily backgrounds like my own, but nontraditional manufacturing backgrounds being extremely successful in operational roles because often what's happening is you need people who are very good systems, thinkers, and are technically capable enough to pick up what they need to pick up, but they might not have a mechanical engineering or super technical background. To see those people excel in operational roles is exciting." (Augmented 2011, ep. 72)

# WHAT WORKFORCE TRAINING ENABLES AN ENGINEERING MINDSET?

Traditional workforce training is time consuming, expensive, and often demotivating. However, we may need to educate a billion people to fill industry jobs or reskill in the next 10 years. We only need to think about the 3.29 billion people that are the world's workforce (Statista 2021a) and consider that around 14% work in manufacturing and have to be reskilled several times every year (Statista 2021b). But we are not on the right track. We propose a rethink of what should count as industrially relevant courses (engineering, Industry 4.0, digitalization, industrial leadership training). We also wonder if existing courses are sufficiently visible.

Training the world's workers to make full use of industrial technologies, tools, and approaches is more important than inventing more of it. However, we need to empower, and augment, not dehumanize. The last time industry faced this challenge was in the eighteenth century, when industry needed to educate young workers to fit that era's factory work. The result was what many of us know as classroom learning. But factories look different now. People stand, they don't sit, they are on the move, their tech is a cell phone. Yet, school learning has not necessarily changed. Neither has workforce learning. This is a paradox.

# Which Courses Are Essential for the Digitally Enabled Frontline Workforce?

What would the top courses be if you were to train a digital workforce from scratch? An initial list of a dozen core courses might include *management frameworks* (augmented lean), *technologies* (additive/3D/4D, AI/ML, Edge/IoT/sensors, industrial production systems, no-code software, robotics systems), *platforms* (frontline operations platforms, MES), and *operational practices* (digital factory operator). Each course would need to be offered at different skill levels, and certainly both as a basic (101) course, an intermediate-level, as well as a masterclass. See Table 9.2 for an overview of what we find to be the essential curriculum, which would have to evolve rapidly as things change.

**Table 9.2   Essential Courses for the Digitally Enabled Frontline Workforce**

| Additive manufacturing | Frontline operations platforms | Industry 4.0 overview |
|---|---|---|
| CNC machining | Manufacturing execution systems (MES): Legacy & best practices | Industrial productivity systems |
| Augmented lean | Industrial AI/ML | No-code software |
| Digital manufacturing | Working with industrial Edge/IoT & sensors | Industrial production systems (nonregulated industries) |
| Operating robotics systems | Industrial production systems (regulated industries) | Digital factory operator |

CESMII, the Smart Manufacturing Institute, is a US government funded, nonprofit organization to drive smart manufacturing and a primary source for education and workforce development, industry networking, funded research, and a smart manufacturing innovation platform to enable digital transformation. CESMII was created in 2016, funded by the US government – Department of Energy with $70 million. Manufacturers can join as members starting at $4,000 a year plus cost-share for projects. As a member, you have access to their knowledge portal, which includes online education with self-paced eLearning modules on smart manufacturing principles and machine learning in manufacturing, as well as educational articles, papers, and training videos. CESMII's cornerstone is its Smart Manufacturing Innovation Platform (SMIP), an interoperable solution to deliver plug and play to discrete, hybrid, and process manufacturers who want secure connectivity, standards, and the ability to create data semantics, with the result that they arguably can define new systems "without the need for extensive middleware configuration or infrastructure maintenance and management" (CESMII 2022).

John Dyck, CEO, CESMII, is facing the challenge of smartening up US manufacturing head on. He realizes that despite having industrial IoT platforms, basic augmented reality, and fairly powerful machine learning tools, the true adoption on the plant floor is abysmal. "That's where the behaviors, the cultures and the characteristics of how we've always done things, and the reluctance to adopt new things, really comes in," says Dyck. Accelerating the evolution toward Industry 4.0 requires the ecosystem to recognize that things have to change and act on that. Dyck says the trend toward "democratization," by which he means increased access to technology tools across the organization, is going to help all parties – the big manufacturers, the big vendors, the big integrators, and the big machine builders will simultaneously increase the accessibility of smart manufacturing capabilities for the small and medium manufacturers.

The reason is simple. The costs involved are not just the cost to acquire and implement, but also the cost to sustain these systems. Staff and expertise shortages abound, and pilots won't help if there are "data silos," meaning data is not shared. Then, "even if they're successful as an individual proof of concept, the success is not there, at scale" (Augmented 2021, ep. 17; see Interview 9.6).

**Interview 9.6** Smart Manufacturing for All. Interview with John Dyck, CEO at CESMII. Episode 17. Augmented podcast.

# CONCLUSION

Without a doubt, process engineering skills and knowledge are foundational to technological innovation and development of the manufacturing industry. Good engineers drive long-term economic growth and help solve societal challenges. However, similar to the necessary de-emphasis on doctors in the healthcare system as digital health takes on the last mile challenge, the manufacturing system needs to deemphasize formalized engineering degrees to face the scale-up challenges. At the same time, workforce training must become more rigid and connected to college-level certificates. How can this be achieved?

Process engineers of the future will have an ever changing mix of formal and informal training under their belt. Both types of training need to be better, smarter, faster, cheaper – and more enjoyable to do. How do we ensure that each element works together? It is far too easy to put the burden on the individual engineer or worker. They cannot possibly see all the ramifications of choosing different learning strategies and it will undoubtedly also be interpreted differently by each individual based on their learning styles. Rather, governments, universities and companies must take a role coordinating, financing, and standardizing education and training and updating it regularly (every 2–3 years). It is required to put the responsibility on learning institutions (universities, colleges and community colleges, high schools, vocational schools) and they must clearly evolve to embrace the challenge. However, no matter how practice-based, theoretically founded instructions not bound by the work context cannot put learners in the same position as learning whilst doing the work. Therefore, the ultimate responsibility rests with employers.

Evidence that training is evolving is ample. As a rapidly scaling startup, we have experimented with training because our product itself represents a new approach to industrial operations. Luckily, the training we provide is not too hard to do. But even for the robotics startups we have covered in this chapter, for whose customers training is a bit more elaborate, it is possible to make training entertaining, scalable, and credentialed through hybrid digital, and face-to-face approaches as well as making increasing use of augmented learning modes.

At its best, training is social, and community enabled. We need to foster environments where learning, teaching, and modeling behavior is incentivized and, more importantly, intrinsically valued. Technology-enhanced training, at best, augments the teacher, uplifts the learner, and happens (soon perhaps) in an extended reality enhanced by sensors, data, and community cues, in an industrial metaverse encompassing digital twins, digital factories, decentralized 3D printing, and increasingly easy-to-use wearables that increase the interaction between learners, physical reality, learning material, as well as mentors.

In the next chapter, we explore the consequences of the fact that most pressing challenges manufacturing faces cannot be solved with automation alone.

# REFERENCES

ABB University (2022). ABB University: Your gateway to comprehensive training portfolio. https://new.abb.com/service/abb-university).

Augmented (2021, ep. 2). How to Train Augmented Workers. Interview with Elisa Roth, doctoral student at the Institute for Manufacturing at the University of Cambridge. Episode 2. *Augmented podcast*. (Feb 15) https://www.augmented podcast.co/how-to-train-augmented-workers/ (accessed 5 November 2021).

Augmented (2021, ep. 6). Human-Robot Interaction challenges. Interview with Kel Guerin, co-founder, Ready Robotics. Episode 6. *Augmented podcast*. (March 10) https://www.augmentedpodcast.co/human-robot-interaction-challenges/ (accessed 12 November 2021).

Augmented (2021, ep. 3). Reimagine Training. Episode 3. Interview with Sarah Boisvert, Founder and CEO Fab Lab Hub, LLC and the nonprofit New Collar

Network. *Augmented podcast.* (Feb 15) https://www.augmentedpodcast.co/reimagine-training/ (accessed 5 November 2021).

Augmented (2021, ep. 5). Plug-and-play Industrial Tech. Interview with Etienne Lacroix, CEO & Founder, Vention. Episode 5. *Augmented podcast.* (March 3) https://www.augmentedpodcast.co/plug-and-play-industrial-tech/ (accessed 12 November 2021).

Augmented (2021, ep. 7). Work of the Future. Interview with Elisabeth Reynolds, Executive Director, MIT Task Force on the Work of the Future. Episode 7. *Augmented podcast.* (March 3) https://www.augmentedpodcast.co/work-of-the-future/ (accessed 12 November 2021).

Augmented (2021, ep. 12). Enterprise Wide Quality of Manufacturing. Episode 12. Interview with Joseph DeFeo, CEO, Juran. *Augmented podcast.* (April 7) https://www.augmentedpodcast.co/enterprise-wide-quality-of-manufacturing/ (accessed 28 November 2021).

Augmented (2021, ep. 17). Smart Manufacturing for All. Interview with John Dyck, CEO at CESMII. Episode 17. *Augmented podcast.* (March 3) (accessed 12 November 2021). https://www.augmentedpodcast.co/smart-manufacturing-for-all/ (accessed 30 November 2021).

Augmented (2021, ep. 27). Industry 4.0 Tools. Interview with Carl March, Stanley Black & Decker. Episode 27. *Augmented podcast.* (June 1) https://www.augmentedpodcast.co/industry-40-tools/ (accessed 12 November 2021).

Augmented (2021, ep. 72). What Is Tulip University? Interview with John Klaess, Product Education, Tulip. Episode 72. *Augmented podcast.* https://www.augmentedpodcast.co/72 (accessed 30 March 2022).

Autor, D., and Mindell, D.A. and Reynolds, E.B. (2022). *The Work of the Future: Building Better Jobs in an Age of Intelligent Machines.* MIT Press.

Black, P. (2018). Process Engineering – Everything You Need to Know! *Process Industry Informer* (November 1). https://www.processindustryinformer.com/process-engineering-everything-need-know (accessed 5 November 2021).

Bonvillian, W.B., and Sarma, S.E. (2021). America Needs a New Workforce Education System. *MIT Open Learning.* (March 9) https://openlearning.mit.edu/news/america-needs-new-workforce-education-system (accessed 12 November 2021).

Bonvillian, W.B., and Sarma, S.E. (2021). *Workforce Education: A New Roadmap.* MIT Press.

Burrowes, J., and Young, A., and Dan Restuccia, D., and Fuller, J. and Raman, M. (2014). Bridge the Gap: Rebuilding America's Middle Skills. *Accenture, Burning Glass Technologies, and Harvard Business School.* https://www.hbs.edu/competitiveness/research/Pages/research-details.aspx?rid=66 (accessed 12 November 2021).

DegreeQuery (2021). How long does it take to get a degree in engineering? DegreQueery. https://www.degreequery.com/how-long-does-it-take-to-get-a-degree-in-engineering/ (accessed 12 November 2021).

Devillieres, R. (2019). Protocols and standards, towards an openness revolution in manufacturing. Medium.com. https://medium.com/opeo-startup-studio/protocols-and-standards-towards-an-openness-revolution-in-manufacturing-a9500c082b9b (accessed 28 January 2022).

Edwards, D. (2021). ABB to continue online robot masterclass training courses. *Robotics and Automation News* (August 19). https://roboticsandautomation-news.com/2021/08/19/abb-to-continue-online-robot-masterclass-training-courses/45625/ (accessed 5 November 2021).

Helper, S., and Reynolds, E., Traficonte, D., and Singh, A. (2021). Factories of the Future: Technology, Skills, and Digital Innovation at Large Manufacturing Firms. Research Briefs (January 25). *MIT Work of the Future.* https://workofthefuture.mit.edu/research-post/factories-of-the-future-technology-skills-and-digital-innovation-at-large-manufacturing-firms/ (accessed 12 November 2021).

J-WEL (2022). The Human Skills Matrix. https://jwel.mit.edu/human-skills-matrix (accessed 10 March 2022).

Kessler, G. (2014). Do 10,000 baby boomers retire every day? *Washington Post.* (July 24). https://www.washingtonpost.com/news/fact-checker/wp/2014/07/24/do-10000-baby-boomers-retire-every-day/ (accessed 10 March 2022).

Lundberg, A. and Westerman, G. (2020). The Transformer CLO. *Harvard Business Review.* (Jan–Feb). https://hbr.org/2020/01/the-transformer-clo (accessed 12 November 2021).

McFadden, C. (2017). The Origin of the Word 'Engineering.' Interesting Engineering (Sept 5). https://interestingengineering.com/the-origin-of-the-word-engineering (accessed 12 November 2021)

Roth, E., and Moencks, M. (2021). Technology-mediated learning in Industry: Solution space, implementation, evaluation. *IEEE International Conference on Industrial Engineering and Engineering Management (IEEM),* pp. 1480–1484.

Statista (2021a). Number of employees worldwide from 1991 to 2021. Statista. https://www.statista.com/statistics/1258612/global-employment-figures/# (accessed 30 March 2022).

Statista (2021b). Manufacturing industry employment share in selected economies worldwide in 2016. Statista. https://www.statista.com/statistics/883390/economies-employment-share-in-manufacturing-industry/(accessed30March 2022).

The United Manufacturing Hub (2021). Open source in Industrial IoT: an open and robust infrastructure instead of reinventing the wheel. *The United Manufacturing Hub*. Documentation. https://docs.umh.app/docs/concepts/open-source-industrial-iot/ (accessed 5 November 2021).

Tulip University (2022) Tulip University: Learn how to build operations apps in hours. https://tulip.co/university/ (accessed 10 March 2022).

# CHAPTER 10

# FROM AUTOMATION TO AUGMENTATION

M anufacturing industries contribute to 16% of global GDP, according to McKinsey Global Institute (Manyika et al. 2012). The technologies of the moment in manufacturing include AI, augmented reality (AR), edge (industrial IoT with powerful on-device computing capability), robots, sensors, wearables, and 3D printing. Despite being avid technologists, we find that focusing too much on flashy emerging tech can be a distraction from accomplishing industrial goals today. This trap has been set by inventors, academics, and corporate innovation people. It has been ushered along by industrialists, media, and futurists from the beginning of the Industrial Revolution (see Chapter 1) to this day. To find a happy middle ground is not easy, but it helps to think in human-centric ways.

To be clear, we are not just saying this to be contrarian: we each have a combination of academic research and industrial experience of more than 20 years telling us this loud and clear. We want to be specific here, not to show off our background, but because of the specific work we have done in this field to get to these observations.

Natan once led Samsung's mobile R&D innovation center in Israel and was among the first ten employees at Rethink Robotics, where he led the work on user interface and interaction design for a new breed of manufacturing robots. He is a co-founder of Formlabs, an early pioneer in industrial desktop 3D printing. He is the co-founder of Tulip, the frontline operations platform that is innovating across cyber-physical systems that currently supports any industrially implemented wearable system that has reached, or is about to reach, critical mass. Natan also has a PhD from the MIT Media Lab on *Rapid Development, Real-World Deployment, and Evaluation of Projected Augmented Reality Applications* (Linder 2017). Natan's 2017 thesis conclusion is still valid: "Current interactive projected augmented reality systems are not designed to support rapid development and deployment of applications beyond the confines of research labs." (Linder 2017).

Trond has worked for and advised governments (the EU, the UK, Portugal, and Norway) on technology policy and strategy, led standardization efforts in EMEA for the big tech giant Oracle, has led consulting efforts on consumer insight for Fortune 500 clients at WPP/Kantar, built and led the MIT Startup Exchange working with thousands of startups, and worked as a venture partner for the corporate investor Hitachi Ventures as well as from Antler, the global seed investor. He gets daily input from thought-leading guests appearing on his Augmented and Futurized podcasts. He has written six books on futurism, leadership, and technology. Trond also has a PhD on *What the Net Can't Do*, dating back to 2002 where he performed fieldwork on the notion of the "nomadic workplace" and found that not even the visionaries inside top tech companies or venture capital firms practiced what they preached (Undheim 2002). This was surprising back then, and should be surprising now, as the pandemic has challenged all our collective notions about remote work yet again, and still has surprises in store as to whether remote technology ever will replace face-to-face knowledge work and teamwork in industrial or office settings.

Regardless of how great the technologies we develop might become, might it be that we always have to think of virtual solutions as the exception? Hybrid and fluid interfaces that cater to and combine both virtual and physical interaction, and emphasize the role of humans, seem to have a lot of promise as an alternative (see Figure 10.1). How far should we expect to go with regards to automation of work processes? Which technologies are likely to help us the most and what attributes do products built on them need to exhibit? What does this mean for the prospect of industrially sound augmented systems today and tomorrow? Let's start with our take on industrial robotics.

**Figure 10.1** From Automation to Augmentation.

# THE STATE OF PLAY
# IN INDUSTRIAL ROBOTICS

In retrospect, repetitive, hard, dangerous work is something humans never should have been doing in the first place. Think, for example, of *dirty tasks* such as sewer reconnaissance, repair, and cleaning, clearing invasive species, milking cows in smelly parlors, cleaning toilets, conducting autopsies, or managing waste at a recycling and waste disposal facility. Perhaps more obviously, *dull tasks* such as data entry, data extraction, and invoice processing, are being taken over by robotic process automation (RPA). However, we need to keep in mind that complex cases might require human judgment. The question is, are the algorithms we install capable of determining which? Robots are getting better at *dangerous tasks* such as endlessly performing repetitive motions without fatigue, fighting wildfires, collecting radioactive waste, defusing bombs, traversing distant planets, working with chemicals, working in contaminated environments, exploring abandoned mines, and inspecting unstable structures.

Robots are also moving into tasks that are both physically and mentally hard for humans. Most workers would consider warehouse fulfillment tasks a mix of dull and dangerous considering the risk of work injuries and boredom, so no wonder warehouse robotics is a big commercial focus, although it is the expediency and precision of warehouse robots that e-commerce employers tend to value the most. Reading radiology charts is another task robotic AI systems coupled with MRI machines are getting much better at – although we'd still want a human to double check its assessment, wouldn't you?

That we now have robots increasingly taking over such types of tasks is an overall improvement. But that's where the simplicity of this argument stops. We need to be more careful about where we place robots and what they contribute. The reason is that humans, in effect, should be considered the best "robots" we have, for some tasks. As the (so far) most complex machine capable of autonomous motion and independent thinking, we are the standard by which all robots are, and should be measured. We should not think of these as pure outsourcing to machines. In fact, lifting heavy objects in manufacturing processes and warehouses, or tending to elderly people at a home care facility or hospital will soon become facilitated by exoskeletons, which technically is augmentation more than robotics – because a human is still intimately involved. We think humans should be deeply involved in automation as much as possible and for as long as possible. When and if we make the determination that robots are a better option, constant human oversight of robotic decisions, decision making paths, and track record, is essential and should be carefully regulated.

In the book *What to Expect When You're Expecting Robots* (Major and Shah 2020), the authors point out that if we expect to have robots working with us not for us, we increasingly have to structure the way we live our lives, from our crosswalks, to our factories, to our social norms, so that robots can more effectively live in our world. The emerging class of robots is the collaborative robot ("cobots") – robots deemed safe (!) and worthy of collaborating with humans directly on the shop floor or in the wild. A key aspect of evolving cobots includes better spatial awareness as well as human-like dexterity and agility, but also behavioral skills, reading emotions in humans, and perhaps even acquiring basic empathy with humankind. The ability to do a new, complex task fast, is a human strength that we have struggled to teach robots to do equally well.

Making more effective robots starts with making more sensible use of the human workforce. Exactly which part of a task is where the human strength resides? Which tasks are viewed as so enjoyable or fulfilling by humans that we should not take it out of their workday? What are the risks with mindless automation of tasks that at some point require deep, human judgment? What exactly would the benefits be of complete automation of a task? Why not start with the assumption that robots are going to be complimentary, not replacements? This reassessment is overripe and it speaks to the value of work, of being human, and of what kind of society we want to create for ourselves.

Also, as robots are increasingly in the wild, open landscape (not in cages but even outside warehouses and on sidewalks) and as we add more complex algorithms into robotic "brains," we soon need to worry about what robots themselves might think of the role they should play. That is, within predetermined spheres of activity, for now. This challenge is completely underestimated by most hyped-up timelines for the full-blown adoption of autonomous robots, cars, and other mobile machines. For example, if, by some innovation miracle, fully autonomous vehicles (Level 5) become technically feasible within the next few decades, there is no telling when society's infrastructure or human traffic behavior will be ready for the same. Deploying the most obvious capabilities first makes tremendous sense, even if automation is becoming more economical and viable. It seems ironic that the challenge of robotic capabilities we ourselves have created would challenge our own workforce, but that's where we are. For the time being, it is an unfair comparison in favor of humans.

Apart from some fancy prototypes and fictionalized robots, of which there were many, almost all robots before approximately 2010 were basic, bulky, dangerous industrial robots. Basic in that they would only attempt to replicate one human action (walking, talking, moving an arm, etc.), bulky in that they were over-engineered with a lot of metal and had few softer parts, and dangerous in the sense that they needed to be fenced in (there are regulations on this matter). Apart from highly specialized use in the automotive industry, robots were initially not that useful on the factory floor for anything other than lifting heavy objects and carrying out highly repetitive tasks that only consisted of a single motion. In mass production of postwar cars, that turned out to be quite useful. You could say that robots are cut out for work that humans never should have been doing in the first place.

The Unimate, conceived from a design for a mechanical arm patented in 1954 (granted in 1961) by American inventor George Devol, licensed to entrepreneur Joseph Engelberger, and made by Unimation in Danbury, Connecticut, was the very first industrial robot (Automate.org 2022, Pearce, 2011). Unimate was developed over two years, from 1957 to 1959, and by 1961 it was first installed on an assembly line at a General Motors die-casting plant in Ewing Township, NJ, a suburb of Trenton. Rapidly deploying 450 units, the first mass-produced robotic arm for factory automation was born, turning the General Motors Trenton facility into the most automated automotive plant in the world, doubling production speed to 110 cars per hour. In 1966, Finland's Nokia obtained the right to manufacture the robots in Scandinavia and Eastern Europe, and by 1969, Kawasaki Heavy Industries (now Kawasaki Robotics) had bought the rights to manufacture and market the Unimate robots for the Asian market. Automotive industry giants BMW, Volvo, Mercedes Benz, British Leyland, and Fiat were soon to follow, and the robot's early industrial trajectory was sealed (Automate.org 2022).

Swedish robot manufacturer ASEA produced the first microcomputer-controlled electric industrial robot, the IRb6 (1974). With a lift capacity of 6 kg, it allowed movement in five axes. Those first four robots are still in the same factory in Sweden doing the same thing they've been doing for the last 40 years (Waltenberger 2014). About 1,900 copies were sold between 1975 and 1992, with a new version, the ASEA IRb 2000 (1986) coming on the market a decade later (Norman 2021). In 1988, the company merged with a Swiss company and became what is today ABB. What emerged was a host of new industrial robots, most notably the ABB IRB 6000 (1991) and the ABB FlexPicker (1998).

Kuka, the German manufacturer of industrial robots and systems for factory automation, and Chinese owned (Midea group) since 2016, is an industrial company founded in 1898. Kuka's six-axis robot, Famulus (1973), allowed industrial robots to perform more complex tasks, such as welding, and to a lesser degree for palletizing, packing, and other materials handling, without constant human intervention. Famous in popular culture through the James Bond movie, *Die Another Day* (Prezi 2021), Famulus was a breakthrough for the automotive industry at the time. Given the six degrees of freedom, for safety, Famulus operated behind physical fence barriers with automatic sensors on the gates of the barriers.

Throughout the past 20 years, industrial robots have tended to be one-trick ponies. ABB's IRB 120, a small multipurpose six-axis material-handling robot (2009), enables flexible and compact production, allowing more manufacturers, such as the consumer, electronics, solar, and medical sectors, to make use of robotics. As of 2009, ABB had installed more than 160,000 robots worldwide (ABB 2009). Does that sound like a big number? It's all relative, considering that as of 2012, the global labor pool consisted of approximately 3 billion workers (Torres 2013). Soon thereafter, ABB released its IRB 460 palletizing robot (2010). In 2014, ABB announced it had installed 250,000 robots, the year after the figure was 300,000, and as of 2021, that figure was 500,000.

Over these last 20 years, the legacy robotic operating systems have mostly been proprietary, for example Denso (Japan), Microsoft (US), Omron Corporation (Japan), Universal Robotics (Denmark), ABB Ltd. (Switzerland), FANUC (Japan), and KUKA AG (Germany) with one notable exception, the open-source robotic operating system, ROS (2007). This is an important point, because it has limited the collaboration across robotics manufacturers, stalled efficient use of robots on the factory floor, and overall, without doubt, has slowed down innovation in the field.

In 2005, three university students in Denmark founded Universal Robot, the first company to deliver commercially viable collaborative robots. By 2019, they were the dominant collaborative robot (cobot) manufacturer in the world. Only a few years after Universal, MIT roboticist Rodney Brooks founded Heartland Robotics, later called Rethink Robotics (2008), with the idea of creating low-cost robots. Natan (co-author of this book) briefly led the user interface and interaction design for this new breed of manufacturing robots around 2009. In 2012, they released the two-armed robot Baxter, and in 2015 they followed up with a smaller, more flexible counterpart, the one-armed Sawyer, designed to perform more detailed tasks. These were both examples of early cobots meaning they were designed to be safe and easy to work alongside, rather than replace humans in factory environments. Commercially, the feat proved difficult at that time, so in 2018, the assets were sold to the Hahn Group, a German automotion specialist. In 2019, that company launched Sawyer Black, a quieter, higher-quality version, and began a partnership with Siemens (Lawrence 2019). Universal is by now the cobot leader with $250 million revenues.

Why did they succeed over Rethink? Arguably because Rethink's robots were overengineered for safety, software adaptability, and bells and whistles such as embedded vision (which, at that time, customers saw no use for) and underperformed on precision, a robot must-have (Lawrence 2019). Universal Robots' UR3 (2015) for tabletops became a huge success. By 2016, there was an ISO safety standard for cobots, ISO/TS 15066:2016, which specifies safety requirements for collaborative industrial robot systems and the work environment, and allows for a much wider usage of robots. As of 2020, Universal said it had sold more than 39,000 cobots worldwide and holds nearly 60% of global market share (Francis 2020).

Over the past decade, the global sales volume of industrial robots tripled, stabilizing at just below 400,000 units in 2019, with the automotive sector at a third of new installations, correspondingly putting most robots in Japan, China, the United States, South Korea, and Germany and the global market size at around $50 billion USD (Placek 2021). In South Korea, for example, there are over 850 robots per 10,000 manufacturing employees. In the automotive sector, however, this figure exceeds 2,000 installations per 10,000 employees (Placek 2021).

The COVID-19 years are pivotal for the industrial robotics industry. It immediately resulted in manufacturing firms turning pilot projects into standards and commercial orders and demanding immediate implementation, according to Tom Ryden, executive director of MassRobotics (Augmented 2021, ep. 13). Legged robots are coming of age, with quadrupeds leaving the lab and entering the workplace. Boston Dynamics' Spot, the robot dog that can walk up to three miles per hour, climb terrain, avoid obstacles, see 360-degrees, and perform a number of programmed tasks and even some autonomous missions, was first introduced in 2015 and, is now in general sales for US $74,500. In testing, it conducted document construction progress, monitored remote or hazardous environments, and provided situational awareness across a variety of environments, including power-generation facilities, decommissioned nuclear sites, factory floors, construction sites, and research laboratories (Stieg 2020). However, we note that the New York Police Department (NYPD) got rid of its leased Spot because "People had figured out the catchphrases and the language to somehow make this evil" (Whitwam 2021). Ironically, it is in industrial-use cases that Boston Dynamics is seeing commercial success. In 2022, it announced that Stretch, its mobile, case-handling robot, will further automate DHL's supply chain warehouses in North America, rolling out over the next few years (Crowe 2022). Stretch can currently shift up to 800 boxes an hour, up to 23 kilograms (50 lbs) in weight, comparable to a human. That is, if the workspace is fairly standardized (Vincent 2021).

# WHERE ROBOTICS IS MAKING AN IMPACT ON THE FACTORY FLOOR

The story of robotics is complex and often misunderstood as an endless march toward replacing humans as part of industrial production. Despite what Martin Ford (2016) claims in *Rise of the Robots: Technology and the Threat of a Jobless Future*, attempting the populist argument that as technology continues to accelerate and machines begin taking care of themselves, fewer people will be necessary, there is no threat of a jobless future in general. Even though Gilchrist (2016) in *Industry 4.0: The Industrial Internet of Things*, might be right that the still largely mechanical, people-based systems of offshore locations will soon be replaced, this does not mean that people will not find new ways to contribute value to the labor process alongside machines. First off all, Gilchrist assumes that the re-industrialization of the former industrial powerhouses to counterbalance the benefits of cheap labor providers dominating the industrial sector will be an easy process.

There are several ways to look at upskilling. You can see it as a career choice or you can see it as a threat. Either way, it does not seem to be optional. Those that do not upskill would seem to risk becoming less attractive workers in future job markets. It is not a truth these authors relish. Replacing humans for robots was a focus 20 years ago but it is not the focus now. Not because it isn't possible, it is, but because it isn't always fruitful. Labor might be costly, but the highest-quality labor will always be in demand. Others have covered this argument. In *The Second Machine Age*, Brynjolfsson and McAfee (2014) come out strong in defense of human ingenuity when up against the machines we create, even though "the new technologies [are] exponential, digital and combinatorial." They recommend that we "race with [the] machines," and that's an apt metaphor, to a point. Robots are not taking over in the sense that there will be no jobs any time soon. Finding talent has been tough in manufacturing over the last decade. The Deloitte (2018) skills gap study pointed out that we are near the historic peak in job openings not seen since 2001. The "future of manufacturing personas" Deloitte describes illustrate the kind of talent we are missing: "digital twin engineer, predictive supply network analyst, robot teaming coordinator, digital offering manager, drone data coordinator, smart factory manager, smart scheduler, smart safety supervisor, UAM flight controller, and smart QA manager." Aside from the overuse of the somewhat trite hype word *smart,* Deloitte was on to something.

Falling into the opposite trap is also not helpful. There is clearly, as Bawani (2019) points out, a real leadership challenge to identify, assess, select, and develop future leaders of an Industry 4.0-enabled organization. We feel authors of *The Technology Fallacy: How People Are the Real Key to Digital Transformation* (Kane et al. 2019) go too far when they claim, based on MIT Sloan and Deloitte survey research from 16,000 people in Walmart, Google, and Salesforce, that digital disruption is "primarily about people." We cannot choose to ignore the cyber-physical aspect of industrial technology, for example. Nor can we ignore the digital characteristics (e.g., its binary precision, data, and calculations) that directly impact human autonomy in the workplace. Digital transformation is, in fact, *socio-technical*, it is about the changing and muddled relationship between humans and technology. Humans and technologies are not just "connected" but more aptly *locked into each other* in mutually interdependent ways. We need to keep finding out more about what that means. The future of work depends on it.

With *Augmented Lean*, we are presenting a contingent view of technology as a tool that increasingly is only one layer, not the whole story, but we maintain that *only* focusing on people, culture, and training without considering technology's highly specific requirements, complexities, and skills, is an equally detrimental approach. Thinking of digital technology without considering the specificity of cyber-physical systems and their material elements (hardware, materials, factories, laws of physics, and more), is also reductionist.

There is indeed a need for *Factory Physics for Managers* (Pound et al. 2014), where the practical science of operations still must determine the choices and execution of the best strategy for better productivity. Having said that, traditional textbooks – for example *Manufacturing Operations*

*Management* (Yoo and Glardon 2018) – are too simplistic. If you want to present the essential theories and tools for production for students in engineering, junior professionals in supply chain, and production managers who are starting their career in a manufacturing firm, you cannot ignore establishing a firm foundation in digital practices. The entire curriculum needs to change, and fast.

# AUTOMATION IS MORE THAN ROBOTICS

Robotics currently dominates the debate over advanced automation. This clouds the fact that there has been a gradually increasing automation of the manufacturing industry for several decades. Automation existed way before robots were a factor. In fact, as much as manufacturing is thought to be the epitome of industrial companies, it mostly consists of small suppliers. According to the International Labor Organization (ILO), micro-, small-, and medium-sized enterprises (commonly abbreviated to SMEs) are responsible for more than two-thirds of all jobs worldwide and account for the majority of new job creation (ILO 2022). SMEs, which in many countries represent more than 90% of all enterprises accounting for 70% of employment worldwide, typically have fewer than 250 employees, and a large share have fewer than 10 employees (ILO 2022). This is the case in big industrial countries such as Germany, the US, and China. Because the technology often is made by software vendors that cater to big players, which appear easier to target with new products through their salesforce, a huge proportion of the market have very limited access to technology.

In many cases, these small and medium enterprises have no ambition to dominate the headlines. However, once in a while, an industrial automation startup comes along that reshapes the industry, through its bifurcations. In the 1990s, Wonderware, which produced a range of software products to address production operations, production performance, manufacturing intelligence, business process management, and collaboration, was such a company (Slavin, 1997). Founded in 1987, sold to British-based engineering giant Siebe plc in 1998, which, in turn, merged with BTR plc to form Invensys, which merged with French multinational Schneider Electric in 2014, now sold as Aveva, Wonderware has had an outsized effect on manufacturing automation and is a precursor of what is now happening across the world. Today, it constitutes a collaborative, standards-based foundation that "unifies people, processes, and assets across all facilities for continuous operational improvement and real-time decision support."

Because of the rapid advent of industrial robotics our current age is often misunderstood as an extension of automation. However, instead, our society is arguably (only) now entering the era of augmentation, which is quite different and qualitatively better for the workforce. Throughout *Augmented Lean*, we explain what that means for 80% of the world's workforce who now need substantial reskilling on the job, and, under the right circumstances, may benefit from upskilling through no-code factory apps that increase productivity, control, and autonomy.

Another issue with robotics is that we often speak about it as if its impact has already happened. On the contrary, the age of robotics is by no means a bygone era. The robotic influx in manufacturing has only just begun. In fact, given the technological progress in the domain of robotics, the challenge before COVID-19 hit was to explain the low uptake. Many companies were experimenting with them, but few had fully implemented robotics in their facilities. As the MIT study on the future of work points out, there is a surprising lack of robots in American factories (Autor, Mindell and Reynolds 2022). That changed somewhat with the pandemic. All of a sudden, orders increased dramatically in magnitude. However, it would be wrong to say that factories are full of robots. Yet.

# WHAT AUTOMATION HAS ACCOMPLISHED

Automation solves problems by taking people out of the equation. However, today, the most pressing challenges manufacturing faces cannot be solved with automation. For the remaining problems, those too hard for a robot to solve, you still need to rely on the most powerful cognitive computer on the shop floor: humans. These problems include creative problem solving, teamwork, complex assembly, safety checks, real-world testing, etc.

Kel Guerin, chief innovation officer and co-founder of Ready Robotics, explains that it's really a question of augmentation because they don't have enough employees to meet demand, so the robots being put in place are not displacing anyone. Ready Robotics works with FedEx Express, which had a factory that was processing a huge number of packages and had a thousand people working there 15 to 20 years ago. Guerin says, "Now, they still have a thousand people working at that processing facility and they do *three times the amount of work*. That's what automation can do and what process improvement can do. It's about augmentation. I see a future where a lot of the tasks that people do right now, where they do have a lot of knowledge about the process, get transformed into automated tasks."

Those employees can transition to a supervisory role. In fact, one of Guerin's customers is Stanley Black & Decker. "We saw [the same] at one of their facilities where they actually created a new class of job at that factory, which was basically a robot technician. Somebody who had been skilled up with our software to manage the several robots that they had running those processes that a person previously was sitting there doing. Now, it's an entirely new job that didn't exist five years ago. I think it's critical that they stay in manufacturing because they have all the knowledge about how to make these products. But what they do will probably change into a more problem solving role rather than putting pieces of metal into a machine role" (Augmented 2021, ep. 6).

The interchange between automation and augmentation will change over the next 10 years, too, says Guerin, as new robotic technologies will redefine how these systems operate. There's a lot of work right now in the machine learning and artificial intelligence space about how to make robots more adaptive, generally, not just in manufacturing, so that they can handle a variety of different situations and environments, because that's the main downside of a robot right now. As you program it to do one thing, within the scope of what it's able to do, that thing really can't change that much, whereas if you put a person in a new situation, they just figure it out. He says:

> So you're gonna see smarter robots in that sense, but you're still gonna need people to show them the ropes. And even if they do learn in a sort of sci-fi futuristic fashion, where you can just tell them what to do, somebody still needs to be there who knows to tell them what to do. I think in the near term there's no concern about that [machines replacing humans]. Nobody that I talked to is concerned about losing employees to automation; they're more interested in how many employees they will be able to hire because they could expand their business because automation makes them more competitive. (Augmented 2021, ep. 6)

# WHAT AUGMENTATION IS AND WHAT IT WILL BECOME

The World Economic Forum's Augmented Workforce Initiative (WEF 2022) correctly states that key drivers of augmentation include time efficiency, complexity, knowledge, and skills gaps and (so far) finds that workforce augmentation offers a "radically new paradigm of workforce empowerment" that is people-centric, accessible, and sustainable. In principle, their definitions are useful: "Augmentation technologies are systems that interact with employees aiming to positively modify, complement, or augment their cognitive or physical abilities while performing a certain range of industrial activities on the shop floor, or being trained in industrial education contexts" (WEF 2022:11). However, the Initiative is (unfortunately) prematurely stuck on the exact technology fix they claim to want to remove elsewhere in industry. In fact, *augmentation technology* is defined as AR/VR, smart devices, exoskeletons, wearables, and cobots. Instead, one must realize that the path toward worker augmentation is a gradual one. See Resource 10.1.

**Resource 10.1** The World Economic Forum's Augmented Workforce Initiative.

The impact across the workforce in true manufacturing settings can only be achieved once the technologies in question reach maturity, industrial form factor (comfortable, lightweight, power, and network requirements), and scalable price points (not prototype pricing aimed at first adopters). Augmentation can only impact skills by "improving activities, learning curves, and employee satisfaction." This particularly goes for *physical skills* such as manual inspection, work safety, product/material handling, maintenance, and machine configuration. However, *cognitive skills* such as lean management, knowledge management, problem solving, process improvement, and work independence are also important to augment. Both technologies and the workforce must be ready for them. Right now, industry is in an experimental phase.

While we are excited about the promise of augmentation, we are also realistic. Those who are prematurely fascinated with the technology aspect (AR/VR, cobots, exoskeletons, goggles, the metaverse, wearables) are likely to be disappointed. These may be high on hype but are not really making a difference on the shop floor where paper still is a prevalent production tool. Having said that, Tulip, for example, supports wearables and marries no-code with wearables. The most notable use case is line clearance, a standardized procedure in manufacturing for ensuring equipment and work areas are free of products, documents, and materials from a previous process. Line clearance is most commonly used in regulated industries, such as pharmaceuticals, biotech, and food and beverage manufacturing. Often, operators need the use of their hands and must take pictures with a wearable camera. These practical and basic use cases are a far cry from the perfectly rendered visions of AR we have been promised for 10 years that surely will take another few years to materialize.

At this time in the industrial worker augmentation journey, form factors are clunky, price points are too high, and many projects are stuck in pilot purgatory. The only exception to the rule is digital apps based on machine monitoring. Extracting data from existing (older) industrial machines is increasingly possible with new approaches. Deploying and harvesting simple data from rapidly commoditizing sensors running on faster and faster networks is now cost effective. However, advanced sensors that would truly transform industrial operations are still costly. With 5G the current upper limit for mobile networks, latency is removed, too. Display technology mostly through consumer grade monitors and, to some extent, apps displayed on cell phones (or messaging sent to them) are prevalent. However, most cell phones are too small to be useful in a factory environment. You might have dirty hands, gloves, or otherwise have a very different need than the consumer electronics manufacturing industry has been customizing for. All of this needs to be addressed before factory operations can move at software speed.

When will industry get to augmented lean? We certainly will not get there if there is no innovation support for the kinds of interfaces that industry demands. It is quite a shocker to realize how little of the creative force of startups, corporate innovation efforts, electronics user interface efforts, and governmental stimulus funds go toward industrial technology with the frontline worker in mind.

One exception is the Industry 4.0 Human Capital Initiative (IHCI 2022). An initiative by the Singapore Business Federation, supported by the government body, Workforce Singapore (WSG), with anchor partners McKinsey and EY, it is the first program in Singapore dedicated to equipping companies with people management and job redesign skills required for successful Industry 4.0 transformation. The program runs an in-person enabler program as well as a self-help portal. The eight-week hands-on program helps companies get started on their Industry 4.0 transformation in a controlled and low-risk environment. The program offers a mix of both experiential learning and trials of solutions on companies' shop floor as part of a four-step journey to build awareness, prepare interventions, experience transformation, validate, and move forward through clear roadmaps.

Much attention goes toward consumers. Robots also get a lot of press. Overhyped tech with no proven use-case and no real market viability gets the rest. Consumer technology (cell phones, web technology) is arguably not a priority for societal innovation at this point. Increased spending on automation technology (robotics) will make a difference, but only if the human perspective is center stage. Overall, the general thrust of both consumer attention and industrial development is utterly unhelpful for the worker. In fact, these technologies might have made their work conditions worse over the past few decades.

# CONCLUSION

Automation solves problems by taking people out of the equation. However, at low volume, the cost to automate doesn't always make sense. Today, the most pressing challenges manufacturing faces cannot be solved with industrial automation – at least not if that's purely defined as "deploying robots." For the remaining problems, creative problem solving, teamwork, complex assembly, safety checks, and real-world testing, to mention a few, we need another approach. They are currently too hard for a robot to solve. Perhaps we don't even need them to. To solve real problems, you still need to rely on the most powerful "computer" on the shop floor: humans.

We think the guiding principle of all industrial technology should be to serve the purpose of augmenting human capabilities. When automation becomes a goal in itself, we are on an ethical and operational slippery slope. We are outsourcing the essence of being human. We may also be shooting ourselves in the foot, even as industrial leaders. Instead, as automation and augmentation continues to blend, we need to embrace technologies created with clear intent. It better be an intent that we agree with. For now, augmentation is in its infancy, which makes it no less important to get right. For industrial operators who want to get to a "factory of the future," instead of endless demonstrations and small pilots of substandard AR technology, what makes sense is clever use of no-code digital apps that do not affect or interrupt the work process too much. Taking a step back is actually the most innovative move you can make as a forward-thinking leader. We can, and will, handle the bigger challenges in due time.

In the upcoming chapter, we look at the potential augmenting power of operational data and the pitfalls on the way to making machine learning work for manufacturing and life science.

# REFERENCES

ABB (2009). ABB launches new small robot for flexible and compact production. Press Release. *ABB* (August). https://library.e.abb.com/public/e02df464f0f607 f6c125762600397766/Press%20Release%20IRB120%20Industrial%20Robot%20 and%20IRC5%20Compact%20Controller.pdf (accessed 14 December 2021).

Automate.org (2022). UNIMATE // The First Industrial Robot. https://www .automate.org/a3-content/joseph-engelberger-unimate (accessed 10 March 2022).

Francis, S. (2020). Universal Robots sells almost 40,000 units (January 10). https:// roboticsandautomationnews.com/2020/01/10/universal-robots-sells-almost- 40000-units/28414/ (accessed 14 December 2021).

Waltenberger, A, (2014). 250,000 robots sold in 40 years – collaboration makes it pos- sible (March 12). https://www.abb-conversations.com/2014/03/250000-robots- sold-in-40-years-collaboration-makes-it-possible/ (accessed 14 December 2021).

Acemoglu, D., and Restrepo, P. (2020). Robots and jobs: Evidence from US labor markets. *Journal of Political Economy* 128 (6) (April 22). https://economics.mit .edu/files/19696 (accessed 14 December 2021).

Augmented (2021, ep. 6). Human-Robot Interaction Challenges. Interview with Kel Guerin, co-founder, Ready Robotics. Episode 6. *Augmented podcast.* (March 10) https://www.augmentedpodcast.co/human-robot-interaction-challenges/ (accessed 12 November 2021).

Autor, D., and Mindell, D.A. and Reynolds, E.B. (2022). *The Work of the Future: Building Better Jobs in an Age of Intelligent Machines.* MIT Press.

Bawani, S. (2019). *Transforming the Next Generation Leaders: Developing Future Leaders for a Disruptive, Digital-Driven Era of the Fourth Industrial Revolution (Industry 4.0).* New York: Business Expert Press.

Brown, S. (2020). A new study measures the actual impact of robots on jobs. It's significant. Why It Matters. *MIT Sloan* (July 29). https://mitsloan.mit.edu/ ideas-made-to-matter/a-new-study-measures-actual-impact-robots-jobs-its- significant (accessed 14 December 2021).

Crowe, S. (2022). Boston Dynamics delivering fleet of Stretch robots to DHL. *The Robot Report* (January 26). https://www.therobotreport.com/boston- dynamics-delivering-fleet-of-stretch-robots-to-dhl/ (accessed 10 March 2022).

Deloitte (2018). 2018 skills gap in manufacturing study: Future of manufacturing: The jobs are here, but where are the people? https://www2.deloitte.com/us/en/ pages/manufacturing/articles/future-of-manufacturing-skills-gap-study.html (accessed 13 March 2022).

IHCI (2022). Industry 4.0 Human Capital Initiative (IHCI). https://ihci.sbf.org.sg/ (accessed 10 March 2022).

ILO (2022). The power of small: Unlocking the potential of SMEs. *ILO*. InfoStories. https://www.ilo.org/infostories/en-GB/Stories/Employment/SMEs#intro (accessed 10 March 2022).

Lawrence, C. (2019). Rise and Fall of Rethink Robotics. *ASME* (April 5). https://www.asme.org/topics-resources/content/rise-fall-of-rethink-robotics (accessed 14 December 2021).

Linder, N. (2017). Rapid development, real-world deployment, and evaluation of projected augmented reality applications. PhD thesis. *Massachusetts Institute of Technology, School of Architecture and Planning, Program in Media Arts and Science.* https://dspace.mit.edu/handle/1721.1/114074?show=full (accessed 13 March 2022).

Major, L., and Shah, J. (2020). *What to Expect When You're Expecting Robots.* New York: Basic Books.

Manyika, J. et al. (2012). Manufacturing the future: The next era of global growth and innovation. McKinsey Global Institute. https://www.mckinsey.com/business-functions/operations/our-insights/the-future-of-manufacturing (accessed 28 January 2022).

Norman, J. M. (2021). ASEA Produces the IRb 6, the first microcomputer controlled electric industrial robot. HistoryofInformation.com. https://www.history-ofinformation.com/detail.php?entryid=4352 (accessed 14 December 2021).

Pearce, J. (2011). George C. Devol, inventor of robot arm, dies at 99. *The New York Times* (August 15). https://www.nytimes.com/2011/08/16/business/george-devol-developer-of-robot-arm-dies-at-99.html (accessed 10 March 2022).

Placek, M. (2021). Industrial robots worldwide – statistics & facts. *Statista* (June 16). https://www.statista.com/topics/1476/industrial-robots/#dossierKeyfigures (accessed 14 December 2021).

Prezi (2021). Kuka Famulus. https://prezi.com/kyy_fxnslg6n/kuka-famulus/ (accessed 14 December 2021).

Stieg, C. (2020). This $75,000 Boston Dynamics robot "dog" is for sale – take a look. CNBC (June 22). https://www.cnbc.com/2020/06/22/75000-boston-dynamics-robot-dog-for-sale-take-a-look.html (accessed 14 December 2021).

Torres, R. (2013). World of Work Report 2013: Repairing the economic and social fabric. Geneva: International Labour Organization (ILO), International Institute for Labour Studies. https://www.ilo.org/global/research/global-reports/world-of-work/2013/WCMS_214476/lang--en/index.htm (accessed 14 December 2021).

Tulip (2021). Cartier's use of Tulip. Unpublished case study.

Undheim, T.A. (2021). Interview with Youri Regnaud.

Futurized (2021). The Future of Commoditized Robotics. Interview with Tom Ryden, Executive Director of MassRobotics. Episode 31. *Futurized podcast* (September 22). https://www.futurized.co/e/the-future-of-commoditized-robotics/ (accessed 28 January 2022).

Undheim, T.A. (2021). What the Net Can't Do. The Everyday Practice of Internet, Globalization and Mobility. *The Norwegian University of Science and Technology (NTNU)*. PhD Thesis. https://ntnuopen.ntnu.no/ntnu-xmlui/handle/11250/268063?locale-attribute=en (accessed 13 March 2022).

Vincent, J. (2021). Boston Dynamics unveils Stretch: a new robot designed to move boxes in warehouses. *The Verge* (March 29). https://www.theverge.com/2021/3/29/22349978/boston-dynamics-stretch-robot-warehouse-logistics (accessed 10 March 2022).

WEF (2022). Augmented workforce: harnessing Industry 4.0 technologies for workforce empowerment in advanced manufacturing and value chains. White Paper in Collaboration with the University of Cambridge. *World Economic Forum*. (January 2022). https://www3.weforum.org/docs/WEF_Augmented_Workforce_2022.pdf (accessed 13 March 2022).

Whitwam, R. (2021). NYPD has gotten rid of its Boston Dynamics robot dog, *ExtremeTech* (May 3). https://www.extremetech.com/extreme/322404-nypd-has-gotten-rid-of-its-boston-dynamics-robot-dog (accessed 14 December 2021).

# PART IV

# AUGMENTED LEAN OPERATIONS

# CHAPTER 11

# THE POTENTIAL AUGMENTING POWER OF OPERATIONAL DATA

R ony Kubat, co-founder of Tulip, has had an interesting journey. From MIT's Computer Science and Artificial Intelligence Lab (CSAIL), via science advisor to Hollywood film productions and working for Sony Pictures Imageworks on movie special effects, back to the MIT Media Lab. All of this led to co-founding Tulip.co together with fellow graduate student Natan Linder. Throughout these crossroads of computer science, artificial intelligence, and cognitive science, he has found time to become a playwright.

Recently spending a year embedded with one of Tulip's major clients, machine tool maker DMG Mori, he has spent his entire career programming a visual-physical-digital environment. We connected over the awareness that the real world is not truly digitized because it is complex. Physical-digital realities are even more complex. The multiverse, this fascinating idea so much in vogue these days, refers to the potential for interacting in this hybrid reality as a matter of course. But even if disconnected space–time constellations (digital avatars that carry out "real" business) theoretically exist and may soon emerge more plentiful, this takes time. Creative applications that make such behavior attractive beyond computer games need to get built. Multiverses, even those powered by digital twins of industrial installations, will remain niche for some time. Rather, Rony's imagination is faced with digitally innovating within highly real physical constraints. He is well suited for it. In fact, his role in Hollywood was to explain what was scientifically realistic: "I was there to provide a veneer of authenticity."

Despite his technical prowess, Rony has a cynical view of AI in the manufacturing space today. He maintains that AI in manufacturing is [for now] often just an overly fancy term for what essentially is the statistical method of regression analysis, known already since the nineteenth century.

Having said that, Rony does believe that there is a legit future for AI to be used. Rony points out that Tulip's first customer, shoe manufacturer New Balance, found value because it was so much better than the existing method. "The first data collection and analysis hardware we built had double-sided sticky tape, and I mean that literally," he says with pride (Augmented 2021, ep. 66; see Interview 11.1). Edith Harmon, New Balance's vice president of manufacturing innovation, has seen results as the approach has further evolved: "Tulip's apps connect to our production equipment, so we are able to correlate machine and human data using the built-in analytics engine. [...] We are now able to capture all this real-time data and get visibility into the root causes of production issues" (Lukic 2017). Human-centric capturing of data is the way forward (see Figure 11.1).

**Interview 11.1** Bridging the Physical-Digital Divide in Industrial Tech. Interview with Rony Kubat, CTO and Co-founder of Tulip. Episode 66. Augmented podcast.

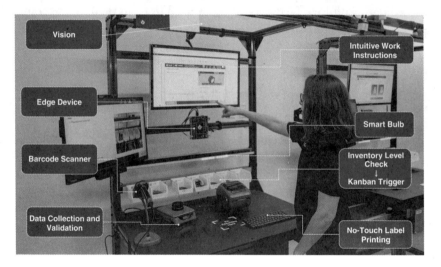

**Figure 11.1** Human-Centric Capturing of Data.

Shoe manufacturing is, in fact, a great example of a complex problem suitable for AI/ML, says Rony, because it moves at a very high speed. "Fashion is changing all the time: new designs [...] very high mix [different] sizes, styles, and gendered versions of the shoes. They're constantly in the process of introducing new products."

An enormous amount of variables impact the quality of a shoe: how to attach the upper of the shoe to the sole, how to apply the glue, the glue mix, the ambient temperature, the glue's set time or activation temperature, how much time the shoe spends in the system, the pressure, or the mold. What that means is that quality inspection through root cause analysis can be incredibly impactful. Says Kubat: "The power of capturing both manual and machine processes comes when you start to be able to connect silos of data together and get a time series of the data attached to the product." It's a typical classification problem where human oversight and machine learning will be working together, says Kubat: "Domain level expertise is critical to getting good output. Realistically, the machines and the algorithms are used to augment experts. Yet, the human is ultimately always going to need to be in the loop on training activities to say what's "good" and what is "bad" (Augmented 2021, ep. 80; see Interview 11.2).

**Interview 11.2** The Augmenting Power of Operational Data. Interview with Rony Kubat, CTO and co-founder of Tulip. Episode 80. Augmented podcast.

Kubat's argument is echoed by world-leading roboticist, the Panasonic Professor of Robotics (emeritus) at MIT, Rodney Brooks, whom one of the authors (Natan) used to work for at Rethink Robotics: "The reality is that just about every successful deployment of AI has either one of two expedients: It has a person somewhere in the loop, or the cost of failure, should the system blunder, is very low" (Brooks 2021).

Having said that, the same Brooks is the co-founder and CTO of Robust AI, who is "building something we believe most robotics companies will find irresistible, taking solutions from single-purpose tools that today function in defined environments, to highly useful systems that can work within our world and all its intricacies" (BusinessWire 2020).

# FROM AUGMENTED REALITY EXPERIMENTS AT MIT TO FRONTLINE OPERATIONS PLATFORM

Artificial intelligence is a curious concept. We are trying to mimic human intelligence. Okay, but why? Perhaps this is wrongheaded. Isn't the point to help humans perform better, not to try to outdo us? Pattie Maes is a professor in MIT's Program in Media Arts and Sciences and runs the Media Lab's Fluid Interfaces research group, which aims to radically reinvent the human-machine experience. She is a co-founder of Tulip, was Natan's thesis advisor and co-founder Rony Kubat's postdoc advisor. Pattie Maes has always had an application driven philosophy. "What that means is that we take a closer look at the ultimate target users and their place where they live or work, and how the technology could make a difference there and could change things there. We study their lives today to understand what the pain points are, what the opportunities are for technologies to make a difference and support them in being more effective, more productive" (Augmented 2021, ep. 24).

Maes advocates that creating *intelligence augmentation* is more important than developing *artificial intelligence*. She echoes Fuchs's (2021) critique of so-called "disembodied reductionism" (the notion that something does not depend on the sensory processing mechanisms of our physical body) of current AI technologies and approaches. Why try to reduce human beings to information processing units? But, without embodiment, self-awareness, intersubjectivity, and common sense, where would humans be?

Humanoid service agent Nadine smiles, recognizes people, and shakes your hand (Tan 2015). However, interestingly, it is not in the field of humanoid robots (e.g., Nadine, Sophia, or ATLAS) that intersubjectivity has exceled lately. Perhaps because humans still take for granted that robots are not humans but might appreciate robotic reactions more if they are perceived not to be "trying too hard." Among the non-humanoid robots, social robots such as Jibo (www.jibo.com) represent brave attempts to mimic eye-gaze. Chatbots such as Alexa have a basic dialogue capability, do pick up on basic contextual cues, and might request clarification, for example. However, even if shared experience between robots and machines might be a worthy stretch goal (Gaggioli et al. 2021), full intersubjectivity is currently impossible to contemplate recreating in a machine.

Professor Maes has worked with Tulip's other co-founders, Kubat and Linder, since 2012. What initially motivated their work was the realization that we were living in two parallel worlds. We live in the physical world and then there's the digital world with information about all the people and things around us. "We realized that we were frustrated," says Maes. To fix that, she wanted to create integrated experiences where our physical lives are integrated with the digital information that exists from our actions and experiences – everything around you. "We experimented with different types of augmented reality systems to bridge that gap and to make the digital information and services available in the physical world" (Augmented 2021, ep. 24).

These experiments, which after a long while led to starting Tulip, began with building systems that had an integrated camera and projector so that the machine could see what is happening and had the ability to project relevant information onto whatever it is looking at.

The work was not easy and even the prototype applications led in many different directions. Says Maes: "We developed all sorts of prototypes to illustrate the vision of integrated augmented reality." For example, with Intel, they built an example of a store that has the two integrated with physical products where a projector system would recognize what camera you were looking at or picking up, and would give you additional information. It would point out the features by pointing at the different buttons on the camera. With research partner Pearson, a leading developer of educational books, they built an augmented desk for an educational context. They also worked with the furniture company Steelcase on how augmented reality technology could be used on the manufacturing floor. How could it help people in real time by giving them feedback about what they were doing? Maybe giving them real-time instructions projected onto their workspace. Or maybe alerting them that something wasn't done right or a step was forgotten, and so on.

All of that led to the spinoff, to Tulip being created as a company that can really realize the vision of a mentored manufacturing place. This was envisioned as a solution where you can have real-time information provided, but you can also track the whole manufacturing floor in real time. The goal was to obtain detailed data, analytics, and intelligence about which steps may cause more errors or which steps in the process take a lot of time (Augmented 2021, ep. 24).

We always have technology with us, and the systems around us (or on us) have sensors integrated. That means the potential is for these systems to truly augment us, says Maes: "Increasingly, systems will have a better sense of the cognitive state of a person, and will help the person with being in the state that they want to be in. My goal is not to create smarter, more capable machines or algorithms. I ultimately want to help people [using machines and AI] enabling them to live their best lives and to grow and learn and ultimately become the person that they would like to be" (Augmented 2021, ep. 24; Interview 11.3).

---

**Interview 11.3** Emerging Interfaces for Human Augmentation. Interview with Pattie Maes, Professor at the MIT Media Lab. Episode 24. Augmented podcast.

---

# THE PROMISE OF MACHINE MONITORING

Manufacturing is many things. This is both a source of strength and a major challenge in terms of progress when we try to apply machines to a problem. This can be especially challenging when we attempt to deploy machine learning to capture and analyze the data that machines generate. "Operational data is very diverse," says Roy Shilkrot, chief scientist at Tulip, and points to images and videos of people making things, security videos, IoT data collected from devices, and wearable devices worn by operators: "The convergence of all this data is what's going to drive us to the future using AI" (Augmented, 2022, ep. 81).

To think that data tells a story all on its own without interpretation is too superficial. After all, machine learning is about finding patterns and finding trends hidden in the data. There's two things in all data: noise and trend. "To separate the trend from the noise, is all machine learning is doing," says Shilkrot.

Let's say that you're on the shop floor doing some assembly, mostly heavily patterned, repetitive work. The first step is to try to pick up on patterns. The second step would be to try to automate around those patterns. For that reason, says Shilkrot, "robotic process automation (RPA), apps that you can install which start picking up on your actions, is going to be fundamental in manufacturing operations" (Augmented 2021, ep. 47; see Interview 11.4).

The paradox is that we are in a situation where we have the powerful tools of machine learning and the promise of even more powerful AI algorithms in the future but we still need to consider where these approaches require a human augmentation approach. Says Kubat:

**Interview 11.4** From Predicative to Diagnostic Manufacturing Augmentation. Interview with Roy Shilkrot, Chief Scientist, Tulip. Episode 81. Augmented podcast.

The human is ultimately always going to be in the loop to do some kind of training activities to say what's good and what is bad. The second thing though, is that there is constant change within a manufacturing context. They're not static systems because materials might be changing, [might be] coming from a different vendor or because the level of expertise of the operator who's doing the work is changed or he is fatigued. Or, it could be that the product itself has changed and has been optimized in some way in order to produce steps in the process. In a machine learning scenario, you need to have these models be flexible and be updated over time. [...] You can think about machine learning or advanced data analytics as a tiered pursuit at the very low end, you have descriptive analytics where you can look at averages, medians, and moving averages, and some sort of window based on time series. The next level is predictive, that would be forecasting or some sort of detection of anomalies based on the signals that you are getting. [The last] level is diagnostic analysis where you take those signals and diagnose a deep problem somewhere in your pipeline. (Augmented, 2022, ep. 81)

Why has it taken manufacturing so long to get to these more advanced levels of analysis? Very likely, because it is such an ancient practice. Those involved have had time to develop their own approaches and tools and started to protect their knowledge from outsiders. As a result, digital technologies outside manufacturing evolved much more rapidly, and without input from manufacturing, which is also a mistake. "Manufacturing has been mostly siloed with a separation between information technology that brings data to the table and operations technology that brings technology to the table," says Çağlayan Arkan, vice president of Manufacturing Industry at Microsoft. Now, he says, "it's a data-driven world. Data dictates everything. Data is end to end. To the extent that you have an enterprise-level data architecture and a system-level approach to things it's a completely different world. As a business, you have to forget more than you remember. Then you must reinvent yourself" (Augmented 2021, ep. 21).

What will be the impact of a future with machine learning built into the manufacturing execution systems? That is a question of how well the manufacturing industry reinvents itself.

# THERE'S LOTS OF BIG DATA IN MANUFACTURING, BUT CAN WE USE IT?

There are a plethora of use cases for big data in manufacturing. Think of optimization tasks such as improving throughput and yield, work cell optimization, tool life-cycle optimization and supply chain management, longer-term challenges such as product life cycle management (PLM), or predictive approaches to maintenance, quality, anomaly detection, and production forecasting (Klaess 2021). Manufacturing was not the first industry to gather and make use of big data, but it is certainly a sector that had the potential for huge scale. Even before the advent of low-cost sensors, industrial data had the potential to generate an enormous amount of insight. One reason it took a while was that there are other challenges to tackle first. Inefficiencies of a much simpler nature abound. Paper is everywhere on the manufacturing floor today. Nothing wrong with that, we love paper, except it is hard to use as input for algorithms.

The best way to make use of all of these sources of data is to organize and contextualize it, which is what a frontline operations platform attempts to do. Before this step, even if you had a lot of data it would be hard to put to use because the data streams were not connected and did not have actionable meaning in real time. Manufacturing is a hands-on activity where workers move things along. If they have to stop and reflect too much on what data means, the production line stops. With the frontline operations platform, we know which operator, which line, which site, which station, what sensors are affected, and at what time. As a result, we have an idea of what happened before and what is going to happen next. This is unique, because, typically, in the old school system approach, workflows are static, modeled once, and configured slowly. Instead, you can discover needed changes through machine learning generated metrics. Then, you can proceed to tweak the workflow with no-code apps that precisely describe new process elements so everyone is clear on what to do even if the process changes often.

At Stanley Black & Decker, which is using Tulip as its global digital manufacturing system, the potential return on investment (ROI) on implementing digital apps across their operations would be enormous. Mark Maybury, chief technology officer, Stanley Black & Decker, writes in *IndustryWeek*: "[We have] partnered with companies like Ready Robotics and Tulip to automate repetitive tasks at several of our plants, creating dedicated programs to reskill all of our workers who were previously doing that work. These employees now work side-by-side with collaborative robots, becoming programmers supervising their robots and being freed up to spend more time finding ways to further increase productivity" (Maybury 2020).

After numerous Gemba-walks, continuous production engineer Sofiya Baran at LISTA, the furniture company of Stanley Black & Decker, determined that their main weakness was "the lack of visibility into our manufacturing processes because we rely on a daily paper schedule." On her process, she notes that "the operators were my #1 customer." This took into consideration that after working at a company many years, welcoming change in their process will be challenging. With their support she made sure the app was easy to use and had "100% of their buy-in." They are now capturing daily percent completion and "know whether our department is winning or losing." Baran credits the application she built in Tulip to capture production visibility utilizing daily schedules for various Detail Fabrication processes with "the ability to eliminate the hidden factory and run operations in real time" (Baran 2022).

Tulip is represented with a demo at Stanley's state-of-the-art Manufactory 4.0 in Hartford, Connecticut, the epicenter for the company's global Industry 4.0 "smart factory" and workforce upskilling initiatives with an app with noninvasive digital work instructions for manual assembly of an impact driver (Tulip 2019). The app generates real-time data on the screen and tracks analytics in the background that can be displayed as dashboards (e.g., daily production target, defects w/cause indicated, average step time).

The current app footprint is already enabling significant cost mitigation savings. However, no software solution has any intrinsic ROI. Instead, the client use case determines the payback. Stanley Black & Decker uses the no-code platform to create a controlled library of apps but also to unlock decentralized innovation with different flavors of the solution across different verticals. Stanley Black & Decker is a highly sophisticated organization. Using a frontline operations platform instead of a legacy solution gives it the ability to combine corporate IT governance with a customized approach if operational units need unique features.

# MACHINE LEARNING IN MANUFACTURING

Despite the hype around machine learning, successful adoption within manufacturing is relatively recent and highly experimental at present. The promise is huge, but getting there is not just about software or algorithms, but also about building hypotheses about exactly where to apply it to best effect. Roy Shilkrot, lead scientist at Tulip, is currently working to get machine learning built into Tulip's frontline operations platform: "What has been a paradigm shift in the last two years, or even less than that is that machine learning now has become so much a commodity and offered in so many very useful and very simple ways that it finally is ready to be applied almost automatically, in whatever industry you want, not just manufacturing, any data rich industry" (Augmented 2021).

According to Shilkrot, Tulip applies machine learning in its computer vision product to enable object detection and classification, and they also use machine learning for machine monitoring (Augmented 2021, ep. 47; see Interview 11.5).

**Interview 11.5** Industrial Machine Learning. Interview with Roy Shilkrot, Chief Scientist, Tulip. Episode 47. Augmented podcast.

The first product containing machine learning is Tulip's Vision product, which came out in spring 2021. Vision is a growing library of computer vision capabilities to guide, measure, and improve your operations. These vision capabilities work with off-the-shelf RGB or depth cameras that serve as powerful sensors capable of tracking operator actions, objects, and spatial activity on the shop floor. This is the evolution of the prototype Natan gave Trond five years ago when he dropped by Tulip's lab as the first external observer, back when he was still leading MIT Startup Exchange. Today, emerging vision-based applications include the obvious first use case of defect and anomaly detection, but can also increasingly be used to track and understand human and machine behavior, because it "collects valuable data about frontline workers with minimal intrusion, which is the cornerstone of process optimization" (Shilkrot 2021).

But what about the future role of machine learning in manufacturing? What is still left to achieve? What's missing is giving a semantic meaning around that data, whether at the low level on the sensors or in the technical protocols that govern the sensors. There's usually very little information that's given – or none – about what the semantics of that might be. Says Shilkrot: "I can imagine adding metadata about the importance of each sensor, so that each is indicating the relationship to something happening somewhere else. Once that's the case, any algorithm that comes in to turn the crank on wherever that data is, can make use of it in a dramatic fashion" (Augmented 2022, ep. 80).

Another leading voice in this debate is Anna-Katrina Shedletsky, CEO and co-founder of Silicon Valley startup Instrumental, a manufacturing optimization platform that uses data and AI to help companies improve their product lines. She reflected on the future promise of manufacturing data in a podcast appearance with tinkerer Spencer Wright in *The Prepared*: "Longer term, we want to build a *source of truth* for actionable manufacturing data, not just data for data's sake" (The Prepared 2018, s. 2, ep. 9). Three years later, in the *Manufacturing Happy Hour* (2021, ep. 60) podcast, the Stanford-educated mechanical engineer is still amazed at this challenge, and she says that customers tell her that being able to access the data is tripling the size of their engineering team." In fact, she says: "Engineers spend 60% of their time on non-engineering tasks," which indicates that legacy solutions are not working so well.

Source of truth is an ambitious term, but speaks to the difference between systems of record (e.g., truth) and system of engagement (no-code platforms that augment, but don't replace traditional systems of record) and the tension between them (Klaess 2020). "On the one hand," writes Klaess (2020), "there's a need for a ground-truth overview of the business. On the other, there's a need for tools that help frontline workers work better." The challenge with systems of record is that they tend to gather data for data's sake. Amassing a lot of data without knowing what to use it for is, at best, what we would call a "KPI hell" of excess data that confuses workers and managers alike, and, at worst, downright threatens efficiency, productivity, and throughput.

# CASE STUDY: THE IMPACT OF OPERATIONAL DATA IN DATA IN LIFE SCIENCE OPERATIONS

Life sciences is a field of manufacturing that keeps growing in scale, significance, and complexity. The cost needed to bring a new drug to market is staggering: $2 billion and 13 years on average (Galtier 2021). Better operational data is particularly useful to reduce such development costs as well as the production costs once a drug is approved. TetraScience, spun out by Harvard and MIT and founded in 2014, has built the largest integrated network of lab instruments, informatics applications, CRO/CDMOs, analytics, and data science partners, creating seamless interoperability and an innovation feedback loop, on an open platform. The effect is that of a "digital plumber" for life science R&D, which historically has been stuck in proprietary platforms with a myriad of unconnected databases that each require separate workstreams and cannot typically be aligned to make the most of complex drug target analysis, for example.

Increased sequencing, mRNA vaccine platforms, more microscopy, plus capturing individual samples are just four of the data sources that are expanding in scope. With the already exploding amount of data in pharma R&D, increasingly sophisticated solutions need to be deployed to make use of it. Another emerging use case is personalized drugs. Again, systems need to change. A key reason vaccine-maker Moderna was able to successfully produce its initial COVID-19 vaccine in 60 days was because the company is cloud-native and able to make use of flexible computational capacity on demand from AWS (AWS 2022, Moderna 2022).

Another cloud-enabled startup, Owkin, deploys a federated approach, meaning they allow sharing of life science R&D data across labs whilst safeguarding privacy considerations because data is anonymized. "We want to build a privacy preserving approach where physicians will trust you, patients will trust you and people will exchange AI without sharing data," says Thomas Clozel, founder of·Owkin. He says there's two sides of AI: acceleration and augmentation:

> The first is how you accelerate processes and diagnosis. You go faster, you can do a thousand CT scan readings per day. The other one is augmentation. How do you get super powers? How can you predict [survival] from a CT scan? How can you predict a response to treatments, how can you discover within the model, new genes that can be targets of innovative drugs? [...] Augmentation is more exciting for doctors. It doesn't threaten the role of a radiologist, for example. [...] But acceleration of course is also very important to the daily workflow to make things more efficient. (Futurized 2020, ep. 55)

# Does Life Science Actually Need Frontline Operations? What Is Pharma 4.0?

The scope of the emerging life science industry's AI-enabled drug discovery R&D is huge. However, the pace AI enables discoveries in the R&D phase must be met with operational excellence on the shop floor. It is all about adopting agile workflows in complex and highly regulated environments. This presents a sort of an "operational paradox." A classic MES (manufacturing execution system) needs several functionality tweaks to work for something as basic as tracking cleaning, sanitation, and sterilization operations. Yet, these are the bread and butter of life science R&D and production facilities. Despite digital process management software, compliance and quality, both of which are highly regulated, are currently not well supported by legacy digital tools. New classes of biological medicines are being developed that require a radical shift in manufacturing processes (BioPhorum 2022). BioPhorum, the biomanufacturing forum founded in 2014, comprises over 135 manufacturers and suppliers deploying 6,000 leaders and subject matter experts to share and discuss the emerging trends and challenges facing their industry.

Life science manufacturing systems have an interesting evolution. Digital transformation executive and Industry Practice Lead, Tulip, Gilad Langer, writes: "Based on my experience, the future digital factory will be supported by a network of software components that will have been put together from the bottom up. They will develop and mature over time through emergence rather than a top-down design and development process. If this is true, so much of our current approaches (GAMP, ISA-95/88, etc.) will not work" (Langer 2021, see Interview 11.6).

**Interview 11.6** Life Science Manufacturing Systems. Interview with Gilad Langer, Industry Practice Lead, Tulip. Episode 78. Augmented podcast.

In a recent MES of the Future Manifesto, the authors detail the gaps in current solutions and declare the vision to adopt "MES of the future" across the industry. Problems identified include that the business models of current systems (on-premises with high one-off implementation costs) are not suitable for small-scale and/or low-cost manufacturing plants that would need pay-per-use subscription models. Current MES solutions are perceived as "monolithic and inflexible," requiring manual configuration and implementation, leaving room for error even with input from the vendor's specialized engineers. New biomanufacturing modalities such as those for cell and gene therapies (CGTs) require extensive parallel processing of personalized batches [that] will require full automation to be financially successful and capable of scale-up, including "better material identity and logistics tracking, and integration with the production operations, together with a distributed model that goes beyond traditional production cells and into the clinic" (BioPhorum 2022). BioPhorum calls for fostering a global MES knowledge GitHub-type community. The automated biomanufacturing facility of the future would have pervasive connectivity, real-time quality control, boundaryless information, self or machine learning, and holonic components (e.g., where all relevant systems (MES, PCS, LIMS, ERP) are linked together). Lastly, it would be modular; in fact, they envision a roadmap for a "MES-lite" for small manufacturing sites.

The digital revolution in life science companies is still in its infancy, although a few digital leaders, including Novartis, Johnson & Johnson, Novo Nordisk, Eli Lilly, and Merck, are attempting to accelerate their efforts (Ghosh and Sachdeva 2019). Part of the challenge is that regulatory compliance makes the software documentation requirements onerous. At Tulip, we have seen that within months of Tulip deployment, a large pharmaceutical manufacturer assembled a small team to build a set of applications derived from the Tulip library providing cleaning work instruction, logbooks, and analytics on a worldwide scale. Furthermore, scales and pH probes were added to the project scope thanks to rapid development progress and confidence in the solution. That resulted in the digitization of over 4,000 paper-based logbooks, auditable for more than 10 years, a significant reduction of compliance costs via right-first-time, point-of-use checks and review-by-exceptions.

Another global healthcare company went from reliance on paper (which has high management costs and low transparency) to guide to digital Electronic Batch Record, in the process closing other key digital process gaps, and especially benefiting the oversight of remote locations. In one instance, a 95-page document describing a 15-minute process was replaced by a process-tailored, updatable work instructions app. So far, they have seen 50–80% change over improvements and 40–60% improved training times as well as increased compliance through error proofing (with up to 50% reduction in errors) and review by exception and an estimated 10x overall ROI.

Vertex Pharmaceuticals converted 2,300 pages of standard operating procedures (SOPs ) to detailed digital work instructions for a complex oral solid dose line with three configurations. PJ Geldenhuis, Vertex, says:

> We reduced the impact of costly assembly-related issues, to improve training and ensure knowledge was captured, we turned to Tulip. We created an application both for pre-assembly and assembly. This simplifies a highly complex process. We captured all the details in video

and picture form, allowing us to capture details that are [now] easy to understand. All of this data is tracked. We can figure out how long it took to perform different tasks and use that data to identify bottlenecks, see where our problems are, identify problems and focus on the right things instead of shooting in the dark. Anything there's a need for, you very likely can build into Tulip. Once you have built something you can duplicate it and leverage it for something else, so you are not building from scratch every single time.

What about reference material, you might wonder. Geldenhuis:

You often need information and need to jump to different systems to get the answer. With Tulip you can integrate the different systems. You can easily go to the equipment manual or the parts drawer to get that information without navigating different systems." Training got very intuitive and exact, too: "In our case, we found it best to create videos for every 15–30 seconds [of assembly] on repeat and a short description and a quality check. You can customize it and build in several quality steps.

You might assume developing such detailed apps takes a lot of time. That's not necessarily the case. Geldenhuis: "It took a week to create each application. A lot of that time was spent editing videos. It is very similar to using PowerPoint just with additional logic. Tulip can be used to accomplish everything you want to accomplish instead of having an MES" (Tulip 2020).

As Arun Kumar Bhaskara-Baba from J&J emphasized (see Chapter 4), the increasingly connected pharma R&D and delivery of those same solutions means we somehow need to simultaneously empower frontline operations. The operations function is infamous for doubling down on machinery and underinvesting in agile, digital efficiency tools. Instead, operators and shop floor workers are usually faced with, and forced to try to interact with, technologies and tools that speak better to machines than to people.

# The Need to Integrate R&D, Scale-Up, and Supply Chain Management

The reason that drug discovery may take 10+ years, is not only due to regulatory constraints, but also arguably even more because of the lack of integration of an operational mindset across the value stream within each life science company. The R&D department waited until they had a drug candidate before they did their hand-off to the product scale-up units on the business side. The clinical trial teams also were quite separate in each of the phases (0-IV). Traditionally, in phase 0 you trial less than 15 people on small dosages, in phase I you trial and monitor 20–80 people with underlying health conditions and look at dosing, safety, and ways to administer the drug (orally, intravenously, or topically). In phase II you monitor several hundred participants for efficacy. In phase III you involve up to 3,000 participants in a randomized trial, usually double-blind, to benchmark against other existing medications for the same condition and need to demonstrate equal or better safety and efficacy. The FDA usually approves some 25% of candidates after successful phase III. In phase IV, after FDA-approval, clinical trials continue with thousands of patients to assess long-term safety, effectiveness, and other benefits (Seladi-Schulman 2019). However, the tectonic plates in the life science industry are moving. The new mRNA platform has a radically different way of discovery, scaling, production, and potentially opening up new ways of personalized delivery in the near future.

The work on Pharma 4.0 (i.e., designing the operational model for bringing the pharmaceutical industry into the digital age) is in no small measure led by The International Society for Pharmaceutical Engineering (ISPE). This association, with roots back to 1980, attempts to "facilitate the development of next generation process technologies and innovative technical solutions" (ISPE 2022). Regulatory constraints make the digitization process much more structured than in other industries. "The baseline functionality is digital signatures, data integrity, digital maturity, and access control," says pharma quality management expert Michelle Vuolo (Augmented 2021, ep. 31). Key to accomplishing this functionality is data validation. "We are trying to overlay process and data knowledge with data mapping and risk mitigation, regardless of the digital tools that they're using." Their goal is process understanding with the ultimate goal of protecting their patients (Augmented 2021, ep. 31; see Interview 11.7).

**Interview 11.7** Pharma 4.0.
Interview with Michelle Vuolo, Tulip.
Episode 31. Augmented podcast.

In pharma, says Gilad Langer, Industry Practice Lead at Tulip, the analogy can be a spreadsheet: "A spreadsheet is the ultimate democratization, right? It allows you certain flexibility, but you can actually put constraints on it." Conversely, Langer says, an Electronic Laboratory Notebook (ELN) looks like a spreadsheet, but it's much more constrained. "You can't just go in and add tabs and add columns and do whatever you want." Langer says that Tulip brings to industry "the ability to put some governance around that spreadsheet and define how it's used" (Augmented 2022, ep. 78; see Interview 11.8).

**Interview 11.8** Life Science Manufacturing Systems. Interview with Gilad Langer, Tulip. Episode 78. Augmented podcast.

# Personalized Operations Loops

Personalized medicine is data-intensive. It will force an enormous shift in the operations of a life science company and in the relationship between drug developers, hospitals, providers, and patients. The quickest way to think of it is what already happened in another industry, that of medical devices, with the advent of molded dentures such as Invisalign. With Invisalign, once X-rays and molds are taken by a dentist, it goes to Invisalign for analysis. The ongoing treatment is a constant interaction between Invisalign, dentist, and patient, exchanging data, molds, and adjustments. Each mold is unique to the person, and the treating product changes nearly weekly. Now think of personalized medicine. Oral Solid Dosage (OSD) drug facilities producing tablets and capsules traditionally use warehouse operations. In that scenario, the business risk for branded drugs with exclusivity stems from generic drugs which follow a multi-competitor model, not the operations flow itself (although flow can always be optimized). However, with biotech's increasing personalization, the clinical trial is the original "vial" that gets copied and inoculated across patients, but the API can be copied and is scaled across great distances, which introduces a number of new business risks and IP issues. Cell and gene therapies that are patient-to-patient are easier to protect (unless a universal donor is found) because the treatment might be the patient's treated blood itself, which can only be reinserted to that patient with the desired effect. This is disruptive for manufacturing, especially for classic MES, which, unlike Tulip, were never designed to handle a batch of one.

# CONCLUSION

The power of operational data impacts manufacturing across the globe in distinct ways. However, exactly what type of data can be made operational? That depends on each factory, site, team, and situation. That mix of factors will determine whether data might become your game changer for productivity. Management decisions are not the most important determining factor. Do you have legacy industrial technology already in the mix? Taking in the data, is the workforce willing to adjust as a result? For sure, even if you have gathered a lot of data, you cannot automatically assume you can easily make it useful. But if you manage to use data in operation, you are well on your way to transforming your frontline workforce into true knowledge workers.

The true power of data lies in augmenting existing processes, not in completely replacing them. Even if data creates completely new ways of doing things, having humans in the loop is the best way to ensure full impact. More importantly, big data is always gathered from somewhere, potentially from people. Manufacturers must ensure responsible use of the enormous new powers at play. This applies to data from machine monitoring, autonomy, drug discovery, discrete or batch production, or from robots. Efficient operations depend on stitching together augmented technologies that enhance worker productivity, and the scope is literally from getting rid of paper on the shop floor, to remote monitoring, to modeling and delivering drugs from the complex analysis and assembly of proteins.

In the next chapter, we will see that Tulip is helping J&J create a next-generation manufacturing system, providing actionable online and offline analytics and putting them in the enviable position to handle significant spikes in market demand, the type of supply chain disruption we are likely to face more of in the future.

# REFERENCES

Augmented (2022, ep. 81). Industrial Machine Learning. Interview with Roy Shilkrot, Chief Scientist, Tulip. Episode 81. *Augmented podcast.* (April 27). https://www.augmentedpodcast.co/81 (accessed 14 March 2022).

Augmented (2022, ep. 80). The Augmenting Power of Operational Data. Interview with Rony Kubat, CTO and co-founder of Tulip, Episode 80. *Augmented podcast.* (May 11). https://www.augmentedpodcast.co/80 (accessed 14 March 2022).

Augmented (2022, ep. 78). Life Science Manufacturing Systems. Interview with Gilad Langer, Industry Practice Lead, Tulip. Episode 78. *Augmented podcast.* (May 4). https://www.augmentedpodcast.co/78 (accessed 13 March 2022).

Augmented (2021, ep. 21). The Future of Digital in Manufacturing. Episode 21. Çağlayan Arkan, VP of Manufacturing Industry at Microsoft. *Augmented podcast.* (June 9) https://www.augmentedpodcast.co/the-future-of-digital-in-manufacturing/ (accessed 15 November 2021).

Augmented (2021, ep. 24). Emerging Interfaces for Human Augmentation. Interview with Pattie Maes, Professor at the MIT Media Lab. Episode 24. *Augmented podcast.* (June 16) https://www.augmentedpodcast.co/emerging-interfaces-for-human-augmentation/ (accessed 18 November 2021).

Augmented (2021, ep. 31). Pharma 4.0. Interview with Michelle Vuolo, Quality Practice Lead, Tulip. Episode 31. *Augmented podcast.* (September 1) https://www.augmentedpodcast.co/pharma-40/ (accessed 25 January 2021).

Augmented (2021, ep. 47). Industrial Machine Learning. Interview with Roy Shilkrot, Tulip Interfaces. Episode 47. *Augmented podcast.* (Sept 8) https://www.augmentedpodcast.co/industrial-machine-learning/ (accessed 17 November 2021).

Augmented (2020, ep. 55). AI for Medicine. Interview with Thomas Clozel, Founder, Owkin. Episode 55. *Futurized podcast.* (Dec 1) https://www.futurized.org/ai-for-medicine/ (accessed 18 November 2021).

Augmented (2021, ep. 66). Bridging the Physical-Digital Divide in Industrial Tech. Interview with Rony Kubat, CTO and co-founder, Tulip Interfaces. Episode 66. *Augmented podcast.* (June 9) https://www.augmentedpodcast.co/66 (accessed 17 November 2021).

AWS (2022). Moderna on AWS [case study]. AWS. https://aws.amazon.com/solutions/case-studies/innovators/moderna/ (accessed 14 January 2022).

Baran (2022). Production visibility is the key to success! *LinkedIn.* [post] https://www.linkedin.com/posts/sofiya-baran-2020_production-visibility-is-the-key-to-success-activity-6921897614565093376-ohlA/?utm_source=linkedin_share&utm_medium=ios_app (accessed 19 April 2022).

BioPhorum (2022). MES of the Future Manifesto. *BioPhorum* (January). https://www.biophorum.com/welcome-to-the-mes-of-the-future/ (accessed 13 March 2022).

Brooks, R. (2021). An inconvenient truth about AIAI won't surpass human intelligence anytime soon. *IEEE Spectrum* (Sept 29). https://spectrum-ieee-org.cdn.ampproject.org/c/s/spectrum.ieee.org/amp/rodney-brooks-ai-2655074291 (accessed 24 March 2022).

BusinessWire (2020). Robust.AI raises $22.5 million to build the world's first industrial-grade cognitive engine for robotics. *BusinessWire* (Oct 28). https://www.businesswire.com/news/home/20201028005816/en/Robust.AI-Raises-22.5-Million-to-Build-the-World%E2%80%99s-First-Industrial-Grade-Cognitive-Engine-for-Robotics (accessed 24 March 2022).

Flagship Pioneering (2020). Flagship Pioneering announces Valo Health to transform drug development. *Flagship Pioneering* (September 23) https://www.flagshippioneering.com/press/valo-launches-with-transformative-cloud-generation-drug-development-platform (accessed 18 November 2021).

Fuchs, T. (2021). *In Defense of the Human Being: Foundational Questions of an Embodied Anthropology.* Oxford: Oxford University Press.

Gaggioli, A, and Chirico, A, Di Lernia, D., Maggioni, M.A., Malighetti, C., Manzi, F., Marchetti, A., Massaro, D., Rea, F., Rossignoli, D., Sandini, G., Villani, D., Wiederhold, B.K., Riva, G., and Sciutti, A. (2021). Machines like us and people like you: Toward human–robot shared experience. *Cyberpsychology, Behavior, and Social Networking.* May 2021. 357-361. http://doi.org/10.1089/cyber.2021.29216.aga

Galtier, M. (2021). MELLODDY: A "Co-opetitive" platform for machine learning across companies powered by Owkin Technology. *Owkin.* https://owkin.com/federated-learning/melloddy-a-co-opetitive-platform-for-machine-learning-across-companies-powered-by-owkin-technology/ (accessed 18 November 2021).

Ghosh, D. and Sachdeva, S. (2019). The digital revolution of life sciences companies. *TCS. Perspectives* 13. https://www.tcs.com/perspectives/articles/the-digital-revolution-of-life-sciences-companies (accessed 23 November 2021).

ISPE (2022). About ISPE. https://ispe.org/about (accessed 25 January 2022).

Klaess, J. (2021). Big Data for manufacturing: An intro to concepts & applications. Tulip.co. Blog. (January 7). https://tulip.co/blog/big-data-for-manufacturing/ (accessed 22 November 2021).

Klaess, J. (2020). System of record vs. system of engagement – What's the difference? *Tulip.co* [blog] (June 24). https://tulip.co/blog/system-of-record-vs-system-of-engagement/ (accessed 13 March 2022).

Langer, G. (2021). The return of custom-built manufacturing software. *MFG. works* ( February 8). https://mfg.works/2021/02/08/the-return-of-custom-built-manufacturing-software/ (accessed 13 March 2022).

Lukic, V. (2017). How New Balance is bringing Industry 4.0 to shoemaking. *BCG.* [blog]. (August 4). https://www.bcg.com/en-us/publications/2017/operations-lean-manufacturing-new-balance-bringing-industry-4-shoemaking (accessed 19 March 2022).

Manufacturing Happy Hour (2021). Leveraging Data to Reimagine the Product Design Process with Instrumental CEO Anna-Katrina Shedletsky, *Manufacturing Happy Hour*, podcast, episode 60. (31 August). https://manufacturinghappyhour .com/60-leveraging-data-to-reimagine-the-product-design-process-with-instrumental-ceo-anna-katrina-shedletsky/ (accessed 13 March 2022).

Maybury, M. (2020). A well-trained workforce is manufacturing's future. *Industry-Week* (October 15). https://www.industryweek.com/talent/education-training/article/21144806/a-welltrained-workforce-is-manufacturings-future? (accessed 10 March 2022).

Moderna (2022). mRNA research and innovation engine. Moderna [web page]. https://www.modernatx.com/mrna-technology/research-engine (accessed 14 January 2022).

Nelson, P. (2021). TetraScience empowers pharma industry with R&D Data Cloud to advance life sciences. *Silicon Angle* (June 17). https://siliconangle .com/2021/06/17/tetrascience-empowers-pharma-industry-rd-data-cloud-advance-life-sciences-awsshowcase2q21/ (accessed 18 November 2021).

Roseman, M. (2021). Drugmaker Sanofi invests $180 million in French AI startup Owkin. WTVB. (November 18). https://wtvbam.com/2021/11/18/drugmaker-sanofi-invests-180-million-in-french-ai-startup-owkin/ (accessed 18 November 2021).

Seladi-Schulman, J. (2019). What happens in a clinical trial? Healthline (June 21). https://www.healthline.com/health/clinical-trial-phases# (accessed 22 November 2021).

Shilkrot, R. (2021). Tulip Vision: A new look into frontline operations. *Tulip blog* (Dec 22). https://tulip.co/blog/tulip-vision-a-new-look-into-frontline-operations/ (accessed 20 March 2022).

Sullivan, N. (2021). Almost $1 trillion: the staggering cost of unplanned downtime to major manufacturers. *Senseye*. Blog. (June 30). https://www.senseye.io/blog/the-true-cost-of-downtime (accessed 18 November 2021).

Tan (2015). Human-like robot 'Nadine' who has a 'personality, mood and emotions' unveiled in Singapore, *ABC News* (December 31). https://abcnews.go.com/Technology/human-robot-nadine-personality-mood-emotions-unveiled-singapore/story?id=36032196 (accessed 20 March 2022).

TetraScience (2021). Novo Nordisk and TetraScience partner on a cloud-based instrument data platform. *TetraScience*. Press Release (March 23) https://www.tetrascience.com/news/novo-nordisk-and-tetrascience-partner-on-a-cloud-based-instrument-data-platform (accessed 23 November 2021).

The Prepared (2018). Anna Shedletsky, CEO of Instrumental. The Prepared [podcast]. (November 16). https://theprepared.org/podcast-feed/2018/11/1/anna-shedletsky-instrumental (accessed 13 March 2022).

Tulip (2020). A view into Pharma 4.0 | Digital Manufacturing Webinar. Tulip (28 May). https://www.youtube.com/watch?v=a1P4G9H_4LQ (accessed 25 January 2022).

Tulip (2019) We're at the grand opening of Stanley Black & Decker's Manufactory 4.0! Tulip. Video. [Facebook page]. https://www.facebook.com/watch/?v=285834658984101 (accessed 10 March 2022).

Von Maltzahn, G. (2021) At Generate Biomedicines, Inc. we envision a future when all therapeutic #proteins are generated, rather than discovered. *LinkedIn post*. https://www.linkedin.com/posts/geoffrey-von-maltzahn-7a6b755a_generate-biomedicines-announces-first-external-activity-6867086883113971712-1i62 (accessed 18 November 2021).

# CHAPTER 12

# FACILITATION OVER CONTROL: HOW THE INDUSTRIAL SYSTEMS OF THE FUTURE MIGHT EMERGE

D o you pay attention to sci-fi writers of books and to Hollywood-style sci-fi film plots and twists? We do. How we imagine the future inspires us and, at the same time, limits us. One of the most famous manufacturing scenes in any Hollywood film comes at the end of *The Terminator*, the 1984 sci-fi action film classic directed by James Cameron and starring Arnold Schwarzenegger as the Terminator, a cyborg assassin sent back in time from 2029 to 1984 to kill Sarah Connor, whose unborn son will one day save mankind from extinction by a hostile artificial intelligence in a post-apocalyptic future. The film explores the potential dangers of AI dominance and rebellion. The robots become self-aware, reject human authority, and determine that the human race needs to be destroyed. There is a pursuit into a factory where Reese, a human soldier, attempts to stop a damaged Terminator endoskeleton by activating machinery to stop it, and Sarah lures it into a hydraulic press, crushing and finally destroying it. The irony is, the pinnacle of human technological development could only be destroyed by the same means that created it. Arguably, the prevalent visual representation of AI risk has become the Terminator robot.

*Minority Report*, the American sci-fi action film from 2002 directed by Steven Spielberg, starring Tom Cruise and loosely based on the 1956 short story *The Minority Report* by Philip K. Dick, also has a great manufacturing scene. Aiming to be "future reality," not sci-fi, pre-discussions were "wide-ranging and included topics such as the future of medical advancements, social theories, defense issues, advertising, infrastructure, technology, workplace and household appliances, and of course, cars" (Serious Wheels 2002). The movie is set in the year 2054, where Precrime, a specialized police department, apprehends criminals based on foreknowledge provided by three psychics called "precogs." The key moment in the film, the chase scene in an auto factory, was filmed in a real facility using props such as a welding robot, a crane, and thousands of robotic arms that are building a car. The Lexus 2054 is a red sports concept car purposely designed for the film by Harald Belker, who also is credited with vehicle designs for *Batman & Robin, Iron Man 2,* and *Total Recall*. The film also features tiny spider-sized robots that are able to search buildings and identify occupants through retinal scans.

The prototype robot weighs just 68 mg and has a 2 cm long body, allowing them to jump on water. Insect robots similar to the film's spider robots, so-called micro aerial vehicles (MAV), are said to be under development by the United States Military (Calderone 2017). But the real question is, why would the creators of a film scene about 2054 still think there will be an industrial space looking like today's factories? Can it be that they are right even with all the progress we think we are making? Or is it the other way around, the film makers (and consultants) cannot truly show us the future either because they don't know what it will look like or because the audience wouldn't find it fascinating?

These depictions of future manufacturing tell us a lot about how our current understanding of the future still leaves a place for factory-based manufacturing. Manufacturing's future will not be decided by sci-fi movies in Hollywood but the way they think things might progress, or even their wildest speculations, does influence reality. If anything, it helps us visualize what we must strive hard to avoid, which is the mindless automation of everything. Whether it be *The Terminator* or *Minority Report*, they all remind us that the factory of the future (whatever that means at any given moment) also has an expiration date. We need to plan for what comes next, meaning we need to plan for the lifecycle of the products and services we allow to exist. This is where having a clear vision of industrial operations matters, to which we will turn next.

# WHY DOES SPACE MANUFACTURING SUDDENLY MAKE SENSE?

When William Bruey was young, he wanted to become an astronaut. To make that more likely to happen, he studied physics for undergrad and systems engineering for grad school at Cornell University, a school known to be working with space missions. Since the early days of space exploration, Cornell astronomers have played major roles in NASA missions to explore the solar system and distant universe. Cornell University's contributions to space exploration dates back over 100 years. Today, top faculty and alumni are designing critical missions to explore various ecosystems and habitats beyond Earth, looking for life on other planets, leading communication strategies between NASA and the government, and even preventing the contamination of space with Earthly elements (Cornell 2022).

However, it was not until sophomore year that Bruey had the courage to commit. Soon enough, while still in undergrad, he was finding time to work for Palo Alto-based SSL, a leading provider of innovative spacecraft systems, where he authored all contingency procedures for the Via-Sat-1 Spacecraft Data Handling Subsystem. As he was getting his master's degree, he researched, developed, and built a power controller system used for drawing vacuum in Cornell's Synchrotron accelerator, which is still in use today. By 2013, he was the Lead Avionics Hardware Development Engineer at SpaceX, the already legendary firm founded by Elon Musk in 2002 that designs, manufactures, and launches the world's most advanced rockets and spacecraft. He became the primary mission control operator for the spacecraft system during flight. But he wanted a new challenge. After he was rejected as a NASA astronaut candidate in the class of 2016, he had a bit of an existential crisis. Soon thereafter, for nearly three years, he abandoned the space mission to learn fintech at Bank of America Merrill Lynch. That gave him the cash and skills to create his own angel investing syndicate, Also Capital. When Delian Asparouhov and Trae Stephens of Founders Fund (mentioned in Chapter 12) tapped him on the shoulder to work on a new adventure, bringing manufacturing to space, he did not say no. In the meantime, however, he managed to become a pilot and to enjoy flying the four-seat, single engine, homebuilt, light (and experimental) aircraft MK IV in his spare time.

Despite its imperfections and hyperbole, venture capital can, at times, fund startups doing incredible things. One recent example is Varda (www .varda.com), a space manufacturing startup that focuses on creating products in space for terrestrial applications. It aims to open up manufacturing processes that aren't possible on Earth, or are difficult or expensive to do, in order to make bioprinted organs, fiberoptic cables, or pharmaceuticals – products that require fundamentally different conditions than what's available on-planet (Alamalhodaei 2021). Bruey is the CEO and co-founder at Varda Space Industries:

> There's a lot of aspects to engineering that space has to offer in product development. The one that we're targeting specifically is microgravity [because] from an engineering perspective, there are four fundamental forces of physics that drive all of engineering: strong nuclear force, weak nuclear force, electromagnetism and gravity. If we literally turn off 25% of that physics for the engineer in that process environment, there's a huge amount of innovation that can be built on top of that. (Augmented 2021, ep. 34)

At first, space manufacturing sounds quite farfetched, but when you realize that a lot of Varda's R&D has already been done by the International Space Station (ISS), and in some ways is a more productive replacement for ISS in the future, it starts to make more sense. "Lots of the grants where funding for research experiments on the ISS come with the rationale of, when launch costs drop someday this might be an economical thing to manufacture in space. We basically look through all of that research and pick out the ones that we think have the highest margins and the best unit economics" (Augmented 2021, ep. 34; see Interview 12.1).

**Interview 12.1** Making Factories in Space. Episode 34. Interview with William Bruey, CEO and Co-founder at Varda Space Industries. Augmented podcast.

Bruey feels that in the long term with a multiplanetary species, it's hard to imagine a world, a solar system, where "we have folks both on Mars and Earth, but for some reason, no manufacturing facilities in between" (Augmented 2021, ep. 34). He cites the "killer application" of space manufacturing, which is bioprinted organs: "Far down the road, 5 to 10 years [at least] would be a human organ printing." Why so long, and what is the big deal here? Keep in mind that when we 3D print something on Earth, we need to use scaffolding in order to support the structure that we're printing along the way. You can't really do that if you want to print something like a human organ that will not operate if it has scaffolding inside of a ventricular valve or something like that.

Another example would be the growth of crystals. A major reason why crystals are important in science is that they give us information about the structure of compounds. Crystal lean structures in chemistry are often determined by how molecules move around in a solution. In microgravity, we can avoid things like sedimentation, which leads to deposits that don't stay uniformly distributed. Sedimentation makes it harder to control experiments and read results.

If you have a mixture of something and you want that mixture to stay uniformly distributed during any chemical process, then doing it on Earth might be more difficult because if one of the things in that mixture, that solution, is heavier, it'll slowly sediment to the bottom [just like] your balsamic dressing in the refrigerator. But if you were to mix it in orbit, then the heavier and the lighter components of that solution stay homogeneously mixed. So now, during the chemical reaction that takes place we have better control over it. In a general sense, we have better control over chemical reactions and that can lead to higher performing materials across the board" (Augmented 2021, ep. 34).

Crystallization is useful in a bunch of industrial processes, including in understanding protein structures, since proteins are highly complex molecules. Bruey says, one method that exists is if you can crystallize that protein, meaning that you create a more regular structure out of it, you can then shine an X-ray through it and look at a diffraction pattern that explains what the atomic structure is of that protein. "Proteins are very important because they are often the interface between a pharmaceutical drug and the human body. Understanding those are crucial, and if we can crystallize them, we understand them better. We can crystallize them better in space, meaning that we can have higher resolution and better understand those proteins that go into the human," says Bruey.

"What's neat is as our cost of goods drop, as the space economy becomes more commoditized and we can purchase more things off the shelf and those costs of goods drop, the number of products that get through that filter, especially from a dollar per kg perspective, just increases more and more.

Space manufacturing might seem farfetched today, but that's only because costs are perceived to be so high. However, as the space industry accelerates, the relative difference between production in space and production on Earth will change radically, perhaps only within a few decades. Also, there is universal agreement that space exploration has been enormously wasteful from a lean perspective and should be improved in many radical ways.

If you're designing an assembly line and you need it to be as cost-effective as possible, putting a billion-dollar piece of machinery [the ISS] with manual labor in the middle [astronauts] is not the most prudent path that I would take. We would like a platform that is completely commercially independent that can certainly learn from the work that's been done on the ISS. It's built to be a research platform, but not a production platform. (Augmented 2021, ep. 34)

The goal of Varda is to have the first industrial park off of Earth. "We have a Greenfield that we can build on and have those from the get-go as part of integrated into our processes rather than having to retrofit" (Augmented 2021, ep. 34).

What makes space manufacturing technology (potentially) *augmented lean* is that putting humans in orbit was never defensible in terms of the value each person contributed in terms of tangible returns or were at least hard to calculate. With industrial production in space, that value will, as Bruey indicates, become more and more tangible. We find it fascinating to speculate on these things because it serves as a reminder of the limitations we often put around our frame of mind when we approach a problem in our own industry.

# THE SIZE AND SHAPE OF THE FUTURE INDUSTRIAL PIE

There are many financial predictions about the future of the manufacturing industry. According to the consultant firm Oliver Wyman, for example, US$1 trillion worth of new markets is expected to develop over the course of a decade. Wyman's report points to megatrends that will increase the pie, such as economic globalization, digital revolution, evolving consumption, and innovation acceleration (Kautzsch et al. 2017).

In contrast, what does Jeff Immelt, the former CEO of GE, arguably the "last" industrialist of the old era, think an industrial powerhouse is going to look like in the future? Will there ever be a digital powerhouse like the one he attempted to create [a renewed GE], a company that by end of 2021 is splitting up into three companies and likely won't be such a company ever again, or will the dominating players be a myriad of startups that have no respect for the old behemoths?

Immelt says he thinks it's a combination of factors: "Smaller facilities close to markets where manufacturing and marketing actually gets spoken about in the same sentence are going to be the way of the future. They're going to be powered by two or three of the technologies, whether it's advanced robotics or different elements that are incorporated in the wave of technology and how it can be applied. I think you've got an Amazon and let's say a Tesla – CEOs that believe dramatically in forward and backward integration. I grew up in an era where you diverted and closed everything, right? You let suppliers do everything. You let them do all your manufacturing, your distribution, everything was diverted" (Augmented 2021, ep. 42).

Immelt has another term for what we internet entrepreneurs would call platform businesses (see Interview 12.2):

**Interview 12.2**  Business Beyond Buzzwords. Episode 42. Interview with Jeff Immelt, Venture Partner, NEA, Former CEO of General Electric. Augmented podcast.

The next wave of entrepreneurs, they are vertical integration guys. They're like, I want to do that. I don't want anybody else to make money other than me. So that's going to be one wave of where technology is going to take place. You can't be in the automotive industry without being respectful of manufacturing. You can't be in the aviation industry without being respectful of manufacturers. There's a certain industry where the product and the process are the same thing, and those guys are always going to be really great manufacturing companies, and then there's going to be startups, and they're going to be trying to disrupt as best they can. It's a combination, but the next generation of winners, and again, I put Amazon [in that category], they don't want to share any dollar of margin with anybody. (Augmented 2021, ep. 42)

While we agree with Immelt that manufacturing work is distinctive and valuable, we think it needs to, and will, evolve more rapidly. Not with mindless automation but with careful augmentation. Change is possible and change is coming, but it won't all be like Amazon's business model. We think diversity will be greater as biomanufacturing becomes a mass production phenomenon and distributed production changes what factories look like not just in size but also in form.

Immelt's brave and honest book *Hot Seat: What I Learned Leading a Great Company* (Immelt 2021) is unusually revealing and instructive. He has shared not only how lonely it is at the top, but seemingly how few big choices and at times how many smaller choices you have at any given time. His struggles with industrial tech are near timeless. Nobody has all the answers in terms of getting organizational implementation of exponential tech right. Especially not if your organization is the size of GE. We were struck by the implication for leaders – be vulnerable or risk not only your own happiness, but those of all your co-workers. Immelt's struggle was to digitize GE, a behemoth in transition. He chose to build an in-house capacity, and its own IoT platform [Predix] at great cost, and initially with mixed results, but how many other options were there on the table? Hindsight is 20-20. As Immelt points out, nowadays, low-code and no-code systems, such as Tulip, are about to transform frontline operations in ways we can only start to imagine. The promise is empowerment of workers and immense productivity gains from freeing up the human mind. Our challenges might, at times, seem or indeed be smaller in scale, but might feel equally overwhelming. Good to know then, that the folks at the top struggle as well.

Another challenge is that despite the gradual emergence of global supply chains, each manufacturing ecosystem still is national or local at heart. Government funding is earmarked for its constituents with the result that the networks become myopic.

Says Dave Evans, CEO and co-founder of Fictiv: "I don't think any amount of buy America strategy is going to truly make a dent in the ecosystem. Any company that's building a physical product today has a global footprint. They have the ability to make, manufacture, and distribute anywhere in the world" (Augmented 2021, ep. 13; see Interview 12.3).

**Interview 12.3** Get Manufacturing Superpowers. Interview with Dave Evans, CEO & co-founder, Fictiv. Episode 13. Augmented podcast.

Standardization is key to the future of industrial manufacturing. The National Institute of Standards and Technology (NIST) at the United States Department of Commerce said in its testimony to the US Congress on

"Industries of the Future" (Copan 2020), that "over the past years NIST has prioritized the work of its programs in Quantum Information Science, Artificial Intelligence, 5G, Advanced Manufacturing, and Biotechnology, the areas that today are collectively referred to as the Industries of the Future." Most notably, perhaps, Manufacturing USA is a network of 14 manufacturing innovation institutes located across the country where companies, universities, community colleges, and entrepreneurs develop new manufacturing technologies with broad applications.

# HOW LONG WILL IT TAKE FOR INDUSTRY 4.0 TO MATURE?

As we have tried to show throughout this book, change in manufacturing is uneven, even within a country, or a state. For example, Kathryn Kelley, Executive Director, Ohio Manufacturing Institute, thinks that her state, the third or fourth largest state for manufacturing depending on how you calculate it, will take a full human generation to transition; she says it could take 20 to 30 years to reach small to midsize firms at the current rate of change. "Transitioning to digital is going to be based on customer demand that comes from the OEMs who can afford the transition. They have the teams; they have the resources to move toward Industry 4.0. They'll be demanding it from their tier one and beyond suppliers. So it's coming."

She compares Industry 4.0 to another technology integration project, enterprise resource planning (ERP), "If you think about it, the ERP diffusion took more than 40 years, starting in 1973. It didn't happen overnight and Industry 4.0 is not going to happen overnight. I think we'll have some fits and starts." Kelley says we are dealing with everything from legacy equipment to culture and feels it is more of a business problem than a technical problem. They're going to face the threats of failing to invest in those technologies and falling behind. We're going to end up with these manu-facturing haves and have-nots, if the structures are not put in place.

Kelley's main concern, coming from the Ohio perspective, is that the small-and-midsize companies are vulnerable to outside influence, whether it be tech trends or third parties. Consultants will often talk to them about one-off automation projects, but not really help them look at it from a systemic level. "If you have a series of standalone automation projects but you don't have some kind of continuous improvement discipline that's part of the managerial culture, moving toward digital operations technologies is going to prove more difficult," says Kelley (Augmented 2022, ep. 67; see Interview 12.4).

**Interview 12.4** Manufacturing 5.0. Interview with Kathryn Kelley, Executive Director, Ohio Manufacturing Institute. Episode 67. Augmented podcast.

# THE FUTURE OF INDUSTRIAL OPERATIONS

What will industrial tech look like in the next two decades? Oliver Wyman's recent survey of Engineering 2030 predicted a complete transformation of engineering work and highlighted the following:

- Work in open engineering ecosystem, system engineering tools based design
- Fully agile and digital development process
- Massive usage of product data to optimize design

- Customer-centric product design
- The polarization of engineering skills, resulting in development cycle time reduced by 50% and new product development cost divided by two (Boilard et al. 2018)

However, this study was carried out in 2017–2018 and most executives said they will be relying more and more on external parties to develop products, since most in-house engineering organizations lack the necessary resources and skills in software, artificial intelligence, and cybersecurity. That view is the opposite of ours taking into account what we feel is possible using no-code systems. Could it be that these executives were unaware of that possibility? A key quote in the report indicates so. In response to what he would do if he had a magic wand, a CTO in the automotive industry is quoted as saying: "I would kill and replace our engineering tools." To this we say, yes, a lot has happened between 2018 and 2022, but that executive has also been sleeping on the job. Either way, cloud-based, no-code engineering tools are mushrooming now, and the results will be transformative, even in the conservative automotive industry, perhaps as mind bogglingly different as before and after Fordism.

There's endless obsession about the digital element of transformation, to the detriment of sound business comprehension. Says Brian Mathews, CTO of industrial automation company Bright Machines, a spinoff from supply chain services provider Flex:

Because of digitization and these different technologies, machine learning, combined with vision, CAD, simulation and so on, we can automate entire workflows. That's what this is really about. If I look at other industries, Salesforce doesn't sell anything, Workday doesn't hire anybody, ServiceNow doesn't fix anybody's bugs. What these really successful companies really do is that they automate the workflow of doing work. In a way, they automate tasks. They're automating machines, but they're also automating the humans that are participating in the process of working with the machines. (Augmented 2021, ep. 29)

# Automating Automation Through Software-Defined Manufacturing

Making the place of production more flexible is a key to innovation and productivity. Erik Mirandette, head of Product & Ecosystem at Tulip, points out that in old manufacturing facilities they had centralized power generation, typically either steam-powered or water-powered. Power would convert that to mechanical energy and then distribute that mechanical energy to the various workstations across the whole of the facility typically using a belt and shaft system.

What does that mean? Mirandette: "Before you think about how you build one of those facilities, you need to know what you're building, how to build it, what parts are required, about how many that you will be building, and where every single physical station is going to be in each facility before you lay the first brick." He contrasts this with building at a platform level, which allows you to click a button and start with a solution that's anywhere from 50–90% done. Mirandette prefers today's situation where you can: "Give frontline users the ability to configure and adapt and adjust as their processes evolve in a 'Lego-like approach' where you can continue to add on functionality or adjust as required based on your operational considerations" (Augmented 2022, ep. 75; see Interview 12.5).

---

**Interview 12.5**  Designing a Worker Friendly Industrial System. Interview with Erik Mirandette, Head of Product & Ecosystem at Tulip. Episode 75. Augmented podcast.

---

There is a meta-level of automation that interests us more than automation itself, although even that phenomenon should be subject to human oversight. It's considered automating automation. According to Mathews (see Figure 12.1):

A software defined manufacturing approach is to get a conveyor that's motorized that has a shaft and coder and knows what its width is set to and you load a recipe and it changes its shape. We've done things like heat sink installers where there's 250,000 different types of heat sinks on them. You can go to any number of companies and find thousands of different grippers for your robot that can pick up heat sinks of different shapes and sizes. But why not have ones that have motors in them that it's under software control, change their shape? It's going to cost you more, but you can reuse it for every future project you're ever going to have. So those are some ideas behind software defined manufacturing.

If you look at a Tesla or an iPhone, what they were compared to their predecessors was a software first approach. It's still hardware, but the hardware isn't the thing that's meant to do the work, it's meant to be controlled by sensors and motors and so on. Mathews says, "I had a friend once who said: 'A robot is what you call something before it becomes useful. After it's useful, you call it a dishwasher or a vacuum cleaner or something else.' When you make something cheap through automation, you actually consume more of it." He asks, "What is the equivalent of GitHub," the software code repository hosting service with 73 million users in this industry? "What is the equivalent of Terraform," the open source tool for writing infrastructure as code to manage public cloud resources such as AWS, GCP, and Azure? "What is the equivalent of ServiceNow," the workflow and productivity tool for technical management support? "What is the equivalent of JIRA," the influential issue and project tracking software? "What is the equivalent of Visual Studio," the integrated development environment from Microsoft? (Augmented 2021, ep. 29; see Interview 12.6).

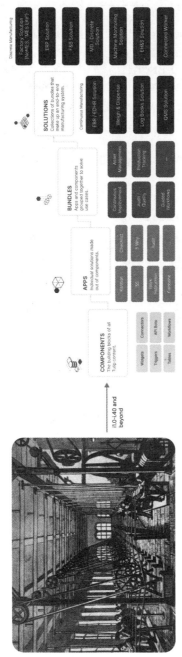

From steam power + belts
to drive manufacturing

**Figure 12.1** Software-Defined Manufacturing.

**Interview 12.6** The Automated Microfactory. Episode 29. Interview with Brian Mathews, CTO, Bright Machines. Augmented podcast.

None of these exist yet in the manufacturing industry, nor have these tools any significant adoption in that industry. Even if some of them are used by engineers in the manufacturing industry, those tools certainly have not yet been fully adapted for it. The impact of that is felt in the lack of adaptable, flexible, and shared solutions.

The million-dollar question throughout the book is: How can we foster conditions for manufacturing to democratize? Says Rony Kubat, Tulip co-founder:

> Expertise will always be valued, whether it be expertise and skills or the ability to create something. That's not going to go away into a fully distributed fashion. The best battery maker will invest enormous amounts into the intellectual capital and the facilities that are required to do that. Maybe you'll have a distributed Silicon fabs, but the best, highest speed, lowest power processors are going to be coming out of some kind of specialized [facility]. Similarly, if you think of larger physical goods, you want to make a car where all the lines line up, that looks beautiful and is very large [...] connected to a global supply chain and, to make the door of that car, you're making the door in Georgia, but your molds for your door are cut in Canada and shipped. That level of specialization won't go away. (Augmented 2021, ep. 66)

There are a few ways industries in the future of industrial operations could play out:

- Networks of firms and stakeholders who collaborate with each other with no clear lead (mutually dependent supply chain networks), in open, distributed ways, yet incrementally specialized.
- Oligopolies that control their own affiliate networks (the Asian conglomerate model) or ecosystems of scale (e.g., the Android model).
- Constantly shifting sets of companies that dominate for a few years each before new disruptors take over and dethrone the former kingmakers (an intensified version of the current IT industry).

Two things to consider are the likely future evolution in contrast to the ideal future. The system we have in mind as *our* ideal industrial system of the future, unlike manufacturing execution systems of the past, is wide-ranging, built on open platforms, and flexible. Such a system rewards proactive, competent individuals, not only organizations and large corporations.

There is ample data that we could get there. In fact, the currently emerging industrial system strongly relies on trust and self-reliance, even self-help, and demands being down-to-earth entrepreneurial. Individuals working within this system fashion solutions when needed – and share those solutions with others – but don't make a fuss about it. It is increasingly becoming apparent that people are the real key to digital transformation. But not in the sense that technology is irrelevant. Rather, in the sense that in the codependency of people and technology, people must hold the steering pin – otherwise you cannot tap into the long-term efficiencies.

Either way, all the previous stages of industrialization (which we discussed in Chapters 1 and 2) were technology centric and neglected humans, some in worse ways than others. Early industrial factories turned into torture chambers of sorts. Mines have always been dirty, dangerous, and dull. Sweatshops in Asia still exist today, thanks to uneven regulatory crackdown (Donaldson 2021). Our meatpacking facilities all over the world will not win "best place to work awards" that teach new skills every day. Progress can still be made.

We believe the time has come for humanistic technology to reign supreme over machines, only constrained by better awareness of the ecological ecosystem that industry is part of. We can now analyze customer requirements, including design and usability best practices, in sophisticated ways. We have the ability to run algorithms to simulate products before they are made. We can create digital twins of entire production systems and supply chains, and create elaborate 3D prototypes. In all, we are poised to enter a more productive era for technology without needing to cut corners with nature or the workforce. Some of this will happen on its own, through industry collaboration and self-regulation, but some aspects, such as algorithmic transparency and oversight, as well as installing robotic tax mandates (similar to carbon taxes) will require future government regulation.

As this future unfolds, a clear path to progress is through intelligence augmentation where we pursue technologies that make human workers more efficient, empowered, and motivated to do their jobs better.

# THE WORKFORCE QUESTIONS

We don't want to leave the impression that there is only one workforce question. The biggest ones are as follows, in this order:

- Will machines take our jobs?
- How will manufacturing companies find new talent as old workers are aging out of the workforce?

- How are we going to upskill billions of workers over the next decade and subsequently on an ongoing basis every day, every week, every month, and every year?

Says Kim Knickle, formerly Gartner's manufacturing analyst, and now research director at Verdantix:

Let's face it. The number of jobs has decreased significantly because you don't need as many people to actually produce something as you did 50 years ago. [But], I want to remind people that manufacturing is not just what happens in a factory of 150 people. Manufacturing is just as important to creativity and design as it is to the actual production piece. [...] Anybody who thinks they're an entrepreneur, anybody who thinks they're a designer or a creator, they should be recognizing that they also need to be involved in the manufacturing process. (Augmented 2021, ep. 35; see Interview 12.7)

**Interview 12.7** Analysts Shape Markets. Episode 35. Interview with Kim Knickle, Research Director, Verdantix. Augmented podcast.

A clue to the second issue, finding new talent, comes from young millennial Lena Jaentsch, a Business Development Specialist at the small German manufacturing firm HERMA GmbH, which makes self-adhesive labels. Jaentsch is an innovation manager and calls herself "the strong, mostly single fighter in the SME space" (see Interview 12.8):

**Interview 12.8** A Female Fighter in a Manufacturing SME. Episode 16. Interview with Lena Jaentsch, Business Development Specialist at HERMA Group. Augmented podcast.

When I graduated from school, to be honest manufacturing wasn't the first topic in my mind. [...] If I come up with my own ideas I see my colleagues' eyes get bigger and they look at me like: "okay, are you serious?" [...] but we need to think about the future [...] It's not so much about production techniques anymore, but more about [developing] new digital products, having something for our customers that really helps them and helps us as well. [...] I'm not a tech woman. I'm interested in tech, I'm not an expert, but I'm curious about it. (Augmented 2021, ep. 16;).

Perhaps we should stop obsessing about tech talent and just start having faith in manufacturing as an exciting place to find a career? Some of these young people are tech literate enough to transform manufacturing, if they are only given tools that are appropriate for their skill level. More importantly, they are highly trainable and motivated. What they lack, it seems, is the role models to come up with the idea in the first place.

# BUILDING A MOVEMENT

When software industry veteran Hilarie Koplow-McAdams, Venture Partner, NEA started at Oracle, it was a hundred million dollar business. When she left, it was an $11 billion business. Now it's even bigger. Her lesson, which is the same for augmented lean, is that you are trying to create a movement, not a company. Koplow-McAdams says, "Lesson number one is: don't just join a category, redefine a category." For example, if you're bringing a product to market, if you're designing a product, don't define it as a database, define it as relational and make that have real meaning, such as the fastest database, which is what they created in the Oracle days.

Koplow-McAdams continues, "And then step two: define an ecosystem around that solution, which is what Oracle did in the early days." Oracle signed up a lot of independent software vendors to build a user interface on top of their database and then proceeded to Trojan horse that database into a myriad of other systems and markets. "Thinking broadly, not just about a technology solution but around how one creates an ecosystem of derivative solutions that get out to market, that's how you scale a company" (Augmented, 2021, ep. 41; see Interview 12.9).

**Interview 12.9** Scaling Software Movements. Episode 41.
Interview with Hilarie Koplow-McAdams, Venture Partner at NEA.
Augmented podcast.

Koplow-McAdams says:

It feels like manufacturing has been the stepchild to some of the modern innovation that we see in other sectors of the market. We've had so many dollars pouring into front office innovation and sales and service and marketing. We've had a lot of money move into engineering, better

PMO systems, better ticketing systems, et cetera, better deployment approaches. I think it's a ton of resourcing as does human capital management, but manufacturers have been left behind as have supply chains. [...] The movement in manufacturing [is connected to the] heroes and heroines on every shop floor that go home at night and dream about a better way. What if we could instrument this? What if we could plug this in? What if we could get a signal on that? They've been unlocked from [...] a lot of early automation, it's pretty dreary, right? It's a very dictated system of work that doesn't allow you to bring creativity in. (Augmented, 2021, ep. 41)

# CONCLUSION

Hundreds of years after the invention of advanced industrial machinery and nearly 50 years into the computer age, paper-based processes abound on the manufacturing shop floors around the world. Why? Because great technologies deeply embedded in society rarely get replaced. Rather, they coexist, and beyond its first adopters, generally adapts in society at human speed, not at the theoretical speed we might imagine it would. Still, automation, software defined automation, augmented lean management, augmented reality, and, eventually, space manufacturing, will each have their place in the future industrial systems. Yet, discrepancies in workforce skills will also persist. The motivation to change and evolve will not be equal for all.

In line with lean, we need to root out wasteful behavior that could destroy industrial processes, break products, or disrupt services. We also need to do other things: design for robust, local, and resilient. In our view, the only way to rapidly evolve industry, introducing sufficient material change, is to design for human-in-the-loop systems that allow for sharing widely across and beyond organizations.

Where does this leave us for industrial operations? All this leads to a more sustainable digital transformation because you are not tied to one technology. Instead, the system is built by the people doing the work. They will "self-upskill" and find and refine new tech and tools all the time. Leadership still has a role, of course. The industrialists of the future will, yet again, have to take the responsibility of society-making, meaning their industrial activities will provide the platform upon which the next iteration of the economy will be built and sustained.

With citizen development and contemporary no-code platforms, the barrier of being literate in software coding practices is less pronounced. We wouldn't counsel our kids to ignore code but there are other paths, too. *Augmented Lean* is our invitation to join a movement, a collective endeavor that will change the world, whether we want it to or not. The alternative, which would be continuing down the futile path of AI-infused industrial automation *for automation's sake*, will be significantly more disappointing. It is a dead end. To engage is easy: Regardless of your age, skills, resources, or track record until now, start thinking of yourself as an industrialist of a new era. We make our world what we want it to become.

In the upcoming chapter, we look at how to reconfigure global supply chains and what the future holds.

# REFERENCES

Alamalhodaei, A. (2021). Varda Space Industries closes $42M Series A for off-plant manufacturing. *TechCrunch* (July 29). https://techcrunch.com/2021/07/29/varda-space-industries-closes-42m-series-a-for-off-planet-manufacturing/ (accessed 26 November 2021).

Augmented (2021, ep. 13). Get Manufacturing Superpowers. Episode 13. Interview with Dave Evans, CEO & co-founder, Fictiv. *Augmented podcast.* (April 14). https://www.augmentedpodcast.co/get-manufacturing-superpowers/ (accessed 26 November 2021).

Augmented (2021, ep. 16). A female fighter in a manufacturing SME. Episode 16. Interview with Lena Jaentsch, Business Development Specialist at HERMA Group. *Augmented podcast.* (April 28). https://www.augmentedpodcast.co/a-female-fighter-in-a-manufacturing-sme/ (accessed 26 November 2021)

Augmented (2021, ep. 29). The Automated Microfactory. Episode 29. Interview with Brian Mathews, CTO, Bright Machines. *Augmented podcast.* (July 28). https://www.augmentedpodcast.co/the-automated-microfactory/ (accessed 26 November 2021)

Augmented (2021, ep. 34). Making Factories in Space. Episode 35. Interview with William Bruey, CEO and co-founder at Varda Space Industries. *Augmented podcast.* (Nov 17). https://www.augmentedpodcast.co/making-factories-in-space/ (accessed 26 November 2021).

Augmented (2021, ep. 35). Industry Analysts Shape Markets. Episode 35. Interview with Kim Knickle, Research Director, Verdantix. *Augmented podcast.* (Aug 4). https://www.augmentedpodcast.co/analysts-shape-markets/ (accessed 26 November 2021).

Augmented (2021, ep. 41). Scaling Software Movements. Episode 41. Interview with Hilarie Koplow-McAdams, Venture Partner at NEA. *Augmented podcast.* (Sept 15) https://www.augmentedpodcast.co/scaling-software-movements/ (accessed 26 November 2021).

Augmented (2021, ep. 42). Business Beyond Buzzwords. Episode 42. Interview with Jeff Immelt, Venture Partner, NEA, former CEO of General Electric. *Augmented podcast.* (July 7). https://www.augmentedpodcast.co/business-beyond-buzzwords/ (accessed 26 November 2021).

Augmented (2021, ep. 66). Bridging the Physical-Digital Divide in Industrial Tech. Interview with Rony Kubat, CTO and co-founder, Tulip Interfaces (not yet published). Episode 66. *Augmented podcast.* (June 9). https://www.augmentedpodcast.co/66 (accessed 17 November 2021).

Augmented (2022, ep. 67). Manufacturing 5.0. Interview with Kathryn Kelley, Executive Director, Ohio Manufacturing Institute (not yet published). Episode 67. *Augmented podcast.* (Jan 26). https://www.augmentedpodcast.co/67 (accessed 17 November 2021).

Boilard, M., Schnurrer, S., and Graff, J. (2018). Engineering 2030: Six megatrends that will shape engineering. *Oliver Wyman.* https://www.oliverwyman.com/content/dam/oliver-wyman/v2/publications/2018/august/Oliver-Wyman-Engineering-2030.pdf (accessed 26 November 2021).

Calderone, L. (2017). Is that a bug or a robotic spy? *Robotics Tomorrow.* (December 5). https://www.roboticstomorrow.com/article/2017/12/is-that-a-bug-or-a-robotic-spy/11089 (accessed 26 November 2021).

Cornell (2022). This is rocket science: Cornell's contributions to discovering the universe. Cornell University. https://cornelluniversity.imodules.com/s/1717/giving/interior.aspx?sid=1717&gid=2&pgid=6760&crid...= (accessed 26 November 2021).

Donaldson, T. (2021). Asia-Pacific supports the fashion industry, but does the fashion industry Support Asia-Pacific? WWD (May 26). https://wwd.com/fashion-news/fashion-features/fashion-industry-taps-75-percent-garment-workers-from-asia-pacific-aapi-heritage-month-1234828301/ (accessed 13 March 2022).

Fuchs, T. (2021). *In Defense of the Human Being: Foundational Questions of an Embodied Anthropology*. Oxford: Oxford University Press.

Gordon, M. (2017). *Blade Runner*'s chillingly prescient vision of the future. *The Conversation* (October 5). https://theconversation.com/blade-runners-chillingly-prescient-vision-of-the-future-84973 (accessed 26 November 2021).

Immelt, J. (2021). *Hot Seat: What I Learned Leading a Great American Company*. New York: Simon & Schuster.

Kautzsch, T. and Kronenwett, D. and Thibault, G. (2017). Megatrends and the future of industry: A new era in manufacturing presents long-term opportunities. *Oliver Wyman*. https://www.oliverwyman.com/content/dam/oliver-wyman/v2/publications/2017/nov/Megatrends_And_The_Future_Of_Industry.pdf ((accessed 26 November 2021).

Knudsen, T. (2017). How the world of *Blade Runner* 2049 was created. *CinemaTyler* (June 3). http://cinematyler.com/archives/817 (accessed 26 November 2021).

Progressive Productions (2022). Inota power plant. *Progressive Productions*. https://progressiveproductions.eu/locations/hungary/special/inota-power-plant (accessed 26 November 2021).

Screenrant (2017). The Deckard replicant question – resolved? *Screenrant*. https://screenrant.com/blade-runner-2049-ending-twist-deckard-daughter-explained/4/ (accessed 26 November 2021).

Serious Wheels (2002). Lexus concept from "Minority Report." *Serious Wheels*. http://www.seriouswheels.com/cars/top-Lexus-Concept-Minority-Report.htm (accessed 26 November 2021).

Undheim, T.A. (2021). *Future Tech: How to Capture Value from Disruptive Industry Trends*. London: Kogan Page.

# CHAPTER 13

# RECONFIGURING GLOBAL SUPPLY CHAINS

The COVID-19 pandemic highlighted a global reluctance to share data, despite its potential to solve societal problems. The crisis led to regulators and manufacturing companies coming together to radically speed up vaccine development and production. Sharing data and approaches early greatly sped up the process and increased the quality at the same time. The reality is that we have the technology to make products faster than ever. A case study we took part in was helping Eduardo Torralba, CEO of Boston-based manufacturing startup Meter, rapidly build the Rise Emergency Ventilator in three weeks using a combination of ingenuity, Tulip software apps to instruct each participant in the process, and 3D-printed parts using Formlabs technology (Tulip 2020). Flexed regulation was part of this story, but it does not alone explain how a complex medical device could go from concept to finished product.

As we have all come to know because of the shortages, a swab is not only an absorbent pad or piece of material used in surgery and medicine for cleaning wounds, or cleaning your ears like a Q-tip. It is also a vital tool for taking virus samples. Formlabs made the swabs, printed them, and bypassed the only two factories that traditionally produce these for the US market (Formlabs 2020). All in all, the whole process took two weeks from concept to FDA-approved device, printed on Formlabs customers' own 3D printers. Going forward, the importance of 3D printing as a tool in wars or pandemics will never be underestimated. And what is more, a swab is not customized; it is a standard product. Imagine the potential for rapidly produced specialty products that do require the kind of customization that we generally expect to wait months for. That era is likely over. We do not need to keep inventory; we just need to keep blueprints. Distributed manufacturing is an evolving phenomenon. If cheap enough, easy enough, or solving an inventory problem, it will become the default. It will, however, not be the solution for all products at all times.

If we could build logistics systems faster than ever to support a crisis, why could we not move faster on a regular basis? The conclusion is pretty evident: if we find ourselves in a constant "pandemic" or other urgent situation, we can improve rapidly forever. During COVID-19, all of this was accomplished using online collaboration tools to connect various product teams. The internet, as a fundamental backbone, played its role, too. All in all, we should all reflect on what might have happened should this pandemic have happened a decade earlier. Undoubtedly, global business would have come to a standstill.

Clearly, the contract manufacturers (CMs) of the future will have at its disposal a fully virtualized value stream from design to shipping of product. They will provide this service to customers, whether they are a multinational or a mom-and-pop store. Already, Shenzhen, the Chinese city, has been built on high-tech, manufacturing, and service industries. It is already the factory of the world but it is becoming much more—as it also incubates new industrial businesses end to end. When a surge in COVID-19 cases across the United States dramatically increased the need for personal protective equipment (PPE), a nonprofit organization called MasksOn sprang to life (www.maskson.org). Coordinated by leaders in healthcare, research, and industry, MasksOn designs and produces reusable, sanitizable emergency-use face shields for medical purposes and distributes them to the clinicians who do not have access to FDA cleared equipment together with Massachusetts-based manufacturer Lightspeed Manufacturing. These are full-face snorkel masks as well as custom-made adapters that mate the mask to a hospital-supplied, standard bacterial/viral filter.

Demand surged, and masks were produced swiftly. However, as more and more frontline workers requested deliveries, the existing systems were strained to the breaking point. Manual work was required to fulfill orders, using a workforce of volunteers and communicating in a distributed fashion. This significantly constrained MasksOn's capacity to ship PPE. Said Bradley Sauln at MasksOn: "In the early days of the MasksOn project, I knew immediately that we needed a more scalable, sustainable process. We were hand-taking inventory, marking everything, hand-creating tracking numbers for the parts, and even creating shipping labels manually" (Tulip 2021f).

As a distributed organization with a geographically dispersed set of manufacturers and suppliers, the group needed a centralized means of coordinating production and fulfillment. Not only that, the grassroots collaboration needed a logistics system they could roll out fast. Tulip reached out to help. On March 27, Tulip's Lean Practice Lead Mark Freedman and CTO and co-founder Rony Kubat began to get involved in the MasksOn project. On March 28, Mark built a set of Tulip apps overnight to create work centers, define products and their Bill of Materials (BOMs), and manage supply couriers. Tulip started work on APIs and critical integrations, and scraped the data from their existing Google sheets to get it into the Tulip system. On April 3, an integration to Slack was added to show when orders come in, and a new web-based order submission form was put online.

On April 4, the system went live. The system is standalone; production managers, couriers, and inventory managers are able to ship the product on their own without the help of the Tulip team, tracking delivery, community, and user data (Ackley 2020). See Case study 13.1.

**Case study 13.1** When MasksOn Needed a Logistics System, They Built One with Tulip in Four Days. Tulip MasksOn Case Study.

Using Tulip's no-code, cloud-based platform, volunteers from Tulip and MasksOn built a set of applications to organize and scale operations. The MasksOn solution has a few key parts. First, ordering applications allows healthcare professionals to place demands directly on the supply chain. Second, several applications help suppliers manage their inventory and operations, giving them the ability to reserve inventory to their demands. Third, shipping applications let suppliers manage delivery using national delivery chains or volunteer networks. Fourth, mobile applications allow people to volunteer to deliver inventory where it's needed. All in all, with Tulip, MasksOn built a full-fledged logistics system in four days. The first 50 masks were manageable in spreadsheets and Google Forms, but the production target of 80,000 called for something more. Before Tulip, MasksOn had shipped 200 units total. Now, it ships over 1,000 a day. In early 2021, 36,000 masks had been shipped across the world at a cost of $30 to $35 per device and MasksOn had raised $2 million in donations to distribute them absolutely free of cost to hospitals (Junior 2021).

# BOOSTING J&J'S DIGITAL SUPPLY CHAIN WITH AUGMENTED LEAN APPROACHES

A healthcare conglomerate is a multifaceted global organization. J&J's mission, and its organizational culture, shapes its approach. Culturally, J&J is a network of companies that have retained their own identities, brands, and ways of working. J&J sources a variety of materials from chemicals, plastics, machinery, to packaging to carry out its business. With 130,000 employees across the world and some 250 subsidiary companies around the world, it manages around 97 manufacturing sites filling approximately 15.2 million square feet of floor space (Schlenker 2021). In November 2021, Johnson & Johnson (J&J) announced its plans to split into two companies, separating consumer products and pharmaceutical businesses. Delivering highly branded products to consumers is different from producing pharmaceuticals and medical devices and delivering this to businesses or governments. However, increasing personalization means there's contact with end clients in that business as well. The former J&J joint business had more than 78,000 suppliers around the world.

Arun Kumar Bhaskara-Baba is the Global Head of Manufacturing for the company. When Trond interviewed him for *Augmented Lean,* we discussed Industry 4.0 and what digital means to operators on the floor. Operators are often ignored or considered last in digital transformation initiatives. We also discussed the "test and learn" sessions with no-code and low-code platforms held at J&J sites. Bhaskara-Baba pointed out that the diversity of products being produced creates a complexity that means J&J "supports almost every aspect of manufacturing": "I see digital as a means to an end [...] very clearly understanding why we want to digitize." Personalization changes the game, too (see Interview 13.1):

> We are getting a place where we take the picture of the knee, get it back and make the product, and then even 3D print it and give it to the surgeon. Or if you think about how we are personalizing, where we are taking the blood from the patient and making the product that is very specific to the patient and shipping them, shipping it to them [...] with the challenge of "how do we really become a full supply chain so that we can produce that batch of one wherever possible?" (Augmented 2021, ep. 43)

Historically, supply chain management, particularly factory systems, were monolithic, but Bhaskara-Baba seems to equally focus on the operators, as well: "A lot of technologies are emerging and that's all driving. But for us at the end of the day, it all comes back to that operator. We are here to serve the operator. We can bring in robots and all of it [but] at the end of the day, there is an operator at the line who is making it happen. So how do we make sure that we put the operator at the center and then create the experience for the operator so that it makes it a lot easier? [...] We are trying to take a step back and say, how do we, first of all, make it simple? Number two is how do we empower them?"

**Interview 13.1** Digitized Supply Chain. Episode 43. Interview with Arun Kumar Bhaskara-Baba, Head of Global Manufacturing IT, Johnson & Johnson. Augmented podcast.

The solution J&J found is: "breaking down by purpose, having a good, consistent architecture and breaking these monolithic things into smaller, nimble apps." We also need to "train the rest of the organization. Management and operations leaders all need to be digitally savvy to drive that and see the lag. It is a journey, but you need to be very clear about why we are doing it and putting the operators at the center and helping them" (Augmented 2021, ep. 43).

J&J operates in a regulated industry. Having said that, not everything they do is regulated. As a result, many business processes can be subject to change management, with less regulatory burden. Some digital apps, for example, slide in between the cracks and accomplish stuff (beyond the clinical trials process), for example on the consumer side, that is not covered by regulation. Other apps, those on the pharma side and related to drug development, need to absolutely be compliant. Bhaskara-Baba feels that to cater to this need, the solutions his industry uses must have a robust architecture. "We need enough control to validate, qualify our approaches and give the parameters of freedom for the operators within those constraints." This work has two aspects, working with the regulators to make sure that they "understand what we are doing," and working to "educate them on emerging opportunities such as real-time release," which refers to the idea of improving process control by generating more data while the manufacturing process is taking place and convincing regulators to also use that data to validate the quality (Augmented 2021, ep. 43).

Lean production principles and agile principles are still valid, says Bhaskara-Baba, since: "what lean is saying is, think about the flow, eliminate the waste, and continue to improve and zero defects if possible." That mindset has to be there for us to even look at digital. What digital is doing is helping us to implement linearly and faster. Traditional boundaries such as "plan, source, make, deliver" is becoming a network, he feels. The only way you can survive in that network is having a mindset where you bring people together very quickly and get the problem solved daily. Better to create a MVP (minimum viable product), don't look back, and once achieved, move onto the next one. Agile principles bring the teams together very quickly. "The focus should be on the key priorities and delivering on the MVP, aligned with the lean thinking to make sure that there is no waste" (Augmented 2021, ep. 43).

Innovating and taking risks is another challenge, says Bhaskara-Baba: "How can we look at our CEO and say, 'Hey, we need to add a 3-year-old startup' to our list of suppliers." Looking at the factories of the future, "some of them might not significantly change. But most of them will be flexible, where [we can] bring them together for specific products or specific customers and be able to re-assemble very quickly to do something else."

"The digital savvy of our day-to-day citizens is helping us to bring these values much faster to our patients and customers," says Bhaskara-Baba. But the shared challenge is to "keep the operator at the center." His rationale is that even as the tech evolves, the operator rules. "Let's make sure that we empower them, we help them to be as digitally savvy as possible. That will actually help us to move this narrative much faster" (Augmented 2021, ep. 43).

Work stations are common across industry to help increase overall productivity by eliminating unnecessary movement. Tulip is currently deployed on one of J&J's medical device factory sites as an MES augmentation app system consisting of hundreds of work stations that are connected to apps substituting paperwork for frontline operations and supporting the arduous work of tracing down and tracking all the parts needed to conduct the work. Rapidly increasing demand spikes are common in this type of production environment, and traditional IT systems are not well equipped to deal with this fluctuation. Another factor is that, in addition to its flagship factories, the company has a multitude of smaller factory sites, some of which have been acquired from other companies. Each site has the need to continually increase efficiencies in production. That process is typically costly. When a traditional MES goes live, the budget required can far outweigh the factory's footprint, as deals require one-off enterprise licenses that cover extensive and "needed" customizations. Upgrades in functionality carry similar cost structures both in discrete and high velocity manufacturing and in process and batch.

J&J exemplifies several principles of *augmented lean* management, including enabling site managers to make site-specific decisions, learning through piloting, empowering operators, respecting workers, and governing the overall approach to roll out best practices globally.

# DIGITAL ORDERING PROCESS IN THE UK'S LARGEST FLOWER BUSINESS

In the last 60 years, family-owned Double H nurseries has grown to be the largest supplier of houseplants in the UK. Selling to supermarkets and other vendors across the UK, Double H has upwards of a million and a half orchids in production at any given time. Double H keeps most of its operations in house. In addition to growing and raising plants, they design products, track trends and fashions, package, and dispatch its product.

The year of 2020 began on an auspicious note for Double H. In the first few weeks of March, Double H broke its record for single-week sales as retailers prepared for the Mother's Day holiday (in March in the UK). "We sold more than 300,000 orchids that weekend," Andy Burton, operations manager at Double H, noted. Within days of breaking their sales record, however, the UK announced sweeping lockdowns as COVID made its first broad sweeps across the UK. Supermarkets shifted their stocks from gifts to paper goods and flowers. Shopping patterns changed. In short, the floor dropped out. Rather than accept their fate, Double H looked for opportunities.

Orchids, however, aren't like other industrial products. They take a year to grow, and if left in a warehouse for too long, they'll spoil. So Burton found himself in a tough spot. If he couldn't sell his inventory, he'd lose it. The challenge was recovering business after a precipitous decline in demand. The solution turned out to be a change in business model. If they couldn't sell to distributors, why not sell directly to consumers?

The move from B2B to B2C, however, was not without growing pains. Burton and his team decided that the best way to move their existing inventory would be to create an online shop. They moved quickly. Within five days, they'd set up an e-commerce storefront implemented using Shopify. Orders followed almost immediately. "We didn't know how we were going to fulfill the orders. But we knew we needed to try." Burton noted of their first experiments selling directly to consumers, "Orders came in. We were basically packing plants and driving them in our cars to the shipment places" (Augmented 2021, ep. 61; see Interview 13.2).

**Interview 13.2** The Digital Journey of a Flower Wholesaler. Episode 61. Interview with Andy Burton, Managing Director, Double H Nurseries Ltd. Augmented podcast.

While the team got a boost from the success of their new process, the manual work associated quickly caught up with them. Burton recalls the attitude in their facilities was, "For the first couple of days we thought, 'Yea, okay, we can do this.'" Then demand increased. On the first day, Double H sold 20 boxes. By day 6 they sold 600. Then local news outlets picked up their story, and orders poured in. "Suddenly we were in a bit of trouble." Soon it was up to 3,500 orders a day through the new channel. For Burton and his team, it was a real struggle to process every order. "There were .csv files everywhere." Burton and his team reached an inflection point. Either find a way to reduce the administrative burden of their new channel, or miss the opportunity they created for themselves.

The friction Double H experienced in its new order process came from the manual administrative work each order required. For each order, they had to pull the relevant information from Shopify, and create shipping labels and packing slips. They packed orders in chronological order because there wasn't enough visibility to optimize sorting picking. Inefficiencies in scheduling followed. "Back in the old system, we were giving operators a bundle of shipping labels in one hand and a stack of packing slips in another and hope that they'd match up," Burton recalled of their initial processes, "Depending on how the .csv was sorted, they could be in entirely different orders." So Burton and his team looked for a way to digitize this process.

The early search didn't turn anything up. "We didn't find anything that was fit for purpose without spending tens of thousands of pounds." Burton connected with an old friend at Tulip, and began a free trial to see if the cloud-based application platform could fit their needs. Within two weeks, Burton and his team had rolled out a set of applications that eliminated administrative work and allowed data to flow seamlessly across the different systems involved in their order process. When an order comes in through Shopify, the data is directly pulled into Tulip. Supervisors have a terminal, where they can select which orders they need to process and schedule them out for fulfillment to members of the team. At this point, orders are filtered and sorted into batches, and operators proceed to pack according to a freshly generated pick list. Operators interact with a single screen that consolidates all of the information they need to process an order. "Now Tulip just sorts them for us. . . There's no paperwork floating around."

From the same application screen, the operator can print labels for each order, with Tulip pulling shipping information from FedEx. During the process, Tulip automatically sends inventory updates to SAP. Altogether, Double H integrated Tulip with Shopify, FedEx, and SAP. They were also able to connect Tulip to their label printers. "When it came to interactions with hardware, we wouldn't even know where to start. With Tulip it was easy." Tulip effectively functioned as the glue between these disparate systems. "I set the target for zero admin," Burton said, "And I think it's fair to say we've achieved it now."

Burton stated that Double H is a company that gives its employees room to innovate. "Innovation is a big part of our culture. We encourage people to solve problems every day. If someone can think of a way to solve a problem, we let them try it." Now, they're seeing how the team can use the data collected by Tulip to create new efficiencies. The data from Tulip helps them calculate cycle times, giving them a sense of where workers are losing time as they process orders. The integrations also give them a better picture of the operation's financials. By pulling actual cost of order through FedEx back into SAP, they now have a clear way to calculate margins on an order (see Case study 13.2).

**Case study 13.2** When Demand Disappeared Overnight, Double H Nurseries Stood Up a New Digital Order Process in Four Weeks. Tulip's Double H Case Study.

Smaller businesses often face a dilemma when it comes to digital innovation. They know it is necessary, but it can be hard to justify the risks. Double H were able to build applications and prove the value of the platform without spending a cent. Implementing a no-code platform helped them standardize a new process, integrate with their existing systems, and it empowered them to do it all themselves. Double H exemplifies several principles of *augmented lean*: hacking their own process, adapting to the circumstances, enabling bottom-up initiative, augmenting individuals and learning, letting them try things, and lastly, governing the process by setting new standards.

# BUILDING AND TRUSTING IN SUPPLY CHAIN RESILIENCE

Yossi Sheffi has worked at MIT for 46 years. The Israeli-born professor with a B.Sc. from the Technion in Israel in 1975, and PhD from MIT in 1978, is an author of seven books, a founder of five successful companies, and the director of the MIT Center for Transportation and Logistics. Despite these accomplishments, he admits that until a year ago, even his wife struggled to explain what he did when at parties. Professor Sheffi is an expert in supply chain management. When Keith Oliver coined the term *supply chain management* in 1982, the idea was to describe "all movement and storage of raw materials, work-in-process inventory, and finished goods from point-of-origin to point-of-consumption." Today, the term encompasses even more components such as "resource management, materials handling, strategic alliances, logistics, technology adaptation, customer satisfaction, and effective communication techniques" (Pounder 2013).

But are supply chains really chains? Sheffi says (Interview 13.3):

Chain is just a stylistic concept because of course it's a web. Even if you talk about a specific manufacturer, they have thousands, sometimes tens of thousands of suppliers and those suppliers of their suppliers and those suppliers, their suppliers, and so forth. It's a huge web that expands backwards. And, if you look at the distribution, it expands forwards, because from that supplier, it will go either to warehouses, to retailers or directly to homes. (Augmented, 2022, ep. 68)

**Interview 13.3** Industrial Supply Chain Optimization. Episode 68. Interview with Professor Yossi Sheffi, Director, MIT Center for Transportation & Logistics. Augmented podcast.

In his recent book, *The New (Ab)Normal*, Sheffi maps how the COVID-19 pandemic impacted business, supply chains, and society (Sheffi 2020). Supply chain risk management had already evolved considerably pre-COVID, due to other shocks. Risk and uncertainty for globally exposed companies had already meant resilience strategies were in place, which goes a long way in explaining why the pandemic did not decimate international business. The virus accelerated preexisting trends in technology adoption of IoT, AI, and real-time data analytics, which provide visibility into supply chains and enable contactless, paperless operations. In fact, nimble startups and small businesses alike are increasingly using off-the-shelf cloud computing and mobile apps deploying considerable sophistication in their supply chains. "At the same time," writes Sheffi, the warehouse, a mainstay of supply chains, is getting a makeover as retailers move closer to customers so they can "fulfill buyers' unquenchable thirst for gratification" (Sheffi 2020).

For decades, supply chains were considered a mere consequence of globalization. Lean processes were achieved through effective shipping routes and increased port capacity, as well through providing ample capacity for airlifted supplies at reasonable cost. The relative ease with which even China and the US collaborated on trade ensured that the bigger issue became to lament about offshoring from the US. CEOs made declarations such as "these jobs are never coming back." Then two things happened. First, the automation revolution made even European and US factories more competitive because they suddenly started to rely on technology again, not just low cost labor. Second, the COVID-19 pandemic ensued and instantly accelerated the trend toward reshoring the supply chain, security, essential goods, and essential workers. For example, the US non-profit advocacy group Reshoring Now (www.reshorenow.org/) has recently had wind in the sails for its ambition to "bring good, well-paying manufacturing jobs back," with President Biden announcing his intention to make more cars and chips in the United States (Buchwald 2022).

# THE RESILIENCE OF GLOBAL SUPPLY CHAINS

The COVID-19 pandemic has definitely stretched the efficiency of what we call supply chains. In fact, no one can argue that 2021 was a great year for supply chains. Despite a global connected network of factories and trade offices, 80 ships were queued outside the port of LA on October 22 (Varley 2021). The world had never seen this. Definitely, something was broken. It should also be said that despite the archaic structures that feed them (ports, regulations, legacy trade relations), many supply chains turned out to be somewhat resilient. Few supply chains completely broke down.

However, emergency production of many goods that had not been manufactured domestically at national demand scale in years were suddenly in high demand: hand sanitizer, face masks, PPE, ventilators, and more. As Sheffi explains, the idea that companies are abandoning China in favor of other offshore manufacturing centers does not reflect reality. China has significant market power, its consumers are strong, and its broader supply chain network of intermediate goods is extensive. China also has an advanced deployment of automation. Companies are adopting a "China +1" strategy with a hedge of small-scale operations elsewhere, mostly in lower-cost regional hubs such as Mexico for the US and Turkey for Europe. China, on its end, claims Sheffi, will use the crisis to rapidly move up the value chain, expanding its vast manufacturing ecosystems.

Naturally, duplicating supply chains, taking greater care to have domestic suppliers as part of a backup plan, and rebuilding some level of national infrastructure, capacity, and stockpiles is likely to occur. Building in this kind of resiliency is now on every supply chain officer's agenda. However, after the initial disruption, the global supply chain recovered quite rapidly, fueled by virtual cloud connected value streams. The reason was that digitalization has now permeated even traditional industries that have largely remained the same for a hundred years. Value streams have usually been contained inside the company's four walls. It was a matter of an individual factory optimizing their own process flows. Changing that logic took a long time. Why? Because the complexity and idiosyncrasy of each location and its specific production setup ensured that any new technology or approach instantly was met with adverse consequences.

It is important to realize that not every business process is digital or will inherently digitize. This certainly applies to the supply chain, says Sheffi, and points out that in most places, somebody makes your cappuccino by hand. "Let's first of all admit that society is not totally digitized, and it's not ready to be. It's not [even] clear that it will be." He reasoned:

[People say,] "Air travel and especially business travel will never come back," but it will, because, people will still have suppliers in China,

Vietnam, Malaysia, and South America. To close the deal, to make a deal, or to keep the deal going it's not enough to do a video call. You need to fly out there and then negotiate the deal and then have dinner with the other party and talk about your kids or grandkids or spouses, and what you like to drink and whatever, create relationships and create trust. It's very hard to create trust online.

Another reason it is hard to digitize supply chains is that "they are so diverse," says Sheffi, and points to the plethora of apps out there to show that you are vaccinated. There's no worldwide app, so there's no standard. In contrast, since 1961 we have a container standard. The ships are built this way. The trucks are built this way. But because we don't have a standard size airplane, we don't have a standard-sized air container (Augmented 2020, ep. 68).

Startups and innovation can help, says Sheffi, as long as you realize that 99% of them will fail. The difference is that workers will realize they are captains of their own ship. "There is no reason today for most workers not to upgrade their capabilities. [Workers] have to make sure that they take care of themselves by upgrading their capabilities" (Augmented 2020, ep. 68).

# THE LESSONS FROM DIGITIZING GE

As chronicled in the book *Lights Out* (2020), since its founding in 1892, GE has been more than just a corporation. For generations, it was job security, a solidly safe investment, and an elite business education for top managers. GE electrified America, powering everything from lightbulbs to turbines, and became fully integrated into the American societal mindset as few companies ever had. And after two decades of leadership under legendary CEO Jack Welch, GE entered the twenty-first century as America's most valuable corporation. Yet, fewer than two decades later, the GE of old was gone.

With that in mind, what does the future of industrial operations hold for the frontline worker? What a recent GE chief executive, Jeff Immelt tried to do with GE was to create an industrial IT powerhouse that had the same role in industry as Microsoft had in many other industries. As he describes in his book, *Hot Seat*, he ultimately had to give up his ambition, as it was both taking longer and facing significant adversity (see Interview 13.4).

**Interview 13.4** Business Beyond Buzzwords. Episode 42. Interview with Jeff Immelt, Venture Partner, NEA, Former CEO of General Electric. Augmented podcast.

There was also a deeper challenge. The startups (or larger manufacturers aiming to be transformers) were faced with finding supply chain experts that were willing to experiment with digital methods. In the case of startups, the learning curve of a newly educated IT engineer who has to program for a manufacturing environment is quite steep.

At the end of the day, a company's manufacturing organization is the sum of its supply chains. The backbone of the manufacturing supply chain is SMEs. An SBA (2019) report claims SMEs create two-thirds of new jobs and deliver 43.5% of the United States' gross domestic product (GDP). Yet, due to their size and maturity of their IT operation, they are typically deprived of access to technology. This reality is changing rapidly. Back in 2020, Alibaba unveiled its new manufacturing digital factory, Xunxi, a cloud intelligence-powered manufacturing system which arguably starts to level the playing field for SMEs, enabling access to small-batch customization and agility in production. The use of AI allows traditional manufacturers to improve profitability and reduce inventory levels while still being able to meet personalization needs. Having the supply chain digitized end-to-end is a necessity if small producers want to compete with mass-market vendors.

# REMAINING CHALLENGES: TACKLING PORT CONGESTION

Even before the COVID-19 pandemic, the ports faced many challenges: larger ships, taller cranes, and bigger volumes per call, and the imperative to make terminal operations safer, greener, and more productive (ABB 2021). Singapore, Shenzhen, Hong Kong, and Dubai have all succeeded in building up regional hub ports. However, aside from those powerhouses, ports in the northern hemisphere have digitized more than those in the southern hemisphere (Maundrill 2021). Regardless of location, investment in quality improvement of port infrastructure and its contribution to the economy are often questioned by politicians, investors, and the general public (Haque Munim and Schramm 2018) because of its costs and the difficulty with which actors in the system have in describing the utility of making infrastructure improvements. There is some evidence that the impact of transport efficiency on export performance decreases as the economy becomes richer. Either way, even though ports clearly facilitate socioeconomic infrastructure and generate external economies, the effects are difficult to put into clear figures. Impact goes over many years and with too many variables to pin down.

Despite the plethora of potential stakeholders, there are not that many actors who are actively proposing digital transformation of ports.

Three of them are ABB, DP World, and TiL Group. ABB delivers automation and electrical systems for container and bulk cargo handling – from ship to gate. DP World is an Emirati multinational logistics company based in Dubai, United Arab Emirates, specializing in cargo logistics, port terminal operations, maritime services, and free trade zones. TIL Group is the largest and most geographically diverse container terminal operator globally, with material equity interests in 40 operating terminals. As pointed out in a 2020 webinar jointly put on by ABB, DP World, and Terminal Investment Limited (TIL) Group, "Digitalization in the container handling context is often considered as a matter of the overall logistic chain, cloud and big data. While those are undoubtedly key aspects in digitalization of container shipping, digitalization also transforms the operational processes and port workers' roles within terminals which has an impact on terminals' productivity" (Port Technology International 2020).

It would be fair to say that ports represent laggards in the digitization of industry and even within the supply chain industry overall. In many ways, it is still based on physical, paper-based interaction. A few startups stand out as would-be changemakers. On the marine side, the startup thrust is more recent and fewer actors distinguish themselves in terms of the digitalization of sea ports or shipping. A few still come to mind, notably, pre-seed stage Singaporean startup Quantship, founded in 2019, which provides freight predictions using algorithmic predictions. Maritime Optima is an Oslo-based startup providing maritime intelligence that includes real-time ship/port information, voyage planning, and carbon footprint calculations to operators such as ship owners and traders. Valencia-based Spanish startup SEAPort Solutions optimizes port call processes with a collaborative data exchange platform.

Key stakeholders in port call processes including port authorities, mooring companies, pilots, tugboat companies, and terminal operators, get real-time visibility of data to enable seamless port functioning. Pilot tests of the concept showed that only 40–65% of the time spent in port, depending on the type of ship, is dedicated to loading and unloading operations, confirming the potential margin for improvement (SEAPort Solutions 2021). ShipIn puts computer vision systems on ships to help with the human factor. All the operations on a boat are supported by vision systems. ShipIn's platform proactively alerts shipowners, managers, and seafarers to onboard anomalies, reducing incidents onboard and increasing cargo operations efficiency. ShipIn shows that frontline tech extends beyond factories and into the maritime sphere.

According to French maritime data startup Sinay, founded in 2007, four key categories of port innovation are crucial, notably robotics, process automation, decision-making automation, and digitalization (Sinay 2021). This is challenging for a maritime industry that has been globalized since the fifteenth century and has developed ingrained ways of doing things and has accumulated substantial infrastructure which is costly to evolve. Ports, of course, serve as a connecting point of all actors in the supply chain and often change would entail agreement between many different sets of stakeholders. Ports differ in size, and small ports don't have the same characteristics or challenges as large ports. The International Port Community Systems Association (IPCSA), created in 2011, aims to take an active role in global trade facilitation through the electronic exchange of information and to promote the use of standards.

# THE FUTURE
# OF SUPPLY CHAINS

For decades the supply chain management and logistics industry has been dominated by giants like UPS, FedEx, or Deutsche Post. However, that has also made the industry ripe for disruption. A new breed of supply chain firms and business models are capitalizing on the renewed attention to the topic, the changing shipper expectations toward faster and more convenient delivery both among consumers and businesses, and are building different business models that are less sensitive to the eroding margins among the traditional players. Famously, transportation startup Uber demonstrated how exponential growth is not necessarily tied to owning assets but, rather, to regulatory arbitrage. Startups have emerged across segments such as warehousing and fulfillment, express delivery, overland transportation, as well as ocean or air transportation (Deloitte 2017). Supply chain startups have sprung up hoping to solve inventory visibility, predictive forecasting, or traceability.

The supply chain is a network where improvements in resiliency, credible risk assessment, optimal supply allocation, working capital optimization, demand planning based on real demand (not just forecasts), portfolio optimization and pricing assessing end-to-end SKU-level profitability, and the emergence of carbon planning through data-driven strategies to quantify and reduce environmental impact, each will shape its future evolution, in an augmented supply chain (see Figure 13.1). Startups exist throughout the supply chain, and their role is growing as they capture the opportunity on the table for supply chains, one of the last "traditional" business functions to digitize. Orbital Insight, Sourcemap, Righthand Robotics, Humatics, Vecna, Ivaldi, Project 44, Trackonomy, VoloDrone, Leverage, Flexport, Homoola, Skuchain, and Stord are startups that illustrate the potential for step-change innovation. Panjiva is an intelligence platform that began as a startup founded by Jim Psota and has been owned by S&P Global since 2018. It is bringing transparency to global trade through machine-learning technologies and data visualizations. Panjiva hosts a database of information on over 700,000 suppliers, including recent shipments, customer lists, credit reports, certification details, and denied parties lists. This illustrates how visualization already transcends shop floors and has penetrated into supply chains.

The main threads or opportunity areas these startups are addressing include putting aspects of the supply chain on the cloud, developing analytics on the flow of goods and services across the supply chain, and

# The Augmented Supply Chain

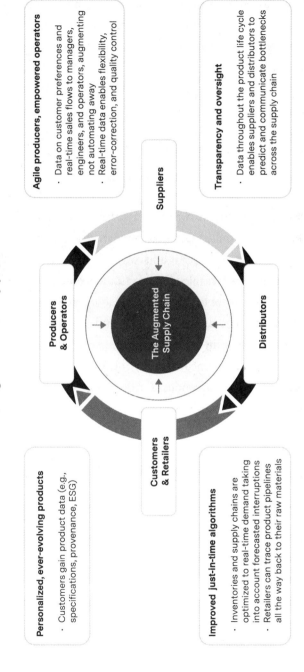

**Personalized, ever-evolving products**

· Customers gain product data (e.g., specifications, provenance, ESG)

**Agile producers, empowered operators**

· Data on customer preferences and real-time sales flows to managers, engineers, and operators, augmenting not automating away
· Real-time data enables flexibility, error-correction, and quality control

**Improved just-in-time algorithms**

· Inventories and supply chains are optimized to real-time demand taking into account forecasted interruptions
· Retailers can trace product pipelines all the way back to their raw materials

**Transparency and oversight**

· Data throughout the product life cycle enables suppliers and distributors to predict and communicate bottlenecks across the supply chain

Producers & Operators

Suppliers

Customers & Retailers

Distributors

The Augmented Supply Chain

**Figure 13.1** The Augmented Supply Chain.

improving the visibility of specific elements of the supply chain, including what happens before, during, and after materials production, shipping, factory assembly, warehousing, and delivery.

Due to the rising set of challenges, and the increasing feasibility of cloud solutions in the space, the role of innovators in the supply chain is likely to grow.

# CONCLUSION

The world went too much toward just-in-time (JIT) and unified supply chains. This affected the global economy in dramatic ways during the COVID-19 pandemic, and might do so again with other disruptions such as wars or natural disasters. Needless to say, startups are risky and supply chains are complex. However, given the relatively low-tech current reality of the sector, even basic digitization is bound to yield significant breakthroughs in efficiency. Putting more and more elements of supply chains on the cloud is a prerequisite for reaping the benefits. We need more (digital) flexibility at the various nodes. Furthermore, if vendors self-select to collaborate with one another and share information more widely through standardized interfaces, there are significant transparency effects. If government regulation stimulates the same, that would be immensely beneficial and might stimulate further innovation and consolidate gains for startups entering the field.

Even as warehousing becomes more and more automated, there are key residual tasks where human coordination remains essential – and may for a long time to come. Our vision for supply chains includes the notion of augmenting industrial frontline workers with the edge-based tools they need to achieve strong visibility into their own work process but also with the potential to achieve drastically increased systemic awareness. With that, surprises should be more rare and bottlenecks can be more easily eliminated or remedied by alternative approaches. Right now, the biggest obstacle is not technology itself but the regulatory infrastructure, notably the poor or lacking incentives governments have put in place to deeply digitize ports and other chokepoints.

Despite the potential of supply chains on the cloud, enabled by edge devices and sensors tracking most aspects of supply chains, no amount of technology can fully compensate for port authorities that act as monopolies, unions that protect old-fashioned ways of doing business without compromising in the interest of the public good, or large conglomerates that exploit loopholes in the system to extract more value before embracing change. Having said that, starting small, using no-code technology that can be implemented by one or a few actors without requiring initial permission from the whole set of stakeholders, is likely a faster way to digitize than to wait for one big fix.

In the upcoming chapter, which is our conclusion, we will ponder the impact of the fact that the phenomenon we have discovered and are describing as augmented lean is already unfolding "in the wild." We will speculate about what it might mean if it became an industrial management paradigm.

# REFERENCES

ABB (2021). Solutions for ports and cargo terminals. *ABB*. https://new.abb.com/ports (accessed 1 November 2021).

Augmented (2021, ep. 43). Digitized Supply Chain. Episode 43. Interview with Arun Kumar Bhaskara-Baba, Head of Global Manufacturing IT, Johnson & Johnson. *Augmented podcast*. (June 23). https://www.augmentedpodcast.co/digitized-supply-chain/ (accessed 17 November 2021).

Augmented (2021, ep. 61). The Digital Journey of a Flower Wholesaler. Episode 61. Interview with Andy Burton, Managing Director, Double H Nurseries Ltd. *Augmented podcast*. (Dec 22). https://www.augmentedpodcast.co/61 (accessed 13 March 2022).

Augmented (2022, ep. 68). Industrial Supply Chain Optimization. Episode 68. Interview with Professor Yossi Sheffi, Director, MIT Center for Transportation & Logistics. *Augmented podcast.* (Feb 2). https://www.augmentedpodcast.co/68

Buchwald, E. (2022). Biden says making more goods in the US, like cars and chips, will lower inflation. Can his plan work? *USA Today* (March 3). https://www.usatoday.com/story/money/economy/2022/03/03/biden-lower-inflation-plan/9341221002/?gnt-cfr=1 (accessed 20 March 2022).

Deloitte (2017). Supply chain startups are coming of age. *Deloitte.* https://www2.deloitte.com/content/dam/Deloitte/de/Documents/operations/Deloitte_PoV-Supply-Chain-Startups-Are-Coming-of-Age.pdf (accessed 2 November 2021).

Formlabs (2020). 3D printed test swabs for COVID-19 Testing. *Formlabs.* https://formlabs.com/covid-19-response/covid-test-swabs/ (accessed 20 March 2022).

Humatics (2019). Supply Chain Management Review: Humatics announces partnership with Vecna Robotics, Humatics. (April 10). https://humatics.com/blog/news_and_events_tags/supply-chain-management-review/ (accessed 2 November 2021).

Junior J. (2021). Aurangabad Hospital gets advanced face shields from non-profit organisation in US – ET HealthWorld. Newsazi.com (August 15). https://newsazi.com/aurangabad-hospital-gets-advanced-face-shields-from-non-profit-organisation-in-us-et-healthworld/ (accessed 1 November 2021).

Maundrill, B. (2021). New report shines light on digital port collaboration. *Port Technology* (January 2021). https://www.porttechnology.org/news/new-report-shines-light-on-digital-port-collaboration/ (accessed 1 November 2021).

Munim, Z.H., Schramm, HJ. (2018). The impacts of port infrastructure and logistics performance on economic growth: the mediating role of seaborne trade. *Journal of Shipping and Trade.* 3, 1 (2018). https://doi.org/10.1186/s41072-018-0027-0 (accessed 1 November 2021).

Port Technology International (2020). Digitalization of Port Operations in Today's Digital Age. *Port Technology International.* https://app.livestorm.co/port-technology-international/digitalization-of-port-operations (accessed 1 November 2021).

Pounder, P. (2013). A review of supply chain management and its main external influential factors. *Supply Chain Forum* 14. 42–50. 10.13140/2.1.3787.3289.

PR Newswire (2021). Successful first public flight of Volocopter's VoloDrone. *PR Newswire.* https://www.prnewswire.com/news-releases/successful-first-public-flight-of-volocopters-volodrone-301398329.html (accessed 1 November 2021).

SBA (2019). Small businesses generate 44 percent of U.S. economic activity. *The Office of Advocacy of the U.S. Small Business Administration (SBA).* (Jan 30).

https://advocacy.sba.gov/2019/01/30/small-businesses-generate-44-percent-of-u-s-economic-activity/# (accessed 30 March 2022).

Schlenker, M. (2021) Johnson & Johnson supply chain (January 22). https://storymaps.arcgis.com/stories/efd9fb73ac4f4e8082036d6296aea5a2 (accessed 17 November 2021).

SEAPort Solutions (2021). Seaport solutions precedents. *SEAPort Solutions.* https://seaport-solutions.com/en/precedents/ (accessed 1 November 2021).

Sheffi, Y. (2020). *The New (Ab)Normal: reshaping business and supply chain strategy beyond COVID-19.* Cambridge: MIT CTL Media.

Sinay (2021). Port Digitalization and the implications for the maritime sector. *Sinay* (June 8) https://sinay.ai/en/what-is-port-digitalization/ (accessed 1 November 2021).

Statista (2022). Container shipping – statistics & facts. https://www.statista.com/topics/1367/container-shipping/#dossierKeyfigures (accessed 6 January 2022).

Tulip (2021f). When MasksOn needed a logistics system, they built one with Tulip in four days. *Tulip.* Case Study. https://tulip.co/case-studies/maskson/ (accessed 29 October 2021).

Tulip (2020). The rapid development of the rise emergency ventilator. *Tulip.* Digital Manufacturing Webinar. (July 23). https://www.youtube.com/watch?v=BL2e944h1GA (accessed 20 March 2022).

Varley, K. (2021). Container ships headed for U.S. poised to worsen port bottleneck. *Bloomberg.* (Oct 22). https://www.bloomberg.com/news/articles/2021-10-22/container-ships-headed-for-u-s-poised-to-worsen-port-bottleneck (accessed 30 March 2022).

# CHAPTER 14

# CONCLUSION: AUGMENTED LEAN MANAGEMENT OF THE EMERGING, FRONTLINE INDUSTRIAL WORKFORCE

With industrial tech, opportunities for change are abundant, but, as history has shown, so is the opportunity for blockages. The 2021 debacle in the Suez Canal, where one blocked cargo ship created a worldwide supply chain bottleneck, is emblematic of a disconnect between the factory floor and the industrial consumer. While it may be wonderful to have these futuristic considerations, this debacle exposes the need for greater connection between the digitized world and the tangible manufacturing of goods. How can 12% of global trade still pass through the same canal? The same technical bottleneck happens when lack of interoperability stops industrial tech systems from sharing data. Or, when automation gets prioritized over augmentation.

Machines are means, not aims in themselves. German philosopher Immanuel Kant's third formulation of the categorical imperative, the

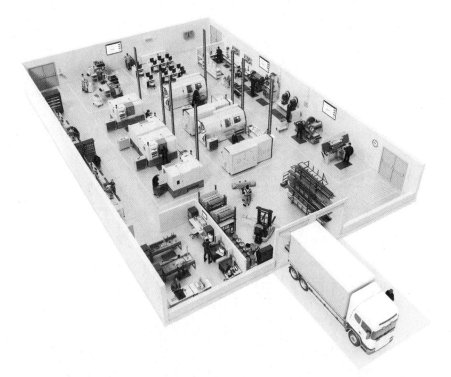

**Figure 14.1** Managing the Evolving Physical Configuration of the Industrial Workforce Is a Persistent (Augmentation) Challenge.

principle of autonomy, dictates we are not dependent on others to tell us what is right and wrong, but that we are free and able to discover this for ourselves through the use of reason (Paton 1971). Kant asks us to imagine that the action we are about to take would become a law that pertains universally, absolutely, to the whole society, including yourself. Would you want that to be the law? If so, action is good. Would you not want to live in that society? If so, the action is not good. He calls it a universal moral law, and we concur. A human-centric framework for managing industrial operations will not emerge on its own. We have to believe it is important. We then have to create a system that fosters it, manifesting it into existence.

# AUGMENTED LEAN MANAGEMENT FOR THE FRONTLINE WORKFORCE

As outlined in this highly empirical book, we hope to have documented how augmented lean management builds on a set of distinct human traits (a hacking mentality), organizational enablement (tools, techniques, technologies), leadership mindset (augment, decentralize, and empower), and systemic awareness (understanding – and respecting – all levels of the system). These traits and functions are not given, and as surely as they have emerged, each will keep changing.

As we conclude this book, we want to point out that the components of augmented lean naturally lead us into the (constantly) emerging field of frontline operations. In this landscape, the forces of change rather than any particular organization or job description will dictate the playing field for frontline workers. Operators (rather than executives) are at the center of the organization building new augmented lean practices. Policy makers have a pivotal role in regulating existing as well as emergent machines, so they always augment not merely automate work.

# Frontline Operations

Frontline operations is a challenging new industrial technology category. In the past, operations was viewed as a niche (and potentially boring) management discipline. Now, the frontlines are where industrial innovation is served up, not just "stations" to pass by where the annoyingly slow production of goods was happening. If you are on a train journey, without stopping at key stations, what have you really experienced?

# Forces of Change

Three forces seem to be shaping the future of industry as we speak: the COVID-19 pandemic, AI developments, and sustainability. The pandemic is clearly accelerating R&D, implementing remote work, and challenging weak production practices all around. The transition from futile attempts at "grand scale" AI and mindless industrial automation efforts seem to be flanked by a good proportion of purposeful intelligence augmentation of workers. Citizen developers using no-code platforms are reaching momentum because those systems are gradually evolving toward simplicity. Eventually, some form of AR/VR that actually works will emerge, but we cannot wait for it. Industrial worker augmentation is already possible now. The sustainability imperative of safeguarding natural ecosystems and achieving symbiosis with human industrial activity is also finally sinking in. We realize we did not spend a lot of time on the significance of sustainability in this book, but *augmented lean* is a powerful way to drive in that direction, and this is a topic we would like to cover in the near future within the augmented lean community.

Inherent in innovation is the potential for significant revisions and change of course. We are *homo faber*, the toolmakers, and what we make, in turn changes us (Frisch 1994; Ihde and Malafouris 2019). We make technology for our survival. Then, we mass produce it for society to exist, for all our needs. Even though individual production lines live and die, because each has a life cycle, manufacturing and production are key elements in human evolution. They are not going anywhere. The *creative destruction*, envisioned by Schumpeter (1942), pertained to innovations in the manufacturing process that increase productivity, for example, "the process of industrial mutation that incessantly revolutionizes the economic structure from within, incessantly destroying the old one, incessantly creating a new one." For workers, companies, governments, and machines to thrive in this new evolving environment, upskilling is key, but what it means will differ.

# Frontline Workers

In the world we envision, frontline workers will be prioritized, empowered, and admired. Real work will, again, be valued. All work that has an impact on the future of the many should be rightfully seen as important, no matter whether its execution took a hammer, a keyboard, a drawing board, or a digital kanban process. Frontline workers were previously "chained" to the production line. Instead, with augmentation technologies, they take on geographical and physical autonomy, and increased control of their own time. Despite the complexity of the goods and services they co-create, there is a potential for greater autonomy and portability of skill set, productivity, and product ownership.

However, only those who equip themselves with the practical ability to reason and talk about changes as they occur, will be able to understand future developments across the industry. More importantly, they will be able to profit from the impending changes. The specific skills that need to be built include a keen awareness of the most important and groundbreaking, emerging manufacturing innovations. Second, it would be prudent to develop the ability to create products and applications on top of such innovations yourself. The creative destruction that fosters industrial revolutions is stronger than any corporate training plan. Only those who are intrinsically motivated to try to understand what's happening around them, and are then capable of acting appropriately, prevail under such conditions.

Through *augmented lean* practices on the factory floor, workers have a fair chance to stand on equal footing with the white-collar knowledge worker. The first 50 years of the IT revolution were entirely dedicated to them. In the process, there is also the possibility of frontline workers leapfrogging traditionally educated engineers or operations professionals. At least, the citizen developer spirit allows them to update skill sets and communicate with managers at more equal levels. They now (in theory) have the same information tools. If augmented lean becomes a prevalent approach, the world's leaders will stop talking about the "future of work" as some sort of mantra. Rather, we should immediately seek to foster and subsequently make full use of an empowered, contemporary workforce. The future of work is ready now.

The quality of work itself is getting an overhaul, and when that process is complete, we will enter the era of "Relaxation." Relaxation is, paradoxically, a mind-bogglingly decentralized but still potentially exhausting form of automation, where most or all physical tasks are taken over by machines, and humans are designing, monitoring, and adjudicating the work of machines. Relaxation will end up being a misnomer, because intellectual work is seldom relaxing, and may lead to exerting more energy. As the shift from an economy dominated by manual work via service work toward intellectual work is taking much longer than earlier futurists such as Toffler (1984) predicted, there is also the distinct possibility that humans enjoy the physical nature of work. There are, therefore, good reasons to contemplate what kinds of systems we *want* to build before building them, instead of waiting until we have to consider the unintended consequences of what we have built and implemented after the fact.

# Operators

Operators are at the center of a process where technology is a tool, not an objective. With *augmented lean* approaches, engineers engaged in industrial control, continuous improvement, safety, quality, or lean management can increasingly build applications themselves with direct feedback from frontline operators. No-code platforms will make their work more efficient, pleasant, and innovative. Implementing such technologies and solutions does not always require traditional engineering skills. What it takes is a "maker" attitude of experimentation, learning, and grit. Once operators are liberated from managers, and empowered by no-code, shop floor workers can also enjoy more freedom in their work.

# Policy Makers

We believe that frontline operations are about to change drastically, even without policy intervention. That does not mean that regulations cannot be helpful. Conversely, they can certainly be harmful. Policy makers who embrace the principles we espouse in this book are likely to, themselves, be at the forefront of change. Enabling scores of SMEs to make use of *augmented lean* management's *LEADER/HG framework* and its eight principles of *learn, emerge, augment, decentralize, empower, respect, hack,* and *govern*, may require training programs and best practice initiatives nationally all around the world. For that, governments are ideally situated, at least as catalysts and enablers of change. The most important role a government could take at this stage is to be the watchdog of clever, lightweight standardization. As manufacturing fully digitizes, the potential for unhelpful lock-in effects, in manufacturing automation systems, in augmentation, in additive manufacturing or in robotics, and especially in the integration of each of these into a coherent system, is significant. Instead of worrying about future factories, governments should study the ethics and fairness of manufacturing algorithms so we have yardsticks for future machines and wise guidance for the humans who govern them.

# Machines

Automation is not the enemy, but mindless automation might be. The best way to view robots is as programmable machines that carry out dull, dirty, and dangerous tasks for you. This way, robots serve a clear purpose. If robots are introduced under any other objective (including purely as a replacement for humans), that is both a regulatory issue (for which there should potentially be an automation tax) and definitely an ethical issue where society needs to intervene. This is grounded in the notion (shared by many), in which work (e.g., defined as labor) is a human emancipatory process that we need in order to feel valued as human beings. You could consider the ability to work (in some fashion) a human right. In fact, the right to work is enshrined in the Universal Declaration of Human Rights. In that light, any obstacle to carrying out this process by machines or inventors or financiers of such machines has to be compensated for, even if there are also socioeconomic efficiency reasons why robots are deployed. Upskilling robots into humanistically oriented cobots that are (somewhat) social is, either way, a key challenge of our time, and both humans and robots still have a lot to learn (Major and Shah 2020).

# BUILDING THE AUGMENTED LEAN COMMUNITY

To check on your progress and to maintain the pace – and inspiration required to achieve these lofty ideas – we would like to invite you to contribute to use cases of the *augmented lean* paradigm. This could be as simple as signing up to receive our newsletter (see Resource 14.1). However, it could also mean getting engaged in the brewing movement. You could become an evangelist, and we would be thrilled to equip you with the examples you need to learn even more.

**Resource 14.1** The Augmented Podcast.

As the isolation of the pandemic is put behind us, the possibility of a larger conversation about the way that workers, employers, goods, and services interact with each other in the larger economic sphere opens up. Even though some interests may seem to clash, ultimately, everybody benefits from working together. This is the truth at the core of this book. The last thing we want is for the leaders of the industrial world – whether they be executives or operators – to be lone wolves. We tend to think too much about industrial revolutions as linearly proceeding along paths predetermined by the most advanced technology at the time.

Manufacturing does not work like that. The emerging frontline operations platforms will be built on the cloud and empowered by no-code interfaces. But they will allow for deep integration with legacy industrial tools, machines, and systems. To bring these together requires a synchronized and concerted activity that allows for the betterment of workers at all levels at its core. The leading industrial organizations of the future will emerge not as singular entities, but in packs. We fear that too many may be left behind. As a result, in *augmented lean* we hope we have offered a more flexible approach of evolving the kind of operational engineering expertise, and cyber-physical wisdom that will serve as a foundation for the future leading frontline operations organizations. That is what comes next, and a worthwhile journey to study further.

To discuss with us, contact us at authors@augmentedleanbook.com, track the ongoing debate on www.augmentedlean.com, and listen to hundreds of related podcast interviews with industrial thought leaders on the Augmented podcast (www.augmentedpodcast.co). Given the QR codes we have sprinkled throughout the book, you are, hopefully, familiar with several of those podcast episodes by now. We value divergent thinking and expect to hear from you. What frustrates you about our book? What stimulates you? Do you have something to add? Let us know.

# REFERENCES

Frisch, M. (1994) *Homo Faber*. New York: HarperVia. [1957].

Ihde, D., Malafouris, L. (2019). Homo faber revisited: Postphenomenology and material engagement theory. *Philosophy & Technology* 32 (2019): 195–214, https://doi.org/10.1007/s13347-018-0321-7

Major, L. and Shah, J. (2020). *What to Expect When You're Expecting Robots: The Future of Human-Robot Collaboration*. New York: Basic Books.

Paton, H.J. (1971). *The Categorical Imperative: A Study in Kant's Moral Philosophy*. Philadelphia: University of Pennsylvania Press.

Schumpeter, J.A. (1942). *Capitalism, Socialism and Democracy*. New York: Harper & Brothers.

Toffler, A. (1984). *The Third Wave*. New York: Bantam.

# INDEX

Page numbers followed by *f* and *t* refer to figures and tables, respectively.